KATYA CENGEL

STRAIT JACKETS

AND LUNCH MONEY

STRAIT JACKETS

JACKETS

AND LUNCH MONEY

KATYA CENGEL

woodhall press
Woodhall Press | Norwalk, CT

woodhall press

Woodhall Press, 81 Old Saugatuck Road, Norwalk, CT 06855
WoodhallPress.com

Cover design: Jessica Dionne
Layout artist: L.J. Mucci

Library of Congress Cataloging-in-Publication Data available

ISBN 978-1-954907-68-3   (paper: alk paper)
ISBN 978-1-954907-69-0   (electronic)

First Edition
Distributed by Independent Publishers Group
(800) 888-4741

Printed in the United States of America

This is a work of creative nonfiction. All of the events in this memoir are true
to the best of the author's memory. Some names and identifying features
have been changed to protect the identity of certain parties. The author in
no way represents any company, corporation, or brand, mentioned herein.

To my sister, and the childhood we shared and lost
And to all the children who never had one to begin with

Contents

Prologue 1

Book I: Remember to Forget

The Prisoners 5
A Taste 13
The Patients 21
Story Time 27
Hunger 35
The Prince 43
The End (Almost) 49
His Subject 57
Admission 65
A Very Special Category 75

Book II: Then and Now

Back Behind Bars 81
Roth 87
The Queen 95
Shadows 103
Number 090 71 51 115
Incredible Shrinking Kids 125
Little Difficult One 133
Escape 141
Antipsychotic 153
Bloodsuckers 161
The Storyteller 177
Those Who Haunt the Mirror 185
By Proxy 195
A Rock Feels No Pain 199

Everybody Loves Dan 207
The Pretenders 213
Dedication... 219
Get Well Soon 223
Reading Between the Lines..227
Extracurricular Activities 229

Book III: After

The Comprehensive Care Unit 235
Scared Straight.. 243
Talk Therapy... 253
Mementos 259
Countdown..261
Priceless 265
Giving Up..267
The Warmth of a Ghost...271
Flowers on Your Grave...277
Fake Santa...281
Haunted Ground 289
Discharge 295
What Might Have Been.. 299
Smoke 303
A Straight Flush...307
To Be Continued... 315
Las Amigas 317
Afterword.. 323

Notes.. 326
Acknowledgments..331
About The Author 332

PROLOGUE

This is the story of what I remember from the time I spent in a psychosomatic unit at a children's hospital at age ten, followed by what I have pieced together thirty years later.

I was there for nearly four months, from early September to late December of 1986. In a child's life, four months is an eternity. It is half of fifth grade. It is Halloween, Thanksgiving, and Christmas, for those who celebrate them. It is multiplication tables. It is sixteen weeks without sleepovers, without soccer games or parents or siblings. It is 120 days without sleeping in your own bed. It is four months of being a patient, not a child. Four months of being institutionalized.

For much of my stay I wore the same outfit, a pair of worn baby-blue pants and a baggy sweatshirt. Patients were allowed to dress in their own clothes. I had one stuffed animal, a tattered-looking bear called Boseys. My sister named it. She made occasional visits. My mother came more often. I refused to see my father. He tried to come twice. I remember that.

Some of the other things I remember: the white strips of cloth they used to tie me down, the crushing isolation that comes when you disappear from society. Loneliness that left me with a fierce independent streak and a commitment to listen to children in need.

Annie might be one of them. She is my "little sister," a sensitive child I was paired with through a mentoring organization. She reads books about funny characters that misunderstand things—and worries that her mother works too hard. Her favorite color is yellow. She is scared of butterflies. She is ten.

This could be Annie's story if we don't listen. It isn't just my story; it is the story of children, both then and now, the story of those who treated us and those who shunned us. Above all else, this is the story of those who couldn't be heard when they needed to be—the children whose problems we hope someone else will solve, the ones whose calls echo in empty rooms. Whether they are in detention facilities or hospitals, foster homes or homes without hope, they are hidden from us. They have been silenced, as I once was.

Now I can ask the questions I couldn't as a child.

I went looking for answers. In some places, I found them. In others, I found holes. Some people—patients, doctors, staff—won't talk. Others couldn't be found. I imagine still others remain in the system, without a voice.

As a journalist, I have a voice, which is why I am writing this now—to document what happened to me—to them. This is a story for all the children whose cries we cannot hear because it hurts too much to listen.

Book I
REMEMBER TO FORGET

THE PRISONERS
2012

It was the straitjacket. I had forgotten it. I am not sure how. Having your arms held forcibly immobile against your body is not something you would think one would forget. It is especially hard to imagine someone like myself, someone who hates to lose control, forgetting having been forced to watch as others took control. But I had forgotten how they overpowered my brain and my will. They took my anger and wrapped me up in it, forcing me to absorb the pain I needed to release.

I was ten years old. A captive. A prisoner. The straitjacket makes you helpless to protect yourself, to defend yourself—to hurt yourself. How do you forget something like that?

I don't know; but I did. I had forgotten about the straitjacket until I saw them forcibly restrain another child, a boy, a teenager. He was fighting them. I didn't want to stare, but I had to look closer. The stiff white contraption that was holding his arms unnaturally at his sides seemed familiar. That's when I remembered. I had seen it before. I had felt it before.

More than two decades had passed, but a memory was coming back. I wasn't sure if it was real. Real was what I was seeing now. A Black teenager incarcerated in a youth detention facility in the greater San Francisco Bay Area for a crime I was not supposed to know being forced into a straitjacket. As an instructor in a weekly writing program at the facility, I had been warned against inquiring about the youths' crimes. I hadn't been volunteering with the program long, but I knew already it was better not to ask too many questions of the children—especially when you had no answers you could give them.

I made that mistake once, asking a boy how he could avoid getting into trouble when he got out. He told me his mom was a prostitute and that she kicked him out when she had customers. I asked about other family members. His older brother was locked up. He had an aunt on the streets, a cousin in the ground, and a father, whereabouts unknown. There were others, but none he could turn to for help staying out of trouble. The way he told it, there was no one on the outside equipped to support him, to house him, to raise him. The adults in his life were a disappointment.

I didn't know what to tell him. I had no solution, no way for him to stay safe, to create a different future. In that I was no different than the other adults around him. I had nothing for him. So, I moved on to the next kid. That is what we do; we focus on the ones we can help, the ones we can save. It makes sense, unless you are one of the children left behind.

My mother won't name them, but she says there were people— friends, family members—I don't know. All I know is what she told me. These people advised her to give up on me, to focus on my sister, the child that was not lost to her. The child she could help.

I did the same with the boy. I left him. I knew from my work as a journalist that it was best not to get too distracted by a single story.

I had become a journalist so I could tell the stories of those who were not being heard. I dove into other people's lives, but I was careful to surface before I got too deep. It was the same thing with the incarcerated youth. I only saw them once a week for a few hours with half a dozen other volunteers. We visited the different groups in pairs, spending less than an hour with each group. I went because I wanted them to know they weren't throwaways, that there were people who cared about what happened to them. I needed them to know this. I needed to know this.

It wasn't what they usually heard. I understand this because for a while I received a similar message. We had that in common, even though in many other ways we couldn't have been more different. Most of them were male. Almost all of them were Black or Latinx. They were in for drug offenses, for robbery, for murder. There was a psych unit, although they called it something different. That was my favorite unit. That's where you would find the transgender kids, Latinx youth born biological males whose mothers kicked them out after they caught them using their eyeliner. There would be girls who weren't afraid to stand in front of their peers and rap, boys who would talk to you about their feelings. The kids in the psych unit were some of the few who actually wrote. They turned their anger at the world into hard-hitting poems and raps.

Then there was the max unit. I wasn't usually assigned that one. The kids there didn't talk much, at least not to me. I remember once trying to engage a quiet boy with a mop of dark hair and sleeves pulled low over his hands. He was hunched over his paper and I thought I could get him to talk to me about what he was writing or drawing. He ignored me. I kept talking.

Finally, another kid pulled me aside. "You know who that is, don't you?"

I shook my head.

"He's the one who killed his parents."

"Oh," I said.

I hadn't been quick enough to hide the surprise on my face. The kid noticed this and used it to his advantage. "I got your back," he said, with the swaggering confidence of a teenager raised on the streets. "I'm looking out for you."

I wondered if I should thank him.

I tried to choose another kid to work with after that. But I was having trouble focusing on the writing prompts we provided the kids at the beginning of each session. I knew some of the youth were in for murder; I just never knew which ones. Now that I knew what that particular boy had done—remembered all the gruesome details I had read in news articles—I had trouble forgetting it. I understood the other kid hadn't been protecting me. He had been testing me.

They liked to challenge us. Once I got into a heated argument with one of them. I shouldn't have. I am the adult. I am the calm and caring "nice lady." Only a few people know about the anger I hide underneath. It isn't as explosive as it was when I was younger. But it's still there, if you know how to look for it. Leave it to another injured animal to sniff it out.

When I was a teenager I used to sometimes suddenly press my foot hard on the gas pedal while driving, accelerating into sharp turns and shooting forward at top speed for short straightaways. I didn't do it for fun. I did it because if I didn't, I felt I would explode. That's how angry I was. That's how fast it hit.

These kids changed just as quickly. One minute I was helping a boy with his writing. The next I was being jostled as another boy launched himself at a third boy. The two boys locked together in a fight. Several guards stepped in close.

"Pepper spray—get back," one of the guards shouted as he began to spray.

I backed into the side of the room, my throat itching, my eyes watering.

"Into your cells," another guard shouted.

The two boys kept fighting, so consumed by anger they didn't notice the pepper spray. The other boys hurried away from the commotion and the pepper spray. They lined up outside their cell doors. A guard let them in and then locked them in. Two other guards were separating the still-entwined fighting teenagers. I watched as they handcuffed the smaller one. He was little, no bigger than a twelve-year-old. He may have been that young; there were a few twelve-year-olds at the facility. Yet the guards were scared of him, scared of what he might do.

He was a child. He also might have been a father. He had done things in his young life that society didn't know how to handle. Here he was not an adolescent. He was an inmate.

In case you were in danger of forgetting, there were plenty of reminders: lockdown, pencil counts, gun lockers, security doors. Still, there were times you forgot, times when you were able to remember they were children as well as inmates.

One of those times happened when I was working with a new boy, trying to help him write about one of that week's writing prompts. Maybe we had taken the easy prompt about a sports star. Maybe we had taken the current events prompt about a legal or political issue. Maybe we were just pretending to write. I can't remember what prompt we used, if we used any. What I remember is his tears.

Teenage boys don't cry. Incarcerated teenage boys definitely don't cry. But this kid was crying. At first it was just a tear or two, his head hunched over his paper. Then there were more, enough that others could see. I waited for the teasing to start, the joking and prodding of the other youth. I waited for the boy to wipe his face and pretend something was caught in his eye. Instead he kept crying. And the others kept quiet. Then he looked up and asked me a question.

"What's going to happen to me?"

I had no idea what to tell him. I was there with him because I was almost as lost as he was. The pain was still inside me and I had no idea how to get it out. For years I had been telling other people's stories. I wrote about gay teenagers growing up in religious families in the South, African immigrants whose families were stuck in refugee camps in Kenya, children left behind in Estonia by Russian military fathers after the collapse of the Soviet Union. The settings, scenes, and sources changed. The silence did not. I tried to fill it with the written word.

The detention facility was different. I did not go there to write. I went to listen.

Then I saw the boy in the straitjacket. That is when I realized their stories were connected to my story—and it was the story I had never told. My story is very different from that of the boy in the jacket: the beginning, the end, even the middle. Being white and middle-class (socially if not always economically), I had privileges he did not. All stories are unique, as unique as the people who live them. Yet there is a connection, the same connection in almost everything I had ever written, the part I had for so long been remembering to forget. It is the pain that no one wanted to see, the hurt that was hidden away. We had disappeared. Concealed in detention facilities and psych units, we were easy to forget, to overlook, to ignore. I wanted society to see us—and their failure.

To bring us back I needed to talk about what happened inside. Aside from my brief visits to the detention facility, I can't say what went on there. What I can say is what happened where I was. It was the one story I had never told because I had never known how to tell it. As a child I did not have the words to express myself, although I did write some things down. I acted out in other ways—with my body, like the boys. The straitjacket silenced the one way we had left to express ourselves. They took that away from us.

After I left the detention facility that day, I called my mother. I didn't trust my memory. I needed to know if it was correct.

It was. She had seen me in a straitjacket. The hospital staff had warned her before she entered my room. I have trouble listening to her describe it. The vision isn't what bothers me. It's the feeling that comes with it—the killing of all communication. Over the years I remembered to forget that feeling. But it must have been there somewhere, leading me toward the stories of others who had been muzzled.

Now that I remembered, I needed to do what I hadn't been able to do before. I had helped others tell their stories; now I needed to tell my own.

Along the way I discovered other things that had happened to me.

I always thought the way the left side of my rib cage juts out at the bottom, almost like an extra breast, was something I was born with, a defect in my biology. My mother told me it wasn't. It developed after. That is what we say: *after*.

My sister always told me I was never the same after the hospital. I thought she said it to hurt me, to make me feel bad for destroying myself, for spending months in a children's psychosomatic unit. She said I was sweet before and angry after.

She was right.

A TASTE
1986

I am pretty sure they were serving pizza that day. I was lucky. I didn't like pizza anyway. I had planned things out the weekend before. Every day my dad gave me a dollar for lunch. If I saved the bills, after a few months, I would have quite a stack. Imagine how happy Dad would be when I gave him all that money! I could pay for gas and food.

Things hadn't been so good recently. Dad didn't have a job and the bills were piling up. Ever since my mom left him back when I was in first grade, four years ago, Dad has been hurting. She took everything. Left him with nothing. That's what he says. It isn't really true, though. Because she left us behind: She left me and Anya behind. That's my sister, Anya.

For the past few years we have been going back and forth every week between Dad's house and wherever Mom is living. In the beginning, when Mom didn't have a place to go, we could only visit her during the day, and not sleep over. Then she started staying in friends' homes when they were on vacation. We got some good deals out of that one. There was the house with the TV and VCR. It even had a pool. We watched *Grease* way too many times.

It gets confusing. At school sometimes we have to fill out papers with our address and phone number and I don't always know what to put. The other kids think I'm slow because I can't remember my home address. I let them think that; it's easier than having to explain.

I memorized my best friend Erin's phone number and address a long time ago. It doesn't change every few weeks like mine. When she answers her phone, strange people don't ask who she is and where the real owners of the house are. I never know what to tell them. Sometimes I just hang up.

Mom will live in a condo soon. If she loses it, we'd have to stay with Dad all the time. Not that I would mind. Well, I mean, I would. But it isn't because I don't love Dad. I do. Only, sometimes it's hard being with him. He hasn't gotten much of what he wanted in life. I'm trying to fix that.

That's why I started saving the dollar bills. I thought they might help. I was pretty proud of myself for my sacrifice (that's a word Dad uses a lot). It felt like not eating lunch was kind of like how you give something up at Lent, although I actually never really do that. But it sounds the same; at least, I think it does. We kind of stopped going to church after the divorce, so I am not really sure about all the rules anymore. I go to a Catholic school, but aside from a lot of the teachers being nuns, we don't really talk much about God and all that stuff.

Anyhow, I felt pretty proud of myself when I walked through the cafeteria line smelling all the warm food and eating nothing. The teachers wouldn't let me go straight to the playground after the bell rang for lunch. That's why I walked past the pizza and hamburgers, even though I knew I wasn't going to buy anything. After my tour of the cafeteria I ran to the playground, which I had to myself for at least fifteen minutes while the other kids were eating. Grown-ups are strange. They make me go to the cafeteria, but no one makes me eat. So, I don't.

At first the hunger pains were hard to ignore. But after a few weeks it got easier. The pain wasn't as sharp, and everything was working out. I even started doing the same thing when I was at my mom's house every other week. I'm tall for my age and have always been skinny. The last time I was at the doctor's I think I weighed around eighty-five pounds. It's probably less now. But I have more money for Dad.

I keep the dollar bills in the dresser I share with Anya. The dresser is lime green. It's so old and bunged-up that Dad let us put stickers on it. I have another stash of bills at my mom's house. I plan to give the money to Dad when the pile gets bigger. I hope it will make him smile.

He hasn't really smiled since Mom left. Although to be truthful, I'm not sure he smiled that much even when she was there. I didn't really notice back then because it wasn't my job. Mom was around so she could take care of Dad. Now there is no one to look after him.

Anya is two years older than me, but she's more interested in her friends and doesn't really pay attention to what's going on at home. I'm the one who makes sure the carpet is vacuumed and we have milk to drink. At least, when there is money to buy stuff.

That's kind of been the problem. Money. Dad hasn't paid tuition at our school. I know this because one of the teachers asked me about it. I can't remember exactly what they said, but I remember what I said. Nothing. What could I say?

When I tried to fix things with the telephone operator I only messed them up more. I was so worried about how I would explain it all to Dad when he got home. I think the electricity had already been turned off. Or maybe that was just a threat and we had electricity still. It gets a bit jumbled up in my head sometimes. I remember the phone call with the operator, though, and how she told me she was going to cut off our phone service for nonpayment. I also remember having to tell Dad about it. He wasn't happy. But then again, he is never happy. I really needed to do something more to help.

I once sold wrapping paper and magazine subscriptions door to door. I'm kind of shy, so it didn't work too well. Saving my lunch money seemed like a better idea. All I had to do was not eat. It was really simple. I started slowly, at first still taking free bites of food from my friends. They were harder to deal with than the adults. One of the first times they gave me trouble, I was huddled with four of them under the trees at the far end of the school playground. Erin was the one sharing. I think she was doing it just for me, but the others pretended.

"These new granola bars taste like fresh cookies. Try some, you guys," Erin said.

She passed a chocolate chip granola bar around our little circle. The other girls took a bite before passing it to me. I smiled and passed it back to Erin.

"Come on, Katya, just taste it," one of the girls coaxed.

"You're getting so skinny, you really should eat," another said, pulling at my baggy navy-blue uniform sweater.

I don't remember exactly how the plan changed. It just did. Not eating Erin's granola bars wouldn't save any money for Dad, but I still couldn't eat.

"Just take a bite. It's really good," Erin said.

She held the granola bar out to me.

I looked at her. Erin had dimples when she smiled, something she hated. Her mom used to fix her long blonde hair into two braids or ponytails, but now she did it herself in a single ponytail. When I slept over at her house, her mom made us pancakes shaped like Mickey Mouse.

I looked down at the granola bar again. I shook my head and swallowed.

"Aren't you hungry?"

Again, I shook my head.

I looked at my friends' puzzled expressions. I was hungry, terribly hungry, but it wasn't a hunger that food could fill.

I think my friends must have told their parents, or the teachers, because rumors spread. My mother, sister, and the witch, otherwise known as Rebecca the psychologist, showed concern. But no one did anything. I guess maybe Rebecca tried. She was the first psychologist I had to see after my parents' divorce. This is how it went.

My dad got the house. Anya and I got suitcases.

Every Friday we packed our bags. Saturday, we unpacked. By Friday we were doing it all over again. Back and forth we went. One week at Mom's house, or wherever she was currently living, and then one week at Dad's. Mom's place tended to be better. Dad's got worse. I worried when I was with Mom how bad it would be at Dad's when I got back. I wondered how many fleas would jump on my legs when I walked through my room, and if there would be anything to eat besides a stale bag of popcorn or frozen dinners. We called the dinners "hot disgust," but I think their real name was Hungry-Man.

Then there were the rules. They were always changing. It was hard to keep track of who wanted us to do what, and which way. Plus, Dad would complain about Mom and I had to figure out if he wanted me to say something to Mom about this, or if it was a secret I was supposed to keep. Mom sometimes had me pass on messages to Dad. He usually ignored them, which made me worry Mom would think I hadn't told him.

I thought it was pretty clear they were the ones who needed a therapist, but the weird thing is, Anya and I were the ones who got stuck with Rebecca. There was some rule about kids and custody. Kids went back and forth. The parents got to stay wherever they wanted. And because they were the ones going back and forth, the kids were the ones who had to see a therapist. Which is how Anya and I ended up with Rebecca. Being two years older than me and better at answering questions, Anya only saw Rebecca a few times. I was a return customer.

Mom liked Rebecca because she was cheap—she hadn't gotten all her training yet. She had long black hair that looked as stiff and dry as a horse's mane. Her face was a fleshy oval with a saggy chin and pouches for cheeks. She was younger than my mom, but too old to remember what it was like to be a kid. She wore loose, flowing dresses with strange pictures on them or pants that hugged her round belly. She wasn't very tall, but her voice was tough, kind of like Alice on *The Brady Bunch*. I hated her staring dark eyes.

I was skinnier and quieter than Anya. But I had always been skinny and quiet. Rebecca hadn't known me since I was a little kid, though, and she thought it was weird that I didn't talk to her. She began to bug me even more than usual during our regular sessions.

"Are the little dolls married?" Rebecca asked.

I looked up from the dollhouse I was playing with and shrugged my shoulders; she would never just let me play. I thought doctors like her were supposed to understand you by watching you, not by asking dumb questions.

I picked up the little baby doll and placed it in the living room of the dollhouse.

"Why is the baby in the living room? Is the baby crying?"

She sounded like an excited child. Would she believe me if I told her I'd put the baby in the living room because it was the easiest room to get to in the fancy dollhouse?

I started to move the little people about, bending their plastic legs so they could sit in the chairs.

"Are the parents happy? Why haven't you used this one?" Rebecca asked.

She wagged a male doll in my face.

I grabbed the doll and shoved him in the bedroom. I hadn't used him because he was ugly. She was probably thinking it was because of Dad or Tyrone, the older boy who'd hurt me. That had happened around the same time as the divorce, and was another thing adults seemed to want me to talk about.

I had kept quiet for months on that one. I was worried because I knew I had done something I wasn't supposed to when Tyrone had brought me into the boys' bathroom. I didn't want to get in trouble, and I didn't want to have a baby. It was the headaches and stomach-aches that gave me away. Finally I told Anya, even though Tyrone told me not to tell. Anya promised not to tell. But she did. Then I had to talk to more people about it. People are always asking me to talk. The thing is, I don't know what they want me to say.

I looked one last time at the dollhouse before getting up from the floor and walking to the couch. I could hear Rebecca's loud steps behind me. I sat down and stared at the clock on the wall, counting the minutes until my mom would come.

"Why did you stop playing?" Rebecca asked.

She actually waited for me to shrug my shoulders before continuing.

"Why have you stopped eating?"

Again, she waited while I shrugged my shoulders.

"Was the happy dollhouse too upsetting?"

I never answered her questions. I never even thought about what they meant. I would sit super still on the couch and stare at the toys in the room. After the dollhouse talk I decided it was easier if I just sat and watched the toys instead of playing with them. I would sit on the edge of the couch, watching the clock and the toys, remembering to shrug my shoulders whenever I noticed Rebecca had gone quiet. I left the talking to Rebecca.

When the time was up, she would follow me into the waiting room so she could update my mom. After the visit with the dollhouse, I started to wonder if Rebecca's imagination was even bigger than mine.

"I see definite improvement," Rebecca whispered to my mother. "Every session she gets a little better."

I hurried away and joined my sister by the door. My mom followed behind with a smile on her face. Mom was the only one who ever left Rebecca's with a smile. She started humming as we walked to the car. She was still humming when we were out on the street. It was kind of annoying that she was happy when I was not.

"Mom, you're wasting your money," I said as I opened the car door. "I hate her. We don't do anything."

I stopped and waited to see if she was listening to me. The humming had stopped.

"Please don't make me go anymore."

"She says you're making progress," Mom said, turning around to face me. She was standing in the street holding her car door open, not noticing the cars whizzing by. Her dark-green suit looked wrinkled. The shoulder pads in her jacket had slipped out of place, and there was a snag in her pantyhose beginning at her right foot. Her shoulders hunched forward and her legs twitched. For the first time I noticed all the wrinkles that lined her eyes and the way she held her mouth tightly shut. I stared at the little bump on her nose, the one I gave her as a baby when I was sitting in her lap and hit her nose with my big head. I looked at the new wrinkles around her mouth and wondered if I had caused those as well.

"Don't worry about the money, Katya," Mom said. "She's cheaper than all the others."

I thought about what she said. Rebecca was cheaper than the others were.

"There's a reason for that," I said.

Anya laughed.

The only thing my sister had gotten out of the few times she'd spent with Rebecca right after the divorce was the free drinks. The one time Rebecca ran out of hot chocolate packets, Anya had to be coaxed to go in. If there wasn't anything in it for her, Anya didn't see why she should go.

THE PATIENTS
2019

The *before* was always missing. I didn't know what the youth at the detention facility had done. Maybe that is as it should be. The *before* wasn't what interested me. It was what was done to me inside—and why—that did. And yet I wouldn't have been inside if what happened before hadn't happened.

Tyrone wasn't why I ended up in the hospital. He was just the first person who taught me adults couldn't be counted on to protect you. I was with my mom when it happened. She was the adult in charge, the parent who had volunteered to watch the younger kids on the playground. I was in first grade. Tyrone was in eighth grade. Mom was in a failing marriage.

Tyrone wanted to show me something. He started walking toward the school building where we both studied, and where eighth graders and first graders were paired as buddies. Tyrone wasn't my buddy. I followed him into the building anyway.

He headed to the boys' bathroom. I didn't want to go there. But I didn't want to disappoint him either. He was bigger than me.

Blue walls. Mine were pink.

He took me into a stall. Then he took down his pants. I don't remember what happened next. Did he lift up my uniform skirt? Did I let him? Did he ask me to touch his penis, and if he did, did I?

What I remember are the blue walls and the promise I made. I wouldn't tell. And I didn't.

It wasn't words that gave me away, it was my body. Headaches and stomachaches said what I couldn't. I worried I might be pregnant, even though there was no penetration. He had molested me; he hadn't raped me. But as a six-year-old I didn't know the difference. What I knew was I had been with a boy doing things I wasn't supposed to be doing. I knew things I shouldn't.

Anya pried it out of me. She promised me as I had promised Tyrone that she wouldn't tell. But Anya didn't keep things inside like I did. After Anya told, I had to repeat my story again to my parents, and then to the police. Tyrone didn't have to do anything. I had to listen to self-defense lectures at school, talks about how to scream and fight back, reminders of how I hadn't done either. The teachers explained that something had happened to a student. They didn't say who. They didn't have to. The kids would sneak looks at me. Talking hadn't helped.

What Tyrone did could have landed him in juvenile detention. It didn't. He was given a second chance. I was the one who ended up in an institution, a juvenile psychosomatic unit. Tyrone was just a small part of how I got there. There is much more to the *before*. And more to what happened inside. To understand the latter I needed to understand juvenile psychiatry—the stigma associated with it, and its relationship to medicine, and, yes, juvenile detention.

In *Child Psychiatry* Leo Kanner cites four factors that played a major role in the development of child psychiatry in the twentieth century. One of them is the development of juvenile courts. Another is the "humanization" of the field. The two others have not fared as well since the 700-plus-page book, considered one of the founding texts in the field, was first published in 1935. There is the mental hygiene movement—the idea that mental illness might be prevented in a similar way to how vaccines prevent diseases. I rather like that one; if only it were that easy. Then there is psychometry, the establishment of tests to serve as a guide for academic placement, which resulted in some students being judged less mentally developed.

Of the two factors still relevant today, humanization is the most accessible. In the early years of psychiatry, Kanner explains that "psychiatric curiosity extended to the mental illness of people rather than to the people who were mentally ill." He goes on to say that what the patient *had* was more important than who they *were*. Over time psychiatrists like Sigmund Freud started to examine present issues in terms of the past, which led to understanding childhood, which in turn led to the formation of child psychiatry. As had been initially the case with adult psychiatry, the focus on child psychiatry did not at first involve actual children. In fact, Kanner notes that Freud published his theory of infantile sexuality in 1905, three years before he saw a child professionally.

Around the same time, toward the tail end of the previous century, in the late 1880s, the first juvenile courts began to appear. The courts were a response to a questioning of the logic of subjecting juveniles to the same punishment as adults. Judges were granted increasing authority as the courts continued to develop, including the ability to remove children from their homes and place them in foster care. In time judges began to question why the children were misbehaving in the first place. That is when they turned to psychologists and psychiatrists, linking justice and juvenile psychiatry in a partnership that continues to this day.

Judges in the juvenile courts were not the only ones who wanted to understand the reasons behind juvenile delinquency. In *Psychiatric Times* Dr. John Schowalter describes how a group of socially concerned women established the Juvenile Psychopathic Institute in 1909 to study the motivations of young offenders. The institute relied on teams composed of a neuropsychiatrist, a psychologist, and a social worker to provide evaluation and treatment strategies, a setup that was copied by child guidance clinics for most of the twentieth century.

They didn't always say it, but the question most professionals wanted answered involved merit. Are the offenders young enough that their behavior can be blamed on something else, making them worthy of reform? Or are they fully at fault and thus unredeemable? It is the same question that plagues not just child psychiatry but psychiatry as a whole. Is there something medically wrong with the mentally ill that merits medical attention and treatment, or are they just acting out, causing their own destruction?

In *The Great Pretender: The Undercover Mission that Changed Our Understanding of Madness*, Susannah Cahalan describes how her care improved after her psychiatric diagnosis was changed to a neurological one. Cahalan says that it was as if a mental illness were her fault, while a physical illness "was something unearned, something 'real.'"

I understand what she is talking about. It is the reason I have trouble watching doomed romance movies about teens dying of cancer. Others feel sympathy. I feel anger. People empathize with the child they can do little to help. Yet the child who is dying inside, who needs attention, is ignored because their disease isn't deemed worthy. When we can do something, we don't. That is what the movies remind me of: the children we ignore, not the ones we can't save.

I am not being completely fair. There have been efforts to change this for children and adults. It was in part to address this attitude that psychiatric care began to move from isolated asylums and institutions, which offered little treatment, toward inclusion in general hospitals, in the 1930s.

Don R. Lipsett explains in *World Psychiatry* that it was believed this change would lessen the stigma of mental illness. It was thought that in general hospitals, patients would be closer to their communities and treated in more "humane" settings. The first full-time children's psychiatric clinic in the United States was established at a pediatric hospital in 1930, when Kanner joined the Harriet Lane Pediatric Clinic at Johns Hopkins University. Studies on the mind–body connection and the return of traumatized soldiers from the battlefields of World War II helped drive the shift from separate hospitals to general hospitals, according to Lipsett. So did the passage of the Community Mental Health Centers Construction Act in 1963, which increased funding for psychiatric beds in general hospitals and expanded the mental health coverage of government insurance programs.

Yet even as people objected to large psychiatric hospitals and demanded their closure, it did not mean they accepted that a mentally ill patient was just as "sick" and blameless for their sickness as a breast cancer patient. The use of pharmaceuticals to treat mental illness did little to change the stigma.

Part of the attempt to again remedy this led to the development of medical-psychiatric or psychosomatic units in the 1980s and 1990s. The idea was to treat medical and psychiatric illnesses together instead of independently, as Dr. Paul Summergrad explained in a *General Hospital Psychiatry* article. In 1994 Summergrad referred to the development of medical-psychiatric or "med-psych" units as the most important conceptual shift in the past decade in terms of general hospital inpatient psychiatric care.

The shift was short-lived. For children it began around 1977, when the first widely cited mention of a children's med-psych unit appears in texts. It came just over two decades after the establishment of the American Academy of Child Psychiatry in 1953. The first children's med-psych unit was at the Children's Hospital Medical Center in Boston. Stanford was next. On July 5, 1978, two years after I was born, the Roth Psychosomatic Unit at Children's Hospital at Stanford opened.

On September 17, 1986, I became patient number 090 71 51.

STORY TIME
1986

There was a mouse living behind the stove at Dad's house and even more fleas living in our bedroom carpet. Anya and I figured out how to hop from our bunk bed to the hallway without stepping on the carpet.

Mom had moved again. Another landlord hadn't liked us kids. We didn't like him either.

It was almost spring, only a month or so until Easter, but at Dad's house the Christmas tree was still up. It was in the corner of the room, brown and dry, the needles piled up on the floor below it. The tinsel and colored-glass decorations looked weird on the branches now that most of the green needles had fallen off. Our Christmas tree, which was supposed to make you happy, was now a dead decoration. It didn't really look out of place. Dad's house was always dark, maybe to match his mood.

He had stopped marking off his job hunt on the calendar months ago. Sometimes he didn't even change the month. It was like he was stuck. At first, I thought it was because Mom had left him and he'd lost his job, but I think it actually started even earlier than that. I think he got stuck when he was just a kid, like me.

We were sitting in the living room. He was eating. I wasn't.

Dad looked at me as he grabbed a handful of stale popcorn.

"Did I ever tell you about the time Grandma Marge broke my piggy bank to get money to drink?" he asked. He never called her Mom. She was always Grandma Marge.

I nodded, but he didn't seem to notice.

"I had saved up enough to buy one of those nice ceramic piggy banks, the kind you can only get the money out of by breaking them. I didn't have much money yet, only a little change..."

I had heard it all before. The time she broke his piggy bank, the time she danced in the snow in her nightgown, all the times she crashed the car with Dad in it. And so many other stupid things she had done when she was drunk—which happened to be most of Dad's childhood. At least that's how he told it.

I decided not to mention the Christmas money Grandma Marge had given me and Anya that year, which he'd made us give him. He'd said he needed it to buy gas so he could drive us to school. He wasn't an alcoholic, but he stole from us just the same.

The shades were down. I couldn't see the sun, or my sister and the neighborhood kids, who I knew were outside playing. I could hear them, though. Anya was laughing at Christina's cheap new perm. The door was only ten feet away: ten feet to sunshine, ten feet to freedom.

Still, I couldn't leave him. If I did, he would have no one. He would never forgive me. Every chance he'd get he would remind me how I went out to play while he was left alone in misery.

That's how it always was. Anya would leave and go play with the Christinas—there were two of them on our street. Whenever I tried to follow, Dad would look at me and say: "Go ahead. Leave your old man here to rot."

It worked. I would stay and watch him smoke his pipe and stare at the white snow on the TV screen. The TV was always on, but usually nothing was actually playing. That didn't seem to bother Dad. Sometimes I would try to clean, but most of the time I just sat real quiet, wondering what it was I needed to do to make the ghost leave and my dad return.

Dad looked at me again.

"Did I ever tell you about my uncle?"

I started to nod my head and then realized I hadn't ever heard any stories about his uncle.

"No, you never told me about your uncle."

He nodded his head and continued. For once he had listened to me.

"I was about your age when it happened. It was all over the papers, small immigrant town, you know."

He took a break to pack more tobacco in his pipe. I wanted to open a window, but I knew Dad wouldn't like that, so I stayed still. He wasn't looking at me anymore. Once he started talking, he stopped looking at me. Sometimes I wondered if he was back in Indiana with Grandma Marge instead of in California with me.

"My dad's brother and his wife had two daughters," he explained. "Even though they didn't live far from us, I didn't see my cousins that often."

He took a puff from his pipe. He was a slow storyteller. I thought about my own cousins. Their dad, my mom's older brother, was a doctor. He was fun. When we went places in his car, he would blast "Burning Down the House" and we would sing along.

Dad didn't do things like that. He made me nervous. I was always scared I would upset him.

He was talking again. I tried to listen, but a sore on my arm was distracting me. I had fallen against a table a week ago and cut my arm. Usually it seemed like cuts healed pretty fast, but this one looked the same as it had right after I fell: red, angry, and now a bit purple as well. I wondered why it was taking so long to heal.

"From what I remember they were pretty girls, a little younger than me, and quite well behaved."

He stopped and looked at the snowy TV screen. He closed his eyes for a minute.

I wondered if he was trying to picture his cousins. Two little girls, kind of like me and Anya. He had never talked about his cousins before. I talked about mine a lot. If I lived in the same town as them, like he did with his cousins, I would probably talk about them even more.

"Yes, they were nice girls, from what little I remember. Anyhow, my uncle went off to the war and when he came back, he was never quite the same—at least, that's what everyone said."

He stopped, as if deciding how to finish the story. I wasn't sure which war he was talking about, but I knew it was better not to ask.

"One night, while his family was sleeping, he killed his wife and then his two little girls."

I stopped picking at my sore. I looked up at Dad, waiting for him to tell me he was joking. But he didn't. Instead he started telling me how it happened, the details, as if that mattered.

"He didn't shoot them; he smothered them with pillows and then hit them with hard objects. After he killed them, he wrote a note about how the world was too awful of a place for his family to live in, and then he shot himself."

Dad took a deep breath before continuing.

"It was all over the papers the next day. That's when the kids started singing, 'Jingle jangle, here comes Cengel,' whenever they saw me."

He was singing, the spit on his lips stretching as he opened his mouth wide for the words.

"That was my new nickname, Jangle, in honor of my uncle's deeds, and because it rhymed. Everyone at school knew. Everyone in the town knew."

He stopped and shook his head.

"He was my father's brother, for goodness' sake. When she wasn't drunk, my mother knew."

I looked at Dad. He was looking at the TV screen. I wanted to bring him back.

"What were they like, your cousins?" I asked.

He didn't answer.

"Dad, what were your cousins like?" I tried again.

My dad turned to look at me, his lips curled down. "I don't remember, Katya. I don't remember."

I tried to think of something to say. Somehow the silence was worse than Dad's words.

His uncle had been sad. Dad was sad. His cousins were about my age when it happened.

Why had he told me?

The girls were killed in their sleep.

I looked at Dad; his large right hand was holding a soda. I had always been scared of his hands. I couldn't remember his hands ever hitting me. Actually, I could hardly remember his hands ever touching me. Besides spankings and a few quick hugs, I had never felt Dad's hands. I always played with Mom's hands, crossing and uncrossing her fingers while she talked to her friends. Dad, with his tall skinny body and hangdog face, I barely touched. My friends were scared of him, especially the ones who had made him mad. I never told them, but he scared me, too, for his silences more than his size.

The girls were killed in their sleep. They hadn't done anything. They were kids. Their father killed them. Their sad father killed them.

I kept the story inside me, like I kept what Tyrone did to me inside. Only this time even Anya didn't get it out of me.

When my mother dropped me off at Dad's house, I would stare at her face, trying to see if I could tell whether she knew about Dad's cousins. I didn't know how to ask her.

I did ask her other things, though.

I was sitting on her bed, watching her choose what suit she would wear to work. It was a holiday, but she still had to work. After she left Dad she took a job as a stockbroker at Merrill Lynch. Sometimes I would go to her office after school, but usually Anya and I just went home. She worked long hours and made just enough to "scrape by." We didn't stay in other people's houses anymore—at least, not exactly. The places we stayed weren't free anymore, and they lasted a little longer. We were renters. We even got a black-and-white TV.

I watched my mother choose a pair of earrings, waiting for her to look at me.

"Mom, I can't live there anymore. I can't live at Dad's house," I said.

It wasn't the first time I'd tried talking to her about Dad. For a few months I had been asking her to get full custody of my sister and me. She wasn't listening. But I kept talking. I didn't know what else to do. Dad was slipping away—and he was taking me with him.

"Katya, we've been through this," she said.

She pulled a blue scarf from her closet door and turned to look at me. It was warm in the room, but I had goose bumps on my arms. Lately it seemed like I was always cold.

"The court awarded joint custody. For me to get full custody, your father would have to basically kill one of you."

She gave a funny laugh but stopped when she saw me, her youngest daughter, sitting on the bed in front of her. There was no laughter on my face.

"Besides, I wouldn't be able to work nearly as hard if I had you and your sister full-time."

My mother pulled out a dark red suit and a cream blouse.

"While you guys are at your dad's, I put in long hours so we can have money. Things would be a lot harder if I had you guys all the time."

My mom pulled the clothes off the hangers and began to put them on.

"Besides, it wouldn't be fair to your dad. It would really upset him if his kids were taken away."

I pulled my face up from the pillow and looked at my mother. She was stabbing her earrings into her ears.

"I have to go. I'm going to be late." She reached out and patted my head. "Make sure you eat well today, okay. Even if it is just Ensure."

I put my head down and nodded into the pillow. I listened for the click-clack of her high-heeled shoes as she walked down the stairs.

"What about me? If you couldn't live with him, why do we have to?" I asked.

When I raised my head from the pillow the room was empty.

May 12, 1953

Whiting Man Beats Wife, Two Children to Death...

Whiting, Ind., (INS)—A Whiting store owner beat his wife and two children to death and then killed himself Monday while police rushed to his home.

Deputy Coroner Peter Stecy said eight notes found in the apartment indicated that Cengel's wife and children were already dead when Cengel telephoned Desk Sgt. Michael Zubeck that he was planning to kill them, and himself.

Dr. Stecy said the notes showed that Mrs. Cengel and the youngsters had been murdered three or four hours before Cengel committed suicide.

One of the notes written in pencil on pieces of paper, read: "I confess to Almighty God with all my heart that it couldn't be helped. Now please bury us all together as we lived."

Hunger
1986

"Anya, Katya, come here," Mom called.

I got up from my spot on the living-room rug and walked to the door. Getting up took quite a bit of energy, but Mom sounded excited, so I figured it was worth it. I stood still a minute, waiting for the stars I always saw now when I first stood up to go away. My sister appeared from the kitchen, a bowl of ice cream in her hands.

"I've got a surprise for you guys."

Mom placed her briefcase by the door and pulled off her shoes.

"What?" Anya asked.

"You know how we've been having competitions at work to win trips to places?"

My sister and I nodded our heads excitedly, waiting for her to continue.

"Well, I won a weekend in Santa Cruz. We're going to spend a weekend at the beach."

"Santa Cruz—it has a boardwalk with rides and stuff, doesn't it?" Anya asked.

"Will we stay in a hotel?" I asked. "One with a pool?"

"Yes, yes," Mom said, smiling at our excitement. "The hotel is right on the beach and it has a pool and a Jacuzzi."

"Thanks, Mom," I said as I touched her hand.

"Yeah, thanks," Anya echoed. "When do we get to go?"

"It's your dad's week next, so we'll have to wait two weeks before we can go."

I told everyone. The trip was all I talked about. It seemed like we never went anywhere, and now finally we were going to go away for a weekend and spend it in a hotel on the beach. For the first time in months I was excited. I thought about something besides how to avoid my next meal. I thought about the trip. I couldn't wait to tell Dad.

"Guess what, Dad? Mom won a trip to Santa Cruz, and we're gonna go the weekend after next. We're gonna stay at a hotel with a pool and room service and the beach."

I stopped talking and looked at my Dad's long face. "What's wrong, Dad?"

"I never get to go anywhere," he said.

He sat in his chair in front of the TV, his long legs stretched in front of him. He wore a pair of wrinkled blue pants and a short-sleeved button-up shirt. His brown hair hung in his face; it looked as if he hadn't combed it since the day before.

"I'm sorry."

"While you guys are off at the beach having fun, I'll be all alone in this house."

He took a long slow swig of his warm soda before continuing. He didn't look at me. His bloodshot eyes were focused on the TV screen in front of him.

"I can't remember the last time I went on a vacation," he said. "I wish I could go to the beach, just spend a weekend relaxing."

He gave a long sigh and put down his soda. Then he looked at me.

He didn't leave it at that. Every chance he got, Dad would talk about his miserable life and how he never got to go on vacation.

It was more than envy. He hated Mom. If he wasn't happy, he didn't want her to be.

I still wanted to go to Santa Cruz. I even planned to eat, or at least drink. I was going to get a hot chocolate from room service. It would probably have whipped cream. I don't really like whipped cream, but I liked the idea of a hot chocolate with a neat swirl of white on top, brought to my room on a tray. That would be special. I pictured sitting on the bed, the knock at the door, the first sip.

But then the picture started to go fuzzy and another one took over. No matter how hard I tried to squint it away, all I saw was Dad sitting in the dark, drinking a warm soda. The imaginary sip of hot chocolate stuck in my throat. My tummy tightened.

I started to fear that if I went to Santa Cruz it would be even worse. Even with a real hot chocolate in my hands I wouldn't be able to feel its warmth. In the room I wouldn't see Anya and Mom; I would see Dad back home alone. I wouldn't be on the beach or in the hotel pool but in the dark living room with him. There wasn't any point in going to a hotel if I was still stuck back at Dad's house.

I wasn't sure how to explain this to Mom. I really wanted to go, but Dad wouldn't let me. He kept pulling me back. If I went while he was pulling me, I would ruin the fun for everyone. Just like Dad did. I couldn't do that to Mom and Anya. If I stayed home maybe Dad would be happy and then I could be happy, happier than if I was in a hotel drinking hot chocolate.

I asked Mom to leave me with Dad.

"I don't understand. Don't you want to swim in the hotel pool and see the beach?" Mom asked.

I did. And I didn't. I didn't know how to tell her this, so I just shook my head and went silent. When words didn't work, I stopped using them.

"Your dad will be fine without you, Katya. He can take care of himself."

I wondered how she knew this. She never went inside the house anymore. She left us at the door when she dropped us off. She hadn't been bitten by the fleas, spotted the mouse behind the stove, or searched for milk that wasn't there.

"Katya, look at me," she said, grabbing my chin so I was facing her. "I'm not going to let your dad ruin this trip. I worked hard for it. You're going, whether you want to or not."

It turns out she wasn't really worried about Dad. She just didn't want to let him win.

I was confused. Everything had gotten twisted. Whatever I did I was going to disappoint one of them. Part of me was glad I didn't have a choice, that I got to go to Santa Cruz. On the drive I even got a little excited as we got closer to the hotel. Then I thought about Dad at home alone without anyone to keep him company and my stomach started to tighten, and I had trouble talking. I couldn't be there and here.

It was too late to go to the pool the first night, and when we woke up the next morning it was raining. We stayed inside waiting for the rain to stop, but it never did. Instead of the beach we went shopping. Anya found a pastel purple shirt that said Santa Cruz. I found a super cute, tie-dye bathing suit. Mom wanted to buy it for me, but it seemed silly getting a bathing suit when it was raining. I also wasn't sure if I deserved a present; Anya and Mom were grumbling about how I was ruining their weekend because I was so gloomy. I think the rain should have taken some of the blame, but I guess it was easier to put it all on me.

Back at the hotel I stayed inside watching the raindrops slip down the window while Mom and Anya went somewhere to explore. Anya talked about room service and the rides on the boardwalk, but I didn't really care about either. My brain was stuck on Dad. I kept thinking about him. Being happy meant forgetting about Dad, which meant feeling guilty. But even if I wanted to, I couldn't forget about him; he kept popping into my head whenever I was just about to do something fun. It made me mad. Then Mom would lecture me for sulking and being a grump. She didn't blame him. She blamed me.

Trying to be happy was exhausting. On the drive back home I decided it might be easier to stop trying.

It wasn't that hard, really. Because I wasn't much fun anymore, no one wanted to be around me. Not eating had become more than a way of saving money for Dad; it was a way out. The hunger I had felt earlier was gone, replaced by a bottomless pit that wouldn't let food in. Even when I wanted to eat, I couldn't. The less I ate, the less energy I had. I stopped doing things, even by myself.

A week passed, and then another. It was warmer now, but instead of taking off clothing I put more on. I wore a baggy green sweatshirt with a whale on it because I was cold, and because I could hide inside it. The sweatshirt covered my goose bumps and the long hairs that stood up on my arms. It seemed like everywhere except my head had more hair than it used to.

"Hi, Linda, it's Karla. I was wondering if Erin wanted to come over for an Easter egg hunt?" My mom asked as she twirled the phone cord in her hand.

I sat on the kitchen floor, hugging my knees, my blue pants hanging off of my legs. I had been wearing the same blue pants and sweatshirt for weeks now. No matter the weather, I was always cold. The outfit grew looser every day.

I didn't care whether Erin could play or not. Alone or with people, my world didn't change. I didn't notice the things around me. I tripped when I walked. I didn't comb my thinning hair. I didn't feel the bruises on my back from bumping into things.

"I see," my mom said.

She looked at me, curled in the corner.

"Could you ask her again?"

My mother waited for an answer, her hand getting stuck in the phone cord as she twirled it round and round.

"Thank you, Linda. I'll do the best I can to make sure they have fun. I'll pick her up around eight on Sunday morning then."

My mom hung up the phone and got down on the floor next to me.

"Erin's going to come for Easter and you guys can have an Easter egg hunt in the backyard."

She used her hands to turn up my face.

I pulled back.

"Did you hear what I said? Erin's going to come."

I squished up further against the wall.

"Erin didn't want to come, did she?" I said. "Her mom is making her come." I pulled my sweatshirt sleeves down over my hands.

"I'm not going to lie to you," Mom said. "You're not a lot of fun to be around right now. But Erin *is* coming. Maybe if you're more fun she'll come more often."

More fun? I felt like leaving the room, but I was too tired to get up. Everything took so much effort. The only thing I had the energy for was planning how to avoid my next meal. I no longer ate any, actually. I just had a few little snacks that were forced on me and did away with the others. I ate so slowly that my mom usually had to leave before I was done. Then I would throw the food away. At Dad's house I just fed it to the dog.

I am pretty sure I failed at being "more fun" when Erin came over for an Easter egg hunt. Mom sure was excited; I guess she thought if *she* was fun, Erin might stay longer.

"Okay, it's all set. You guys can start looking," my mom said as she flung open the front door.

Erin scurried toward the door and then turned around. "Aren't you coming?"

I shrugged my shoulders and slowly shuffled toward the door.

"Go ahead, Erin. Katya will come soon."

My mother nudged Erin out the door. Then she grabbed my arm and pulled me toward the door.

"Erin is going to find all the eggs."

I shrugged my shoulders and walked outside, standing by my mom's side, watching as Erin peeked in the bushes for eggs.

"I think there might be one in that tree," Mom said, pointing to a bright pink plastic egg in the lemon tree in front of us. It was too obvious for a ten-year-old, more like it had been hidden for a little kid.

I walked to the tree and carefully took the egg from its not very hidden hiding place. I put it in my bag and walked back to my mother.

That morning the scale read seventy-four pounds.

THE PRINCE
2018

It was a meat grinder. That's what my great-uncle used to kill his family. He used a shotgun on himself. In one newspaper account there is a picture of two policemen holding the weapons, tentative smiles, just slivers really, on their faces. The shotgun is the length of a tall cane, so long it stretches beyond the border of the photo. The meat grinder is smaller, about the size of a square box of tissues. The photo above the police officers shows the crowds gathered outside my great-uncle's apartment. Boys in neat, *Leave It to Beaver*–style haircuts and women in dresses with big prints stand facing the building. Men with hands on their hips are gathered in small groups.

There are no photos of Joseph, thirty-two, his wife Mary, thirty, or their two kids, Mary Jo, four, and Jackie, two. The children were younger than my father remembered. In newspaper accounts it isn't clear if Jackie was a boy or a girl. My great-uncle Joseph is the focus of all the stories. Before he killed himself, he called the police and told them he "was tired of living."

The first time I wrote about my dad's nightmare was when I was in college. That is also when I wrote about the Roth Psychosomatic Unit. I was trying to figure out who I was. Writing was what I used. The murder was a short story; Roth was a manuscript. It was that simple. I became a writer because of Roth.

The truth, of course, is more complicated.

I had always told stories. When I was little, they were about animals. In college, it was Roth. A professor told me I had a strong voice. I told him it was because I had something to say. I wanted to talk about how the children of Roth had been cast aside the same way problem children continued to be cast aside. Roth, and everything that happened before, had given me a mission, to tell the stories of those who had no voice.

It would take two decades as a journalist, telling the stories of others who were hurting, before I understood that to tell the story of Roth, I needed to know how those in charge saw it. I saw Roth from the inside. As a patient I did not realize—or care—that my experience came during a unique time in child psychiatry. It turns out that those in charge viewed Roth as a sort of utopia that was cut short. We can agree on that: The concept of treating mind and body together in a children's psychosomatic unit was a short-lived experiment. Not because it wasn't successful—that is still up for debate. It met its demise because insurance companies balked at paying for long-term stays for patients who after an initial period were deemed medically stable, for the most part. Money was the deciding factor. What was best for the patients had little to do with it.

There are still a few pediatric med-psych units left, but it is hard to compare them to their earlier incarnations; at least, that is what those who work in the field tell me. I can't talk to the patients. Privacy, they say. Silence is what I hear.

That is why I am telling this story from the patient perspective. My perspective. Yet I am still a journalist, and I know no story is complete unless it has all sides. I need to look at this from both the inside and the outside. That is why I want to hear from Dr. Hans Steiner, the former head psychiatrist of the Roth Unit. The man who once decided my fate, as well as the fate of everyone else on the Unit. Rarely seen yet always present, not unlike the wizard in *The Wizard of Oz*. There were those who believed the wizard could fix them. And those who feared him, possibly for the same reason. I belonged to the second group.

By the time I arrived at Roth in the mid-1980s, Dr. Steiner no longer did much day-to-day overseeing of the Unit. Later he will tell me that at that point, it was running "on autopilot," and he just performed occasional quality checks. Nevertheless, his presence was felt. Few decisions were made without him. Nurses, counselors, students, staff, patients—they all fell under his domain. I saw him infrequently, but I heard his name mentioned on an almost daily basis.

A former counselor uses the term "the Prince" to describe him. I find it fitting. Dr. Steiner was from the Old World, after all—Austria. Tall, lean, tan, he was the epitome of health, everything we patients were not. I remember how the teenage girls on the Unit used to gather around and giggle when he made an appearance. They liked him. I didn't. Granted, I liked very few people back then, especially doctors. I wanted to die. Doctors wanted me to live. The relationship was doomed from the start.

But with Dr. Steiner there was something else as well. I disliked the power he held, the way everyone looked up to him and the way I felt he looked down on the rest of us. A prince and his subjects—and we were subjects in more ways than one. Stanford was a teaching hospital. We were the patients the students needed to study, the cases the doctors and professors referenced in their papers.

The main Roth Unit articles were written before my time. I am not in any of them. That doesn't mean they don't offer clues. In one Dr. Steiner outlines the setup and demographics of the fourteen-bed unit during its first two years of existence. There were an equal number of male and female patients who ranged in age from one to twenty years old. They stayed for an average of forty days and were treated for a number of disorders, including asthma, poorly controlled diabetes, eating disorders, schizophrenic spectrum disorder, conversion reaction, rheumatoid arthritis, seizure disorders, and depression. Whatever their particular disorder, what all the patients had in common was the psychosomatic component—psychological factors were affecting physical illness.

In a subsequent article, Steiner breaks psychosomatic disorders into three types. The first type he covers is when physical illness results in a psychological disturbance. He cites the example of a child with a chronic physical illness developing suicidal depression. The second type he mentions is when psychological disturbance interferes with treatment of a physical illness, using the example of a diabetic who experiences fluctuations in blood sugar due to stress. The third type is when a psychological disturbance causes a physical illness, such as anorexia.

That is where I fit in, category three. Not that I knew it at the time. What I did know was that there were a number of children with different illnesses and a large number of staff to support them. According to Dr. Steiner's articles, the staff-to-patient ratio ranged from two-to-one to three-to-one. The staff included five psychiatrists, two pediatricians, a social worker, and pediatric and psychiatric nurses and paraprofessionals—what I like to call "counselors." I remember the staff assigned to me well, but only their first names. Dr. Steiner is one of the few whose last name I recall. I still fear the Wizard, but I am also pulled to his power, and hold out hope that he will have the answers I wasn't ready to hear as a child. Thus, it is with Dr. Steiner that I begin my search.

He is relatively easy to find. He is still associated with Stanford University and also has a private practice locally. Meeting him face-to-face is a different matter. I don't think about that before I e-mail him. I am so focused on finding him, on finding answers, that I forget how much I used to fear seeing him.

He answers my e-mail the way older people with vision problems sometimes do, in large, all-capital letters. When I knew him in the 1980s, he was in his early forties, the same age I am now, which places him in his early seventies today. We agree to meet on the Stanford campus on a summer day at one p.m. He chooses the time and location. I choose the day.

It is only after we have made the appointment that I recognize he has chosen a mealtime. It is a natural thing to do—except when meeting someone with an eating disorder. That was not my diagnosis. I never exactly had one. I had the non-diagnosis of "Deferred," followed by "Eating disorder secondary to underlying emotional state." I attempted to starve myself to death.

Eating was clearly an issue. He knows that. Many of the patients on the Unit had eating disorders.

I wonder if he is testing me. Will he be watching to see how I handle my food, looking for signs of lingering illness or full recovery?

In the days leading up to the meeting I become increasingly anxious about having to eat in front of him. Eating is still difficult for me, especially when I am uncomfortable. Dr. Steiner is a memory from my hospital stay, an association which makes me instantly uncomfortable. I remember being restrained and force-fed through a tube. A nurse would sit beside me and watch. I hated that part the most, that the nurse was there watching me lose control. She may have been the one watching, but it was on Dr. Steiner's orders that I was force-fed. He was the one in control. I hated him for his power.

That hadn't changed, only now I felt I had the right to know what that power had allowed him to learn about me and the others.

At a lunch meeting I worry I will become one of his patients again, a case he is observing to see how I act around food. I don't want to be the subject again. Yet to reschedule for a different time would reveal that I am still uneasy around him and around food, two things I don't want him to know. I want to be the one getting information, not giving it. I want to strip him of power the way Dorothy did with the Wizard of Oz. This is my story, not his.

THE END (ALMOST)
1986

I don't know how the time passed, but it did. Not eating was all I thought about. That's the funny thing: Although I wasn't eating, my life was all about food. All my energy was focused on food. My every thought was about food and calories.

School ended and Mom sent me and Anya away for the summer to live with our grandparents in LA. She did that a lot. Sent us away. It was easier for her to work when we weren't around. It was easier for me to starve when she wasn't around.

Not long after we arrived my uncle and aunt took us to Catalina Island with their kids, my cousins. After days of watching me slink around with the grown-ups, a shadow that never spoke, my uncle and aunt agreed I could go back early and stay with my grandparents.

My cousins seemed relieved. Like my friends at home, they didn't know how to deal with a kid who never smiled or laughed. They would follow me around in the arcade. I would put a quarter in a game and then walk away without playing it. I only put the money in because if I didn't, then my aunt would ask me why I hadn't spent it. I wore the same blue sweatshirt no matter how warm it was. I shrank when anyone got too close. The only words I ever said were "I don't care."

And I didn't. I didn't care about anything. I was numb. My clothes must have smelled but I didn't notice. No one else got close enough to care.

When I got back to LA, my grandma tried.

"Katya, please. Just a little, just a bite," she pleaded.

She followed me into her guest room. A cooking apron was tied around her waist.

"Maybe you'd rather something else, like peanut butter and jelly? You always liked peanut butter."

I shook my head and pulled my knees closer to my chest.

"How can you do this to your mother? She loves you so much," my grandmother said.

She sat down next to me, her words beginning to catch in her throat.

"You're really hurting your mother. How can you be so selfish? Please, Katya."

She stopped talking, her voice silenced by defeat. I heard a choking noise coming from her. I looked up. She was crying. I had never seen my grandmother cry. She was tough, even tougher than my grandpa, who had been a fighter pilot in the navy. My grandma's dad had also been in the navy. He was a doctor. When she was a kid her father was stationed in Haiti and Turkey. She watched a person get eaten by a shark in Haiti, and she was kidnapped in Turkey. The kidnapping didn't last long, but still—not many people can say they've been kidnapped. While still a kid in Haiti she used to ride a donkey into the bush to help her dad talk to the locals, her French being better than his.

She didn't talk about her brother and sister. Something happened and they were erased. Another thing she didn't talk about was what it was like when my grandpa was off fighting in the war. I guess she didn't see any reason to look back, to spend time on things she couldn't fix. She was more practical than emotional. That is why it was weird to see her crying.

For a minute I felt something as I watched her tears, but the minute passed quickly and once again I felt nothing. I felt no hunger, no sadness, and no excitement. I felt nothing but cold and tired.

After being at our grandparents' we were sent to stay with Dad for a month, while Mom went to New York to work.

We watched while she packed.

"Anya, I have to ask you to watch your sister. Your father doesn't seem able to," she said. "Watch and make sure she eats, please. Like you've been doing all along."

My mother patted my sister on the shoulder and then looked over to the corner where I was curled up.

"I'm trusting you, Anya. You're the only one who is always with her. I can't be with her when she is at your dad's house. Right now, she weighs sixty-eight pounds. She can't lose any more weight."

I watched my sister nod her head and turn to look at me.

When I was born, she called me her baby. When I got older, she dressed me up and taught me how to play games with her. She gave me the nickname Woofys, because I liked dogs. Now, before she was even a teenager, she was my parent.

She pushed her stringy blonde hair behind her ears. Her lips were set, her eyes steady.

"I know, Mom."

I pretended not to be listening, but I knew from my mom's voice that I was in trouble. It was hard to concentrate on what she said sometimes. I was so cold and tired. I had read about people freezing to death. They fall asleep and never wake up. I wondered if that would happen to me.

Rebecca also must have been asked to look out for me, because she started telling me scary stories.

"You know where they're going to send you?" she asked. She leaned in close, her long black hair almost touching my face. "They'll put you in the hospital. Have they told you that? Do you know what it's like in the hospital?"

She was so close I could see the small hairs on her face. I pulled back, sinking further into the soft couch. I fiddled with my fingers, pretending not to listen, but what she was saying scared me. So far no one had threatened the hospital. No one had said anything about my future.

I already knew my future. I could feel it in my constant shivering, in my slow movements.

I was dying.

A small part of me still wanted to live, but it was buried down below all my games, all the ways I had come up with to protect myself. It was the part that wished I didn't push people away; it was the part that wanted to feel the touch of people, the warmth of food. It was a part I couldn't reach because I had buried it.

"There are no TVs in the rooms," she said. "No, the hospital is not a fun place."

Rebecca sat back in her chair, giving me space to breathe.

"In the hospital you won't have the option of eating. Nope, they won't let you eat."

I looked up at her.

"Got you there. You're thinking, 'What do you mean, they don't let you eat?' Thinking it sounds pretty good to you, huh? Well, you know what they do instead? You know how they get food in you?"

I shook my head. She was enjoying the attention I was giving her a bit too much. I guess she felt she was doing her job, finally getting a reaction out of me.

"They put a tube down your nose. It hurts, but they force this tube down your nose and feed you that way."

Rebecca smirked.

"So, if you don't want to end up with a tube being pushed down your nose, you better start eating."

I looked at her, for once meeting her eyes. Where had she come up with such a nightmare to scare me, I wondered. Did she lie awake at night and think of the most horrible ways to feed a person, or did it just come naturally to her, these scare tactics? And how would a tube in your nose reach your stomach?

No, I didn't want to think about it. It wasn't possible. Any smart doctor would just put a tube down your throat or something.

The doorbell that meant the end of the session stopped my thoughts. I jumped up.

"Remember that, Katya," Rebecca said, as she held the door for me. "Remember how you're going to be fed if you don't start eating. It's a big tube."

Mom wasn't happy when she got back from New York at the end of the summer and came to pick us up.

"Denny, I asked you to make sure she ate. That's all I asked," Mom said.

She stood on the sidewalk in front of Dad's house. He was in front of her, his hunched back and long face making him seem small. Mom's anger made her seem like the bully.

Anya smooshed her nose against the car window. We had been shut into the backseat of my mom's parked car before the argument began.

"They're talking about you, Woofys," Anya said.

I shrugged my shoulders and hugged Boseys to my chest.

"Mom's mad 'cause you lost more weight while she was gone." My sister turned from the window and looked at me. "I told you she would be mad. I guess you can hear them, though. Mom sure is yelling loud enough."

Anya smooshed her face back against the window.

"One simple thing, Denny. To make sure your daughter ate." My mother stopped for breath. "Are you even listening to me?"

My father mumbled something and backed up closer to the house.

My mom walked toward him, not letting him escape.

"Have you looked at her?" she said, pointing at the car. "Do you even see her? Her friends ask me what's wrong. Even strangers come up to me, concerned. But do you even notice?"

My mother was pointing at me now.

"Look at her. Before I left at least there was some flesh on her face. Now there's no flesh around the bridge of her nose. Doesn't it seem strange to you that even your daughter's *nose* has lost weight?"

My mom stopped to take another breath. She looked back at my father.

He had backed up to the front porch steps now, his curved frame making him look like he was fleeing a madwoman.

"Stretch pants. They're supposed to be tight, Denny. Her blue stretch pants, when I bought them for her, they hugged her legs. Now they're baggy! Her damn stretch pants look like sweatpants, they're so baggy. She's a bundle of bones."

My mother shook her head and walked toward the car.

My father moved to the porch. He raised his hand and began to wave good-bye to us.

My mother opened her door and looked at my father one last time.

"Do you even care? Do you even care, Denny?"

My father's lips did not move. His large hand just kept waving back and forth.

The first thing my mother did when we got home was push me onto the scale.

Sixty-six pounds.

That's what it said. I didn't look at the numbers, she told me.

She couldn't tell me what was reflected in the mirror. She couldn't see.

I avoided mirrors. Whenever I felt my image being caught in glass, I walked away. I didn't want to see what wasn't there.

The tip of a ponytail tickled my face.

"Are you okay?" Erin asked.

She was bent over me. I was at the bottom of the main staircase at school. I shook my head no and felt for my feet. They were tucked in front of me.

"How did I get here?" I asked.

My voice sounded strange, like it was coming from somewhere far away.

"You were at the landing, looking down, and then all of a sudden you kinda just barreled over and fell forward."

Erin rolled her eyes in her head and tipped forward on her tiptoes. "Like this, and then next thing I know you're at the bottom of the stairs."

I remembered then.

I had been at the top of the stairway. The little spots on the brown carpet seemed to be dancing and my legs didn't seem to want to move. I had waited until after the first rush following the ringing of the recess bell so I wouldn't have to fight the pack of scrambling legs and pushing arms making their way to the playground.

The sun shone through the open doors at the bottom of the stairs. Down there, ten steps away, Erin waited for me. None of the other kids played with me anymore, except Erin, and that was only because her mom made her.

I had taken a breath and shut my eyes, wondering when it had gotten so hard to walk down the stairs. I'd picked up my right foot and looked down at Erin. The dark blue of her uniform seemed to be spreading, like a blob. Soon all I saw was a blue blackness.

That was where my memory stopped. Everything went black. It stayed that way until I was at the bottom of the stairs and Erin's voice pulled me back from wherever I had been.

I grabbed Erin's hand. My heart must have stopped. Mom had warned me about this. She said that's what happens when you don't eat. She told me that is how I would die.

Now I knew she was right.

What I didn't know is why I had come back—and when the blackness would return. Forever.

His Subject
2018

When Dr. Steiner tells me that I'm breaking his heart, I am glad. Then I realize he isn't talking about me as a person. He is talking about my words. He is talking about Roth.

That's not the first time Dr. Steiner lets me down on the day we meet. It starts before he even arrives, with a text. He is running fifteen minutes late.

I quietly curse him for the extra money I will now need to add to the parking meter. In the years since I was hospitalized, Silicon Valley has sprouted up around Stanford. Nothing here is cheap. It never really was, but now it's astronomically unaffordable for pretty much anyone outside the tech and start-up industries. Parking is costing me six dollars. The delay means more than just extra money, though; it means more time to be nervous.

As I wait, I text my mother to commiserate. She is not fond of Dr. Steiner. Fairly or not, she holds him largely responsible for what happened to me in the hospital, and for what almost happened to me after. He in turn holds her and my father responsible for the fact that I almost died and ended up in the hospital in the first place.

I see both sides. But since the hospital, my mother has been there for me, and it is to her that I now turn to strategize. After I note with relief that no food is being served on the deck, we come up with a plan. I find a corner table and sit down facing the entrance so I can spot Dr. Steiner when he enters.

It doesn't work. As soon as he shows up Dr. Steiner motions for me to follow him inside. He doesn't even come over to the table, just gestures from a distance.

I get up and follow him.

So much for my effort to take control of the situation.

Up close I realize he is not the giant I remember. Instead of the Wizard of Oz or the Prince, I find an old man. He is about my height, six feet tall, or a little shorter, due to a slight hunch. He wears a checkered long-sleeved shirt open at the collar and a gold chain around his neck, a combo that strikes me as European. His eyes are blue, his hair white, his tanned skin a little leathery.

As we walk toward a table he asks if I want to eat or just do drinks. "Just drinks," I say.

We are seated—and he asks for lunch menus. He orders a seafood salad.

I wonder if he heard me. Even though my stomach is all tangled up I order a beet salad. When my salad arrives, I manage to spend almost as much time eating it as pushing it around my plate.

I am surprised to discover that I almost enjoy listening to Dr. Steiner. He is an interesting guy, something he knows a little too well. He is happy to answer questions, although the answers are more general than I would like. I record them in a notebook, which serves both as a buffer between us and as a distraction from my anxiety.

He has his own questions. He wants to know if I was in any of his studies. The question surprises me. I thought he would be worried about how a former psychosomatic patient would react to being included in a study without their prior knowledge. Instead he seems to be confident I will be pleased at having been written about. I am not. I am offended, at first.

Then I realize he isn't treating me that differently than how I would treat a former source. I also assume most of the sources I write about are proud of the fact that they appeared in my articles.

There is a difference, though. The sources I interviewed gave me permission to write about them. I like to believe I included their voices. That was the point.

For Dr. Steiner, the patients did not exist outside of the medical realm. They were subjects, not sources. Statistics and numbers, not names. With so little of the individual in the studies, I am not sure I would recognize myself. The year in which the study was written would probably be the biggest indicator as to whether I am one of the nameless cases mentioned. If I am, my voice was not there.

Now I use it not to answer him but to ask a question of my own. I ask about the old hospital building. I know they have built a new hospital, but I don't know what happened to the old one-story building where I spent part of my childhood. Dr Steiner does, and he isn't happy about it. That is when he delivers the line.

"You're breaking my heart again," he says.

He explains that the old building was demolished. His heartache has nothing to do with a ten-year-old child wanting to die and everything to do with a building. The hospital's demolition was the primary source of his heartache; my revisiting that destruction is secondary. My own heartache—whatever it was that landed a young child in a psychosomatic ward—has nothing to do with any of it.

I feel silenced, the same way I was silenced thirty years ago.

I remember the biggest gulf between us—our relationship to Roth. I was sent to Roth. Dr. Steiner helped create it.

He arrived in the late 1970s and had hired staff and gotten the program running within a year. Although he speaks of Roth mainly as a solo experience, which is how I remember it, the Unit was based on the connection between mind and body, which means it was run by two people: Dr. Steiner and pediatrician Dr. Iris Litt. It isn't until later that I track down Dr. Litt. For now, I must rely on Dr. Steiner's recollections and writings.

Teams were put together to deal with the different illnesses. Pediatric care was not to be separated from psychiatric care. Dr. Steiner believed, and still believes, that psychiatrists and psychologists shouldn't have to worry that a patient will have a heart attack.

He is not speaking theoretically, he tells me now. Early in his training, while working on a psychiatric ward in New York, he watched as a young female patient suddenly keeled over and turned blue.

"I didn't know what the hell was going on," he says.

He and his colleagues started CPR, but it was too late. The woman died.

"So that immediately gave me the idea, 'What the hell is she doing on the psych ward? Why isn't there an internist right here?'" he says.

He doesn't tell me her name or anything else about her. The story isn't about her; it is about how her death inspired him.

It was then that he decided he would do things differently, a decision that led him to med-psych wards. They were still a new idea at the time, especially in pediatrics, where there was a clear separation between psychiatry and medicine, a separation that didn't make a lot of sense to Dr. Steiner. He estimates that 10 percent to 30 percent of the problems pediatricians were consulted on at the time were psychiatric. Of those, he believes pediatricians recognized maybe a quarter of the issues, and referred a quarter of those they recognized to a psychiatrist for treatment. The rest of the problems would be explained away by the pediatrician.

The difficulty, he explains, is that pediatricians "are trained to look for normal development," while psychiatrists are "trained to look for bad things." To get the full picture for children with physiological and psychological symptoms, they need to collaborate. Before med-psych units, this didn't happen. Children with both kinds of symptoms had to choose between pediatric or psychiatric treatment.

A noncompliant diabetic might be treated medically, but the reasons why they were not taking care of themselves would not be addressed. For eating disorders, the "why" was looked into through psychiatric treatment, but the physical deterioration was left largely unchecked.

Steiner finds this treatment so inadequate as to be almost laughable. A patient can talk all they want, he explains, but if their body is wasting away, it isn't serving much purpose, especially because malnourished people do not think well. When the Roth Unit opened, the average death rate for eating disorders was 5 percent.

"I said we're going to have zero. None," he says. "And we did."

During my time at Roth, anorexics were more common than bulimics. This seems to have been true throughout the history of the Unit. In his second Roth article, Steiner lists "starvational state" as the most common diagnosis, followed by asthma and diabetes, failure to thrive, and seizure disorders. Recurrent vomiting or bulimia was present in just 1 percent of patients during the first year and ten months of the Unit's operation.

Eating disorders were Roth's mainstay, and Steiner became an expert in their care, penning at least one book and several studies on the topic. He believes about 30 percent of anorexics have post-traumatic stress disorder (PTSD). They start out as anxious children, he says, and become more anxious due to counterproductive parental involvement or other factors. Along the way they discover "the great tranquilizer of nature"—starvation. Not full starvation, that doesn't work so well, but semi-starvation, which acts as a sort of sedative. When semi-starved, people become tired and docile.

I remember that feeling. When you are starving, you have very little energy to fight. Which is exactly why semi-starvation is what they used in prison camps and concentration camps.

"They would half starve them, enough so they could work, but not so much that they could feel things like outrage and so forth," says Dr. Steiner.

The sedating effect helps explain why people become anorexic. It also means the logical pediatric response of getting anorexics to gain weight is not as simple as it sounds. As the weight returns, so does the anxiety and fear, both of which can manifest themselves in aggressive behavior. And now that the patient is being fed, they suddenly have energy to fight.

"If I frighten you enough by any means, you will try and fight with me," says Dr. Steiner.

And the patients did. The bulimics tended to be more aggressive than the anorexics. There were staff members who ended up with black eyes. They tolerated the abuse in part because they were told that fighting was a good thing. The prognosis for the kids who fought back was much better than for the ones who didn't.

"If kids are noncompliant, then they're in there," says Dr. Steiner, meaning they are still inside their bodies and haven't given up completely.

I tell him I sometimes fought back.

He tells me he remembers. "You were a pill," he says.

That is why they used the straitjacket on me. I kept pulling out the tube they stuck up my nose and down into my stomach to force-feed me. The straitjacket made it impossible for me to do this. While it may have solved the outside problem, it didn't solve the underlying issue—why I was pulling the tube out in the first place.

There are gentler methods—medication, talk therapy, exercise—most of them coming through psychiatry and not pediatrics. They tried some of those on me, as well, but my case was difficult because of my age.

Dr. Steiner gets into this at our second meeting.

Admission
1986

I followed the nurse into the room. She was walking so slowly that I stepped on her heels. All the nurses, receptionists, and doctors did stuff slowly around me, as if I was a piece of glass that was about to fall from the table and break.

"You need to put this gown on and then wait for me to come back, okay?" the nurse said, slowly and quietly. "Do you need any help?"

I shook my head and waited for her to leave. It only took a minute to take off my clothes, and then I knew I would wait ages for anyone to come back. That is what happened here; you waited—first in the waiting room, and then in the exam room. My doctor was always late.

I quickly took off my pants and shirt and then moved toward the door so I could listen to the noises outside in the hall.

"Have you weighed her yet?"

It was my doctor's voice. I could hear the shuffling of papers as she pulled my chart from the slot on the door.

"No. I thought that maybe you wanted to do that," the nurse said. "I know you wanted extra time with her, and I thought—"

"Yeah, that's fine," my doctor said, knocking on the door.

The door swung open and Dr. Always Late bounced in. "How are you doing, Katya?"

Before I could answer she was on to another question. In the short time she had known me, she had learned not to wait for my shrugs. I liked her for that.

"Have you been eating at all? Ensure, or anything?"

This time she waited. She was older than my mom, but still energetic. Her dark hair was curly and a bit wild, kind of like a kid's. Instead of fancy jewelry, she had a stethoscope covered with clip-on animals.

I looked away from the Winnie the Pooh poster on the wall and faced her. I didn't look at her eyes. I tried not to look at anyone's eyes.

"Well, I guess we'll find out," she said. "Let's go down the hall and check your weight."

With that Dr. Always Late swung open the door and walked quickly down the hall.

I followed behind, pulling the blue paper gown tight around my shivering body.

The scale was the only thing that seemed real. I stepped on it and bent my head while Dr. Always Late fixed the settings, slowly moving the balance further and further to the left. When she finally stopped fiddling with it, she sighed and murmured "Fifty-five pounds."

"Come on," said the doctor, tapping me on the shoulder. "Let's go back to the room."

She turned and walked back toward the exam room, her steps slower and choppier than they had been when we walked to the scale. She held the door open for me and looked at her watch.

"You go ahead and get dressed and then go into my office," she said. "As soon as my last patient is gone, I will get your mom and we'll join you in there."

She began to shut the door and then stopped. "You know where my office is, right?"

I nodded my head and pointed to the door at the end of the hall.

After she shut the door I put my shirt and pants back on. My fingers were numb with cold. As soon as I had shoved my shoes on, I walked out of the room and entered Dr. Always Late's office. I had been her patient less than a year, but I had already visited her office once before. It was a big room, much bigger than the exam rooms. Pictures were everywhere: smiling kids, crying babies, laughing adults. Every face had some sort of expression.

I sat down on a big soft chair that was in the corner by a bookshelf. The chair was not close to the desk, where I knew Dr. Always Late and my mom would be sitting. I curled up and waited for them to come.

"She's lost more weight again, Karla..."

I jolted awake and looked up.

Dr. Always Late was sitting behind her desk and my mom was sitting across from her. I hadn't even heard them come in.

"How much this time?" my mom asked.

She looked over at me, not seeming to care that I was now awake.

"Too much," my doctor said. "Here, take a look at this."

She held out a chart for my mom. "It's a graph of height and weight. Her height is way above average. Her weight is *way* below average."

"Should we send her to a hospital?" my mom asked.

"No, not yet. But I do want you to start thinking about where you will send her if it becomes necessary. I know Children's Hospital at Stanford has a good program."

No one talked for a minute, as if by staying quiet Mom and Dr. Always Late could stop time and keep the hospital far away from me. Then Dr. Always Late started explaining things.

"Placement is going to be hard, so I would rather avoid it. You see, she is so young. She would be lumped with a group of much older girls with eating disorders. It might be hard on her. She could develop worse habits…"

I picked up a book from the bookshelf. They were just going to talk about me without ever talking to me. They would decide my future without me. In my ten years of life I had learned to expect as much from grown-ups.

"This is what I want you to do, Karla. I want you to go home and pack a suitcase for her, just a few overnight things, and put it by the door. Then I want you guys to work on eating for the next week. If she has gained one pound by next week, then we won't admit her. But if she hasn't gained any weight by then, we'll admit her to the program I think is best. A colleague of mine is a big fan of the program at Stanford, but Oakland also has a good one."

My mom nodded her head and turned to look at me.

"Did you hear that, Katya? If you gain weight by next week, you won't have to go to the hospital."

I nodded my head.

I wasn't going to the hospital. And I wasn't going to gain any weight. No one had asked me about this. School had started back, and that was the only place I was going.

I put the book back and walked toward the door.

Dr. Always Late grabbed me by the shoulder and spun me around.

"Do you understand how serious this is, Katya? Your life is in danger. I want you to really make an effort this next week, okay? Otherwise you're going to go to the hospital."

"I don't want to go," I said, my voice sounding funny from lack of use.

"I know," she said. "That's why you have to do this—why you have to gain weight."

Dad didn't seem too worried when Mom talked to him later that week.

I was spying on them from an upstairs window at Mom's house. They stood outside the front door.

"Did you talk with Katya's doctor?" Mom asked.

"Yes," Dad said. He leaned in closer, so he was almost standing over her. "She says Katya and I are both sensitive," he said.

It was always about him.

"She talked to you for over an hour, Denny," my mom said. "And all she talked about was that Katya is a little sensitive?"

"Yes, that was what she said," Dad said, more confident now. "No big deal, really. She's just lost a bit of weight. Lots of thin people in my family."

"She's dying, Denny!" my mom shouted.

"Calm down," my dad said. Except he wasn't calm. Now his voice was loud, too. "I don't need this. I don't need to listen to you attack me."

I don't remember how the argument ended. I do remember the phone conversation Mom had with Dr. Always Late afterwards. I listened in on the other phone.

"What the hell did you tell him?" my mom shouted as soon as Dr. Always Late picked up the phone.

"What are you talking about?" my doctor shot back. "I told him the same things we discussed. That his daughter was very sick and in danger of dying."

There was that silence again. Mom and Dr. Always Late had a lot of those when they talked. Then the doctor took a deep breath and lowered her voice. "What did he say to you, Karla?"

"That you said she was 'sensitive.' That nothing was really wrong—Katya's just a 'little thin.' "

"Wow! Did he not hear a word I said? I'm sorry. I don't know what he heard, but that is not what I said." Dr. Always Late paused. "I'm sorry. I thought I made myself clear. I thought I reached him—that he understood. I thought he cared."

I didn't try to gain weight that week, but with my mom always watching over me, a few calories must have snuck in.

"You did it. You gained a pound." Dr. Always Late smiled at me as she slid the scale back to zero.

I nodded my head and pulled the paper gown tight around my goose-bump-covered skin. "Can I go now?"

"Go back to the room and get dressed and then meet your mother and me in the office, okay?"

"Can't I go home?"

"Very soon. I just want to meet with you and your mother first."

When I got to the office, they were both already there. Dr. Always Late sat at her desk, a large folder in front of her. My mom sat in the easy chair opposite her.

I took a spot at the edge of the desk.

"She's kept her promise and gained a pound. She's fifty-six pounds now, but—"

I didn't let her finish. "You said I wouldn't have to go to the hospital." I walked forward and leaned on the desk. "You promised if I gained a pound I could stay at home, as long as I kept gaining weight." I turned to look at my mom. "I gained a pound, Mom."

"Great. Only about fifty more to go," my mom said.

My mother placed her hands on the desk and looked at Dr. Always Late.

"She has heavy bones, you know. She is still in serious danger, isn't she?"

70

"Yes. I looked at her chart and all of the figures. She is dangerously underweight. Even if she gains weight, we can't leave her at home. She needs to be monitored. I think you're right. I think we should admit her. We're playing games with her life. She needs to be watched more closely."

I glared at my mother. She was the one who had changed my doctor's mind. She was the one who had decided I should go to the hospital.

"I'm not going," I said. I looked at the doctor. "You *promised* me. I gained the weight."

My mother pushed back her chair and stood up. Long fingernails dug into my shoulders.

"We're not talking about a single pound, Katya. We're talking about your life."

"It won't be for long," Dr. Always Late interrupted. "You already packed your PJs and stuff, right? It's only for a couple of days. Until you're out of the danger area."

I pulled away from my mom and backed toward the door. "You promised. You promised me."

"It will only be for a few days," said Dr. Always Late again. "You'll be back home before you know it."

———

"Do you have Boseys?" Anya asked as she picked up my small backpack.

"No."

I stood at my bedroom window watching kids doing tricks on their skateboards outside.

"It's only for a couple of days," I said. "Boseys can stay here."

71

I turned around and walked toward the door.

"But Boseys will miss you."

I looked back in time to see my sister sneak my teddy bear into my backpack.

"We have to go, you guys. I want to hit the road before rush hour," Mom shouted up the stairs.

Anya put the backpack on her back and walked past me and down the stairs. Halfway down, she turned around to check that I was still behind her.

"Do you have your PJs and toothbrush and everything?" my mom asked.

I nodded my head. It felt more like I was going on a sleepover than to the hospital.

I walked out the door and waited by the car. It would be a long drive to Stanford. Dr. Always Late had chosen Stanford because another doctor told her it was good. No one planned on me staying at the hospital long, so the hour-and-a-half drive from our condo in Berkeley didn't seem that important.

The car ride was silent, my mom concentrating on driving, my sister rechecking my stuff.

I watched the signs out of the window, trying to remember all the directions so I could run away. All the little towns and houses on the side of the freeway seemed to blur together. Trees merged and signs seemed to say the same things. I didn't see anything except blurs of color and shapes whizzing by. After about twenty minutes I gave up and just watched the world cruise by.

Palo Alto was clean and organized, filled with shopping malls and giggling kids.

When we got out of the car, I lowered my head and followed my sister's footsteps, careful to avoid the people in the parking lot. I could tell by the way their shoes slowed that they were watching me.

My sister's white Ked shoes stopped. I looked up. The entrance sign above the big doors told me we were there.

I followed my sister in. I wouldn't be following her out.

A VERY SPECIAL CATEGORY
2018

I am in Dr. Steiner's office, the place where he still sees patients on a part-time basis. I take the seat closest to the door, what he calls the "flight seat." He tells me to come closer. I move, not because I am a patient listening to a doctor, but because I am trying to prove I am no longer the scared patient that wants to exit immediately, although part of me wants nothing more. I take my notebook out, using it for protection once again.

Eating disorders are usually triggered by puberty, says Dr. Steiner. Which makes younger patients unusual and harder to treat, because there is much more at play than just puberty.

"Your age put you in a very special category," says Dr. Steiner. "That's actually the amazing thing about you. Usually when you have this early onset, it's not so good."

He doesn't need to tell me what that means. With young children, success is less assured. Dr. Steiner's protégé, psychiatrist Dr. Bernard

Kahan, later backs this up. For Dr. Steiner, family involvement in the cases of younger patients was an "integral part of the treatment."

It didn't quite work out that way with me.

"As I recall, that was an issue with you," he says. "It was just so destructive. That makes it so hard, and so slow to resolve, because you don't have parents to work with."

Earlier, after we discovered we were both writers, Dr. Steiner and I talked about our current projects. Dr. Steiner's paper about the trauma child refugees in Europe suffer; my book on Cambodian survivors of the Killing Fields and the trauma they pass on to their children. That post-traumatic stress disorder (PTSD) can be passed down is not a new idea. As far back as 2000, researchers working with the adult children of Holocaust survivors found that they were more likely to develop PTSD after traumatic experiences than those who were not the offspring of Holocaust survivors. Further research has shown that adult children of Holocaust survivors who suffer with PTSD have a higher rate of PTSD themselves than those who survived the Holocaust and didn't suffer from PTSD. It is not just social and emotional stress they suffer from, being raised by a parent with PTSD as a result of trauma; they also have a higher risk of developing PTSD themselves due to physical changes, according to researchers.

The trauma my family suffered in no way compares to the Holocaust or genocide. Still, I wonder if my father could have suffered from PTSD and have passed it on to me, not just through his stories, but through his genes as well. I don't ask Dr. Steiner this. I haven't told him about my great-uncle. He hasn't earned the right to hear that story.

In the hospital records he gives me, I learn that family therapy was a failure in my case, so the hospital stopped doing it. I wonder how Dr. Steiner dealt with failure. How he dealt with the girl that he tells me was admitted to Roth twenty-eight times. The boy with a heart transplant who drank so much water his heart failed.

He had a wife, has a wife, he mentions her name several times as if I know her, as if we are old friends and not formerly patient and doctor. He has grown children. I ask him if raising his kids while working at Roth was challenging. He says that by then he had "a pretty good grip." "Not to say it didn't affect me, but I could contain it," he says. His words sound clinical and distant. I realize "contain it" refers to the emotions he felt when he saw our pain.

When he was younger, he found it harder. It was the same for me in journalism. I was too close to the first sources I wrote about, wanting to donate my own bone marrow to one, almost dating another. In time I learned how to gain their trust while still keeping a distance. It is a balancing act I still struggle with.

Dr. Steiner's cool-cat thing could all be an act, a facade. Only, I'm not sure it is.

He decided he wanted to be a psychiatrist when he was sixteen, after his English teacher assigned Sigmund Freud's *The Interpretation of Dreams*. Getting paid to listen to people's dreams and trying to figure them out sounded like a lot of fun to him. He had always been intrigued by people's stories and he realized being interested in people's lives was one of the main things a psychiatrist needed to be. Basically, they sit and listen, not unlike a journalist. The task is the same, he explains; it's what psychiatrists and journalists do with the story that is different.

"We use words to heal," he says. "Ideally, you use words to show the truth."

Book II

THEN AND NOW

BACK BEHIND BARS
2008

The hospital kept me alive. But there was a cost. Institutionalization leaves a mark. I spent the first decade after my release trying to escape the stain. The second decade I became a journalist. I thought telling the stories of those who had been overlooked was enough.

Then I met Crystal.

That is when I first began to look back. It took time and another teenager, this one in California, but the journey got under way there at a youth detention center in Kentucky. That's what eventually led me back to Roth, the place that changed my life.

It's Saturday. The visiting area at Morehead Youth Development Center should be packed. At least, that's what I thought, or maybe just hoped.

In reality, the cafeteria where visits are conducted at the youth detention facility for girls is filled not with guests, but with staff. I am the only visitor. I know the location of the center in rural Kentucky makes it difficult for some families to reach it, but not all of them.

If I can spend two hours driving here from Louisville on my day off, surely a few parents could spend an hour driving from Lexington. I don't expect them to drive the five hours from Paducah or almost four from Owensboro, but some of them must be from the numerous surrounding towns.

Yet there are no parents. No friends. No relatives. Just me.

I am thirty-two and working as a features reporter at a daily newspaper in Louisville. I have a mortgage, a long-term boyfriend, and a 401(k). I eat. Breakfast, lunch, dinner, all of them. I don't belong to the shadows anymore. I visit them instead. That's why I am here today. I wrote about a program that pairs retired racing greyhounds that need to learn how to be pets with girls at the center who train them. I am here now to see one of those girls.

Crystal is sixteen but looks younger. Small and slight, she is talkative and open. There is a sweetness about her that makes me want to convince her that there are people in the world who care about her. That is why I came. That's what I tell myself, anyway. As with the youth in the California juvenile detention facility I will visit more than half a decade later, I visit because I want the kids inside to know there are people outside who haven't given up on them.

Crystal seems surprised that I have come just to see her and not for a story or some other purpose. I bring her a few books from my own childhood, ones about kids who have imperfect lives. She told me once she wanted to be a lawyer. I thought it would be good for her to read as many books as possible.

I don't know what she thinks of the books, or if she will ever read them. I want her to have something of mine, as if giving her a few of my old books offers her tangible proof that I care about her. Maybe that will be enough to make a difference in her life, to help her get out of here and become a lawyer. I know she has grown up fast, but I also feel there is a part of her that still needs to be a kid.

I glimpsed that part while writing about the greyhound program. For twelve weeks the girls at the center prepared the dogs for adoption. They taught the greyhounds about all the things they hadn't known at the racetrack: windows, stairs, cars, leashes. Every few weeks I would check in on the dogs and the girls, telling the story of the program through a single dog, EF He's My-leader, otherwise known as Leader, or Rascal.

Two girls were assigned to Rascal, Crystal and Twanda. They decided they would call him Rascal when he was bad and Leader when he was good. That was one of the first decisions they made. They had been preparing for the dog's arrival for some time, and even wrote about him in their journals before they met him. Twanda filled a page with complete thoughts and sentences. She decorated the page with stars, smiley faces, and hearts with arrows through them. Crystal wrote only a few short bursts of text: "I worry Rascals will be depressed. I hope he likes me. I know I'll like him."

Later she tells me she has been away from home for several years. How long exactly she has been gone is hard to pin down because her answers tend to vary. She is here because she ran away from her "last placement." That's what she says at first. Later she adds to her story, slowly, and then almost breathlessly, letting the words tumble out. She steals, she says, from houses. Maybe that is why she is here. Maybe it isn't. I know her truth is slippery. But then maybe mine is too. I don't tell her what really attracted me to the greyhound story. I am not sure I know.

She is eager to please and even easier to quote. She offers an explanation for why she chose to work with Rascal that sums up the situation nicely. Her voice has the hesitancy and informality of a typical teenager.

"They basically came from somewhere rough, and then they go to a new family and, well, I felt they were kind of like me, so I felt I could help them while I'm getting help too."

Later, when calling the dog two different names proves confusing, Crystal asks Rascal what he wants to be called. She tells him to blink once if he wants to be called Rascal and twice if he doesn't. Crystal insists he blinks once. Rascal it is. The girls draw up a contract for Rascal modeled after their own contracts with the center. When Rascal misbehaves, they put a paw print on his contract. In the beginning there are a lot of paw prints. Most of the write-ups are for peeing inside.

Rascal learns how to climb stairs and walk on a leash halfway through his training. Crystal is released around the same time. She hasn't lived with her mother in three years and she is both excited and scared to go home. On her last day at the center she constantly repeats her name to Rascal, so he won't forget it. If all goes as planned, she won't see him again.

That isn't how it works out, though. Crystal is back at the center before Rascal graduates from the program. She made it two weeks outside. Then she broke the rules of her release. She is still at the center after the story on Rascal runs.

I decide to keep the connection going. I give her my cell phone number.

She calls sometimes. Her mother calls as well, asking if I will bring her to see Crystal. Her mother lives in Lexington, an hour away from the center, but has transportation issues. I pick her mother up on my way to the center. The ride there is awkward, the ride back even worse. Crystal's mother is suspicious of me. I am suspicious of her. I wonder what happened to Crystal at home to make her want to escape.

After Crystal is released and is getting into trouble again, her mother tells me that Crystal can't be trusted. She claims Crystal uses people. I know she is trying to warn me, but it still seems like a callous thing for a mother to say.

Crystal turns seventeen, and then eighteen. I can't track her through the Morehead center anymore. She has graduated from youth detention. If she gets in trouble now, the consequences will follow her for life. She stops calling, and I no longer feel comfortable calling her mother's number. We lose track of each other.

The next juvenile detention facility I visit is in the San Francisco Bay Area, the one where I see the boy being put in a straitjacket. The center is far bigger than the one in Kentucky, with hundreds, even thousands, of kids, compared to the thirty at Morehead. The setting is urban, not rural, and the doors are locked, both outside the building and inside it. At Morehead the girls could walk freely around the halls and even leave the building to sit on the grass outside. At the California facility the youth can't move more than a few feet without running into a locked door. I volunteer at the facility for a year, enough time to see the kids who have been released come back, just like Crystal did.

One girl I work with is shot a week after she is released. She lives, but it is a reminder that the world outside isn't safe for them. Inside they survive, but they are stained. The mark of institutionalization is on all of us. That is what led me to them and what leads me back to Roth in 2018, more than thirty years after I left it. It is then that I finally start looking for what I realize I was after all along.

Like any good journalist I am in search of answers. The questions I have are simple: I want to know what happened to the other patients, what happened to the staff, what happened to Roth—and what happened to me. I also want to know what could have happened to me and what happens to kids like me now. It all seems pretty straightforward.

It isn't.

In searching for the answers I unearth things I wasn't expecting, like the links with the justice system. After my initial research I didn't think I would discover more connections between incarcerated kids and Roth. But I did. They start at the very beginning, with the pediatrician who first ran Roth alongside Dr. Steiner.

Roth
1986

"What do we have here?" the admitting nurse asked. She sat behind her large desk and shuffled papers until she found a small note.

"Ah. You must be Karla"—she looked at my sister and then at me—"and this must be Katya. Sit down. We have some paperwork to go over first."

She handed a stack of papers to my mother and McDonald's magic pads to my sister and me. I watched my mom press the pen onto the papers, jabbing the answers in the blank white spaces. Although I didn't say so, I was sort of happy to be at the hospital. The fact that I was here was proof the grown-ups had noticed me and finally done something. It was like they had at last realized that something was wrong.

After the physical exam, the nurse said she was surprised I was still alive. Based on her figures, my heart should have stopped a week or more before.

The blackout. It should have ended there.

A tray with a brownie and a plate of macaroni and cheese was put in front of me. I was hungry. I am not sure how it happened, but I wanted to eat. Maybe it was the smell of macaroni and cheese, my favorite, back when I had favorites. If I ate, though, I thought they might change their minds and send me home. That is what I feared—and hoped for—most. I watched the cheesy noodles grow cold.

After about an hour Anya started picking at the plate. She hated macaroni and cheese, but dinnertime had passed, and she hadn't had anything to eat. She was hungry. I watched her screw up her face as she spooned the cold macaroni into her mouth. I wished I could have done that. I wished eating could be so easy for me. But even if I had tried to eat the macaroni and cheese, I don't think I could have. My stomach wasn't used to that much food, and wouldn't have known what to do with it.

When the paperwork was done, they put a wheelchair in front of me. I pushed it away and stood up. Stars blocked my vision, but I was used to that.

"I can walk," I said, reaching for the desk to support myself.

The nurse, my mother, and my sister looked up. I hadn't said anything other than "I don't know" all evening.

"Your heart is unstable," the nurse said.

She gently pushed me into the wheelchair. My mom just stared as the nurse wheeled me down the hall. I watched her face all evening, looking for the grief I feared, yet wanted, to see. My only power over my mom was the pain I was causing her.

I was placed in a high bed, in a large room with five other beds separated by yellow curtains. The witch, Rebecca, had been right; there were no TVs. Doctors and nurses told me their names as they pushed needles into me and hooked up machines. A heart monitor and various other connections tied me to the bed.

With tears forming in her eyes, my mom protested as yet another person came up to my bed.

"Her nose is so cute," my mom said.

I was confused until I saw the tube. Then I realized they would force food down me by pushing a clear tube up my nose and down into my stomach. Rebecca had been right—again. They really were going to feed me through my nose.

As the nurse greased the end of the tube, my mom left the room. Anya stayed.

In a fake cheerful voice Anya told me about my new home.

"The girl across from you, her name is Amanda," she said. "She's eleven, and was admitted right before you."

At twelve, my sister had already lost faith in the world. As she talked her green eyes did not leave the nurses. My mother trusted the hospital. Not my sister. She wasn't sure about the adult world. Anya was scared that if she left me, no one would take care of me.

She had a point. After all, I was there because no one had been taking care of me. Anya was there to make sure that now, someone did. Dressed in a pastel pink sweatshirt and tight jeans, her blonde hair in a feathered bob and her full lips smeared with lip gloss, she looked pretty. Not cute. No one would ever make that mistake with Anya. She might have been only twelve, but there was already a prickliness to her that kept people away. She stood at the side of my bed, a quiet presence whose darting eyes caused the nurses to avoid her glance.

I watched as the largest nurse pushed the tube up my nose. I pulled away, but her fleshy hands grasped my skinny arms and I stopped fighting. My mother came in to look once more before leaving for the night. I could see by her blotchy red face that she had been crying. I was glad. She still wore her navy-blue work suit. Her makeup that had been neatly done that morning was now in strangely colored blotches on her face. Her tightly permed black hair, high cheekbones, thin dark lips, and unsteady long legs on high heels gave her a tragic look. While my sister's face showed fear, my mother's showed sadness. My sister's dry eyes were those of a fighter. My mother's eyes were those of a martyr.

I was tied down, hooked up, connected to all sorts of machines. On my left side was some sort of heart machine, and on my right was the hanger for my tube feedings. On top of me were heavy itchy blankets that flattened me to the bed.

For the first time in months I felt safe. I drifted off, staring at the yellow curtains around me, listening to the voices, knowing there were people looking out for me.

"Come on, it isn't that bad," the night nurse said. "Just put the thermometer in your mouth."

I went back to sleep only to be woken an hour later for my temperature to be taken again, and another hour later, the same thing again. The breaks in my sleep continued all night.

Morning turned into night, then night to day. My yellow curtains stayed shut, blocking out most of the light from the window at the other end of the room. Days usually broken up by chores and mealtimes (even if I didn't eat anything) now slipped away through the bleeps of the machines. Nurses' hands fixing my blankets, voices outside my room, the blackness of my aloneness were my only distractions.

A tiredness as heavy as the wool blankets pressed down on me, leaving me no energy to fight. The most I could do when they forced a thermometer down my throat was turn my head away. I never spoke. I spent the time somewhere between deep sleep and wakefulness. I thought about nothing, not the future or the past. My body had finally given up. I was drifting between life and death, too tired to understand that the tubes and machines were the only things holding me to this world—and there was no guarantee they would succeed.

———

Several days must have passed. I needed to pee. I couldn't remember how I had peed before this point. Had I used the bedpan? Had I not had to go pee because I was too dehydrated? I looked down at the sheets and my face burned. Had I wet my bed? I didn't know. I couldn't remember.

I pushed back the heavy covers and pulled my head up. Dizziness took over, and I sat still, focusing on my feet until I could see straight.

I looked at my legs stretched in front of me and told them to move. Slowly I slid them across the bed and onto the cold floor. With my hands pulling at the bedsheets, I pushed myself forward, leaning against the bed. I took a deep breath and looked toward the door, which I could see through a crack in the curtain. It was more than ten feet away.

Slowly I straightened my body and let my hands fall to my sides. I moved my right foot and then my left. The door was closer. My heart raced and I felt my legs begin to wobble. Just a little further. Just a little more. But my body wasn't listening. My legs were bending and my head was spinning. I collapsed on the floor.

There was no way I would make it to the bathroom. I couldn't remember exactly where it was, and I couldn't even take the ten steps to the door. I hugged my arms around my chest, trying to ease the shivers I felt. I looked at the bed behind me; it was so high off the ground, too high to reach again, especially because my legs wouldn't move. Little sobs filled my chest as I reached a hand for the scratchy blanket on my bed. Even the blanket was too heavy to pull down. I had escaped its crushing weight only to be trapped by my own weakness. Tears of frustration and exhaustion trickled down my face.

"Lordy Lord. What are you doing in a heap on the floor?" one of the nurses asked when she found me.

I looked up, my eyes damp, sobs choking my voice. I shook my head and tried to explain, but I had no voice. My mind wouldn't make words.

"Well, let's get you back up where you belong," the nurse said, bending down and encircling me in her arms. "Were you trying to go somewhere? I'm surprised you got as far as you did in your state."

She lifted me and tucked me under the covers. "There we go, all set."

I grabbed for her hand and tried to push the words from my mouth. No sound would come out.

"It's okay," she said.

She pulled her hand from me and patted my head down onto the pillow.

"I'm not mad at you for getting up," she said. "Now rest, okay. You've used up a lot of energy on your little adventure."

I pushed my head up and shook it slowly.

"I have to..." I took a deep breath and tried again. "I have to go pee."

"Oh. Why didn't you say so?"

The nurse laughed as she started disconnecting me from the machines. I watched her and figured out that the tube hanging out of my nose was hooked to a hanger. Without moving the hanger, I wouldn't have been able to reach the door.

"We have to unhook you and then we can go," she said.

After she finished with all the machines, she scooped me up in her arms and moved toward the door.

"There's a wheelchair for this, but right now I might as well just carry you," she said.

In the hall I looked around. I didn't recognize anything.

We turned right into an open door only about twenty feet from my room. The nurse carried me to a stall and put me on the toilet seat. She never shut the stall door. She watched me as I peed, careful to make sure I didn't fall over or try anything sneaky. When I was done, I straightened and she picked me up and carried me to the sink to wash my hands, and then back to my room.

As she hooked me back up to the machines, she explained how things worked at my new home.

"From now on when you need to go to the bathroom, you tell a nurse and they'll get the wheelchair and wheel you there," she said, pointing at the wheelchair in the corner of the room. "Okay?"

I nodded my head and shut my eyes.

When had going to the bathroom gotten to be so tiring? Luckily, I didn't seem to need to pee very often. I planned on using the bathroom only when absolutely necessary. I knew if I was really tired, I could use the little yellow plastic bedpan, but I wasn't really sure how to pee lying down. I didn't understand how it worked, and I was too embarrassed to ask. Small tears trickled down as I pushed my head into the pillow, too tired to figure out the mystery.

"Wake her up," the head night nurse said. Her stubby hands gestured at the bed as she moved toward the door.

"Shouldn't I wait until you have the water ready?" the other nurse asked, looking at my silent form curled under a huge pile of blankets. She thought I was still sleeping, but their voices had woken me.

"Whatever you want. It's gonna take longer than you think, though. That one's a little fighter."

The other nurse turned back to the bed and slowly reached a hand toward me. She gently nudged me. I curled up tighter, hiding my head beneath the covers.

"Honey, you've gotta get up. Come on now, it's not that bad. You just need to take a hot bath so you can get warm again."

She was nicer than the other nurse, but nothing else stood out. They were all strong, dependable, and kind, even if it was sometimes a rough kindness. I saw them through a cloud of sleep and confusion that blurred them together.

I opened my eyes and mumbled something about not being cold, and why couldn't they just put more blankets on me or turn that dumb heat machine up.

"Your temperature has gotten too low. It's not safe. Come on, it won't be that bad," Sweet Nurse said.

She took me from my bed and wheeled me into the bathroom where I was lowered into a warm bath. The two nurses didn't turn away. They sat by the side of the tub splashing water on my bare chest. Sweet Nurse splashed the water lightly, biting her red lips as she saw the unhealed sores and hollow areas on my body. I sat in the water, sleepily trying to fight them, mumbling "How much longer?" whenever I was able to keep my eyes open for more than a minute. Sweet Nurse pushed my bangs from my face and told me it wouldn't be long; even Boss Nurse started to murmur encouragement.

"It's not going up," Sweet Nurse said, once again pulling the thermometer from my mouth.

"I know. There isn't anything else we can do, just keep her in here and hope it changes," Boss Nurse replied, her rough hands patting my head for the first time.

THE QUEEN
2019

When your temperature drops too low, your organs fail. If nothing is done, you die.

I didn't.

That is where Dr. Iris Litt comes in.

The same former counselor who had dubbed Dr. Steiner the Prince nicknamed Dr. Litt the Queen. Oddly enough, she does have royal connections. In 1993, when Dr. Litt was the director of Stanford's Institute for Research on Women and Gender, the institute gave Queen Sirikit of Thailand a Woman of the Year Award. When the queen came to California to accept the award, Dr. Litt got to know her and later visited her in Thailand.

Dr. Litt doesn't mention any of this unless you ask. She has class—lots of it. Even dressed in a velour tracksuit with a Christmas-stocking pin, she somehow manages to look chic. She also keeps the conversation clearly on topic, steering things toward the clinical and away from the personal. According to Dr. Litt, our interview is not about her.

She is wrong. The interview is about Roth, and her story and that of the Unit are intertwined. Roth was a medical-psychiatric unit. Steiner was the psychiatric half, and Litt was the medical half.

On paper Dr. Litt is impressive. As I read about the more than 150 scholarly publications she has authored, her recognition by the National Library of Medicine, and her role as a charter member in the Society for Adolescent Medicine (now, the Society for Adolescent Health and Medicine), I try to recall any interactions I might have had with her. I can't. But she made Roth what it was, so my time there was inevitably shaped by her.

The counselor who referred to her as the Queen talks about her with reverence. As a woman, I am inspired by her accomplishments in what was then a male-dominated field. But it isn't her research, titles, or roles in medicine that matter to me—it is her person. Because for me, it is all personal.

I meet her at a French-style café in Menlo Park on a cool December day. The city is minutes from Stanford, where Litt still holds emerita and active positions in research, directing, and chairing. She is retired, but medicine remains a large part of her life. It has been that way since childhood. As a little girl Litt would tell people the doll she was pushing in a carriage had pneumonia. Then she would inform them that she was treating it with sulfadiazine and aspirin. She was barely old enough to attend school, yet Litt already knew the medications in use at the time.

Nevertheless, it was far from a given that she would become a doctor. When Litt entered medical school in 1961, most schools would allow women to account for only 10 percent of the class. Some schools took less. As a woman at a medical school you were made to understand that you were taking a man's spot. That was the attitude then, and there were no laws to protect against it. Nine years after Litt entered medical school, women still made up only 11 percent of those accepted into medical school. Even Litt's father, a general practitioner, told her the medical profession was no place for a woman. He took her on house calls with him when she was a child and let her work in his office, but he didn't want her to follow him into medicine. He thought she should be a teacher, like her mother.

Litt did actually work briefly as a teacher. It was while teaching science to junior high school students in the time between college and medical school that she was drawn to adolescent medicine. More accurately, drawn to teenagers. The age group most adults dreaded fascinated her. The problem was, there wasn't really such a thing as adolescent medicine at the time; Litt had to help create it. In 1976 she founded the Division of Adolescent Medicine at Stanford. I was born the same year.

Litt's work with adolescent medicine began even earlier—in the juvenile justice system. It was a love of medicine and not troubled teens that led to her job designing and running a health-care program at New York City's Juvenile Detention Center. The justice work was what she had to do in order to do what she really wanted, which was to work at the then-new adolescent program at Albert Einstein College of Medicine and Montefiore Medical Center. Although the thought of working with youth offenders scared her, Dr. Litt managed to create a model there, and later, at the Adolescent Remand Center at Rikers Island Prison, which helped to establish the national standard for prison health care. It also led her toward psychiatry and the larger field of behavioral sciences, which in turn led her to Stanford, and Roth.

The incarcerated kids were a means to an end. She was not interested in them. They were just what she had to do to get the job she wanted. She is honest about this. Honest about being scared. She assumes I will understand. I do. And I don't. She considers me a part of her world. We belong on the outside.

But it isn't as simple for me. Once you have been inside, you can't let it go that easily. If you make it out, you have a responsibility to let others know what it is like for those you left behind. That was what the hospital gave me: a drive and a purpose. Dr. Litt found her purpose following her father. I found mine in an institution, the one she helped run.

She hasn't even gotten around to talking about Roth yet, and already I am defensive, angry. I don't let it show. I am a trained journalist. I know how to listen. That is what I do as she tells me about the fascinating contrast between the two groups she was treating: the kids at the detention center and the ones at the medical center. At the detention center she dealt with patients who used drugs and alcohol without thinking about the harm they were causing their bodies. At the medical center she dealt with the same basic demographic, minus the justice component. Only these children were refusing to take the drugs that would help fight their chronic illnesses. Dr. Litt wanted to understand the thought process of the teenagers. It was an age group she had learned little about in her medical training. When a job at Stanford offered her the chance to work collaboratively with psychiatry, psychology, and sociology, among other disciplines, she thought she might be able to find some answers.

Today the justice system plays an even more prominent role in mental illness. In *The Great Pretender*, Susannah Cahalan writes that before changing attitudes toward institutionalization in the 1960s and 1970s resulted in the closure of many state psychiatric hospitals, about 5 percent of the jail population was considered mentally ill. Today it is 20 percent or higher, according to Cahalan. When it comes to juveniles, the story is similar, with the rate of mental health issues in incarcerated minors a lot higher than for the general population, says Dr. Richard Shaw, a psychiatry and pediatrics professor at Stanford University.

It shouldn't come as a surprise, then, that juvenile courts are among the places Steiner mentions as sources of referrals to Roth in his second Roth article. Other places they come from include pediatric and psychiatric clinics and emergency rooms, private practitioners, Child Protective Services, and community hospitals and clinics, as well as a few self-referrals.

Yet I am still surprised to see a direct link between Roth patients and juvenile detention offenders. I wonder if any of the kids I knew came from the courts. The tuff teenager with her anger and penchant for running away seems a possibility. Although all of this literature comes from Steiner, interestingly, Roth was originally someone else's experiment.

Thomas Anders, then chair of Child and Adolescent Psychiatry at Stanford, got the Roth Unit off the ground a few years after Litt arrived. Steiner soon took over the psychiatry part while Litt handled the medical side. The medical component began at admittance when patients were given a medical assessment. If no major medical issues came up in the assessment, then Dr. Litt and her pediatric team might not be involved further. If there were medical issues, they would continue to treat the patient alongside Dr. Steiner and his people. Decisions were made jointly, with everyone providing input.

The combining of medical and psychiatric meant a broad range of children with different diagnoses could be treated in one group. In a paper co-written by Dr. Sandra B. Sexson and Dr. Bernard Kahan, early findings indicate that the combined-treatment model showed less morbidity. Stigma also seemed to be diminished.

It isn't something any of the professionals like to talk about, but there it is in the paper—the stigma associated with the psychiatric half of a med-psych unit. When Dr. Kahan ran a med-psych unit at Emory in Atlanta in the late 1980s and early 1990s, he noticed that medical staff would acknowledge the need for such a unit, but insist that none of their patients needed psychiatric care. They also seemed to have difficulty considering it a medical unit.

Kahan's account reminds me of Roth and how visitors treated us. We were different than the kids on the other units, and not in a good way. At Emory there was a perception the med-psych unit was isolated from the rest of the hospital and closed off, even though it was not. Kahan writes there was a need to "work hard to combat stigma." Closed psychiatric units tended to give medical doctors what Kahan calls the "heebie-jeebies." That is one of the reasons Roth was designed to be open and unlocked. It is an aspect former staff members almost never fail to mention. It meant patients had to be preselected to rule out extremely violent cases. The same was true on the eight-bed Emory unit. Even so, the Emory unit featured shatterproof windows, breakaway curtain and shower rods, and safe electrical outlets.

Dr. Litt doesn't fit the description of the medical doctors Kahan describes in his reports. She was not scared off by the psych side of things. On the contrary, she wanted collaboration with other disciplines. In Dr. Steiner she found a partner. Together they both began to specialize in patients with eating disorders, a demographic which over the years came to dominate Roth. On the medical side, Litt wanted to know how malnutrition during childhood, in particular, puberty, affected development. She and her colleagues noticed that girls who lost significant weight tended to lose or delay their menstrual cycles. In the absence of menstruation, they had low estrogen levels similar to those experienced by women after menopause. Dr. Litt wanted to know whether these girls would have problems with bone density in the same way postmenopausal women did. It turned out they did, and that this would put them at risk for osteoporosis later in life.

At Roth I remember having a bone scan. I didn't think much about it at the time. It wasn't a problem for young people. But what happens to us in our youth can impact us when we are old. That is a big part of what Dr. Litt wants physicians to keep in mind—what they're doing now has implications for the future. Early intervention is key in preventing problems later in life. With underweight adolescent girls, that means increasing body weight and estrogen so they produce the bone density they will need later. If it isn't produced then, they can never make it up.

In other words, I'm screwed.

I don't know if I ever had a follow-up bone scan. Dr. Litt explains that follow-up studies at Roth were tough. Once they leave, former patients don't want to revisit what was a very difficult period in their life.

I wonder if that is why she agreed to meet me—so she has a chance to follow up on data that was never collected? She certainly peppers me with questions, first about my occupation and then about my hospital stay. I reveal little about myself medically or socially. There isn't much to say about the latter. There is no ring on my finger, and she doesn't inquire about the children I never had, nor the father and sister I rarely hear from. Instead she tells me about her family and how they are her most important accomplishment: her husband, her children, and her grandchildren. It is what you are supposed to say—and what I may never be able to say.

She is unable to tell me why eating disorders happen. According to her, there are so many things that lead to problems in eating that it is a mistake to make any blanket statement.

I realize then that I was not asking in general.

I was asking about me.

SHADOWS
1986

My mom held out a paper grocery bag.

"I brought you some more clothes," she said. "Underwear, socks, and some different pants."

I stared at the chest of drawers in my hospital room. It had been empty so far. I hadn't taken any more than the clothes I was wearing, a nightgown, and one change of underwear and socks.

"Here's a clean pair of pants." My mom held a pair of turquoise stretch pants out toward me. "Why don't you put them on?"

"I like what I'm wearing," I said, backing away from the fuzz-covered pants.

"You haven't changed those pants the whole time you've been here."

I shrugged my shoulders and looked down at the light blue pants I wore. They were comfy, as was the green sweatshirt I had been wearing since the first day I was admitted.

"I'll just take them home and wash them, and you can have them right back." My mom moved closer and tugged at the top of my pants.

"I'm going home soon anyhow, what does it matter?" I looked at my mom, wondering how she lived with her lies. The "few days" had already stretched into one, and then two, weeks.

She did what grown-ups are so good at: She ignored me. She reached into the bag, searching for a different pair of pants.

"These are nice and soft, light blue like the ones you're wearing," she said.

I sat down on the bed and let her take over. I hated to feel another security taken away; the clothes that had hidden me for so long were now being removed. When they came back, they wouldn't be the same, their smell would be different, their feel would be stiffer, and their protection would be less. I tried to explain this to my mom, but she only understood the embarrassment of wearing the same clothes for more than a week. It wasn't her body that had to be stripped before a stiff pair of pants was pulled over her legs. I watched as my mom unpacked the bag of clean clothes and then pushed my dirty blue pants to the bottom of the bag. To her the dirty pants were something to hide. To me they were one of my few comforts. They were a constant in a world that had already changed too much.

Dan was the one who helped me learn about a bigger thing I had already lost. He was one of the two aides or counselors who watched over me. Most adults were too busy with their own issues to worry about kids. They'd pretend to care, but they didn't—not really.

Dan was different. He didn't do the doomsday talk like Rebecca and Mom, and he didn't ask for something I couldn't give him, like Dad. He just hung out with me. His jokes were a bit corny, but he was there with me, and not in his own world.

The first time he came into my room and peeked behind the curtain I thought he might be lost. He was that different from all the nurses and doctors who had been looking after me so far, with their charts and notes and rules and regulations. With his relaxed jeans and tousled, sun-streaked hair, Dan looked like he was about to head to the beach. He came in, introduced himself, asked if he could sit down, and then asked me how I was doing. He didn't say it in the quick way adults usually do, when they are already moving on to the next question. He said it like he really wanted to hear my answer. He looked at me and smiled, and when I didn't say anything, he didn't act hurt or annoyed, he just said something silly. After a while he left. But he came back later that day, and the next day, and the day after that.

If Dan wasn't with me, then Sherri was. The nurses and doctors were there as well, but it is Dan and Sherri who I remember best. They were the ones who explained what was going on, what all the machines and tests meant.

"It won't be that bad," Dan said, straightening an IV in my arm. "I'll hold your hand the whole time. They just push you through this tunnel."

"Do I have to go all the way in?" I pushed his hands away from the IV and started to walk toward the door. There was a sharp pain in my right arm. I had forgotten to take the hanger filled with liquid with me.

Dan quickly pushed the hanger toward me. "No, it's just your head that goes in; the rest of you sticks out."

"Oh. Why do I need to have a CAT scan anyway?" I asked as I turned toward Dan.

Dan pulled at his blue jeans, keeping his eyes on the ground as his lips began to move. "They do it so they can see if there is anything wrong in your brain."

He pushed a wheelchair toward me and for once I didn't protest. I also wanted to see what was wrong with my brain—what was eating at my insides.

Outside of the hospital, the only meaning food had for me was how to avoid it. Inside it was different. In the hospital, food meant Ensure. Each week I was given a little more. The increase was tiny, but every added drop felt like a rock that would weigh me down. I couldn't block out the change. I had to lie silent and watch each drip slide down the tube. I had to feel it fill my stomach. It made me feel helpless, powerless. On good days I would turn my head away and wait for it to end; on bad days I would squirm, pulling and messing with the tube so the food wouldn't flow.

Watching and waiting for my belly to fill hurt. It meant I had failed. I had lost control. It also meant that someone was taking care of me. I didn't have to worry. I think it was the mix of happiness and anger that tore my insides up most, making every drop matter.

Food was so much more than food. It wasn't just my mind that had trouble with the Ensure. My stomach did, too. I had forgotten how to digest food.

When I couldn't control the food going in, I would try to control other things.

There was a big machine at the base of my bed that was turned on at night. It heated my bed from below through a special pad. When you are skinny, your body can't keep warm. That is why the nurses turned the machine on at night while I was sleeping. I would turn it off. A night nurse would turn it back on. Later, when I had more energy and they had figured out my trick, I left the machine on but pulled the warm pad beneath my blankets out. I hid it in one of the empty beds. After a few days they noticed and brought it back. Next time I wheeled the whole machine away. After a while they stopped bringing it back. I had won. The thing was, I liked the machine; without it, I was cold.

It was even easier to ditch Dad.

Once I wasn't tied down to my bed with machines, people started to visit—people besides my mom. In the beginning my mom came almost every day, and Anya and my grandma came every other day. I hadn't seen Dad since before I was admitted. I didn't miss him, and I don't think I wanted to see him.

Of course, that didn't matter. No one bothered asking me what I wanted. Dad wanted to visit, so he did.

The hospital staff was excited. Visits with family were viewed as "progress," and a good thing. When my mom and sister came to visit, they sat on my bed, wandered around the Unit, and chatted with Amanda and my other roommates.

Dad's visit was different. He never made it to my room. Instead, someone unlocked the group meeting room and shut us in there. Before leaving us alone they handed me a cup of strawberry Ensure. It had a straw in it. They didn't trust me to drink on my own, but Dad was there. They thought he would police me.

I knew better.

Dad sat on the couch. I stood close to the door. I was trying to decide how to throw out my Ensure. Thinking about the Ensure made it easier for me to ignore him. I wasn't trying to be mean; it's just that when he wasn't around, I was able to be happy, at least a little bit. It was like without him there, I could breathe.

Dad picked a storybook off the cluttered table.

"This is a neat room," he said. He sat hunched over on the couch. He looked around at the bookcase filled with toys, the window that looked onto trees, and the beanbag in the corner.

I shrugged my shoulders and began to pour my drink into the trash can. I poured slowly, waiting for Dad to stop me. He didn't get up. He raised his head and looked at me.

"Don't do that, Katya," he said.

I kept pouring.

"Why not?" I asked.

The pink liquid trickled into the trash can.

"You're supposed to drink it," he said.

The drink was almost gone.

That's when he slowly slid across the couch to where I stood. His large right hand loosely took my wrist. I looked at him. His grip was light. I pulled away, dropping the cup into the trash. In his eyes I didn't see my mom's hurt or my sister's fear. Instead I saw annoyance, a sense of duty in case the nurses were watching. It was like before, when he would tell me to eat, and then, when I didn't, he would eat my food for me. He didn't really want me to get better; he just pretended he did when other people were watching. He said the words for my sister. He ate my leftovers for himself.

I turned away from him. Then I ran back to my room.

I refused to see him after that.

He tried to come once more. Legally they couldn't keep him from visiting me.

My counselor Sherri helped me avoid him. When we found out he was going to be coming, we spent all day scheming. That may sound fun, but it wasn't. The last thing I wanted to do was hurt my dad. I didn't want to turn his visit into a game of cat-and-mouse. It was just that it hurt so much to see him. I think it was because I cared about him and I was having trouble ignoring the fact that he didn't seem to care about me.

Sherri came up with the idea of having me hide in a stall in the girls' bathroom. Sherri was stricter than Dan, but she was also more protective. Dan would let me get away with things; he would bend the rules a bit and go easy on me when he could. Sherri stuck to the rules because she felt they were good for me. The first time Dad came, she made sure I visited with him. After that visit, when I curled up in a tight ball on my bed and retreated back into "I don't knows," she decided I didn't need to see him again.

When she saw me shaking on the day of Dad's second visit, she told me to go ahead into my hiding place even though it was still a half-hour before visiting time. There wasn't anyone there to bother me. Girls weren't allowed to stay in the bathroom for long, in case they tried to throw up. Sherri had cleared it with staff beforehand, explaining why I should be allowed to stay in a bathroom stall. Whenever a girl came in to pee, I asked her for an update. Had my dad arrived? The girl would go out and look and report back. To them, what I was asking didn't seem weird. Many of them had spent time hiding from men in bathrooms.

I heard his voice first. He was arguing with Sherri, asking her why I wouldn't come out, why I wouldn't see him. She stayed calm and firm. Much as I liked Dan, I knew he might have buckled. Sherri wouldn't. She told Dad I didn't want to see him. She told him I was hiding in the girls' bathroom and she was not going to force me to come out. Dad called into the bathroom, asking if anyone else was in there. The bathroom was empty.

I heard him shuffle in. Sherri had counted on her words keeping him away. She couldn't physically stop him. Even if she'd had the authority, which I don't think she did, she was too small. Dad was six-foot-four, and Sherri wasn't much taller than me.

I held the stall door shut but it couldn't protect me from his voice. He stood there a while, waiting for me to come out. He talked to me. I held my breath. He questioned me. I had to breathe. He laughed. I shook.

Finally, it was over. He gave up and left.

I stayed in the stall until Sherri came in and told me he was gone. When I asked her to double-check for me, she did.

When I finally opened the stall door, she was standing there, ready to wrap her arms around me. I wanted to fall into her, but I was also mad at her. She had promised to protect me, but she couldn't. Dad had made it into the bathroom—not the stall, but the bathroom. I had to listen to him while Sherri stood outside, unable to protect me, another adult who had let me down.

Not completely, of course. I knew that if she hadn't been there at all, Dad would have gone further. He was as stubborn as me. But he was also proud, and he didn't like being ignored in front of an audience. He cared too much about what other people thought. Calling to a child who was so scared of you she wouldn't leave the bathroom stall was too embarrassing for him.

He didn't come back.

He tried calling on the telephone. There was a pay phone at the end of the hall where you could talk to your family and friends. One of the counselors would usually answer it and find whomever the phone call was for.

My dad wasn't really calling for me. His questions were always the same.

"Why won't your sister talk to me? Why doesn't she want to live with me? I'm all alone. Why are you doing this?"

He never let me answer, so it must have been a while before he realized he was shouting at the empty hall of the hospital, the public telephone hanging off the hook. By then I was already back in my room, staring at the wall.

I tried not to think about how alone he must have felt. I knew if I did, I wouldn't be able to escape. He'd pull me right back down into the darkness.

My mother came almost every day, dragging herself off work early to make the long drive to visit me. On weekends my sister came with her, but on weekdays, Mom came alone, a tired woman who was about to lose her job for leaving work early so often.

Although I was improving and had made some friends, I wasn't healthy—nowhere near it. I was still dying. I had lost a lot of weight and I was fighting every pound they tried to put back on me. My heart rate was still erratic, my temperature low, my muscles in danger of being eaten.

Of course, I didn't see it that way. That is because I didn't look. My mom was the one who forced me to notice.

One day after following me into the bathroom she pushed me in front of the mirror. I wriggled out of her grasp, but her nails dug into my wrists and I was forced to look in the mirror. There were mirrors in front of all the sinks. We were never allowed to stay in the bathroom long, so few girls ever stared at their reflections.

I didn't look in the mirror while brushing my teeth because I didn't brush my teeth. I had braces and knew keeping my teeth clean was important but toothpaste had calories. When I brushed my hair, it came out in handfuls, so I didn't brush it anymore. I seldom went to the sink because as soon as the water ran, the nurses watched. Running water could cover so many things. I never had to look in the mirror, but it was always there in the background. The mirror haunted me just as my image haunted it.

But my mom was tired of ghosts. My mom wanted her daughter back.

She held me in front of the mirror. "What do you see?" she demanded. She pulled my chin away from my chest and pushed me closer to the glass. "Tell me what you see."

I looked, but what I saw was not all there. I saw something, but I wasn't sure if it was me. Looking back at me from the mirror was a girl with eyes bigger than any I'd ever seen. There were wrinkles on her face where her skin sagged around empty cheeks. The top of her nose caved in around the bone, and a long plastic tube filled with stomach acid dangled from her right nostril. Her light brown hair was not full anymore. It was falling out in patches. Her arms, hidden under a baggy sweatshirt, were more hairy than usual and contained little cuts that would not heal.

The girl who looked back at me scared me. But it wasn't me. I didn't feel connected to the skeleton in the mirror.

Anorexics are as blind to their bodies as they are to their emotions. A mirror isn't a reflection of reality. It's an image. The image is of something that shouldn't be there. It is an image of someone who doesn't want to exist. In the mirror are the ghosts who haunt the living.

My mother yanked at my hair. "It's falling out," she said. She began to cry.

I pulled away from her and raised a hand to my hair. There was so much less than I remembered. Because I didn't brush my hair, I hadn't noticed quite how much I was losing.

"Will I go bald?" I asked. I had a little vanity left. "Will it all fall out?"

"Probably," my mother said. She let go of me and let out a long sigh.

That's when I refused to see my mother.

I think she was secretly relieved. She would be able to hold on to her job a little longer.

TREATMENT SUMMARY:

On 9/17/86 to 10/3/86, the patient was admitted to the Roth Psychosomatic Unit. She has been followed by Adolescent Medicine. The patient's vital signs have been periodically unstable. The patient was begun on a caloric and fluid minimum requirements. Initially, the patient was able to take 1,000 calories and 1,500 cc of fluids orally. She did well on this approach, with slight weight gain. Her caloric minimums were increased to 1,500 calories. However, the patient has been unable to tolerate this increase. Thus, an NG tube was inserted into the patient on 10/1/86/ At this point, the patient is unwilling to eat p.o., and thus is receiving NG tube feedings nightly. The patient has showed weight gain on this approach.

Emotionally, the patient has remained clinically depressed. Her mood remains markedly low with sad to irritable affect. She continues to display psychomotor retardation with poor eye contact. The patient continues to deny active suicidal ideation at the present time. However, she continues to respond to direct questions with "I don't know", and is unable to engage with both peers and staff. She remains regressed in her behavior. Individual psychotherapy has been initiated and is in progress. A family assessment is currently being undertaken and a family therapist has been assigned to work with the family in order to fully understand the interpersonal conflicts that exist and its relationship to the patient's current emotional state. The patient is also involved in group therapy, as well as recreational activity. A specific behavior modification program is currently in progress.

The treatment goals at this point are to improve her weight gain, and to achieve medical stability, to continue the psychiatric evaluation and to assess the need for antidepressant medication. A complete family assessment is underway.

It does appear that baseline laboratories and studies have been drawn on the patient. Thyroid function studies appear to be normal. Electrolytes are within normal range, as well as a CBC. A serum prolactin level was also normal. Thus, at this point in time, it does not appear that an organic etiology can explain the patient's current medical condition.

Treatment thus far has included developing a behavior modification program and continued NG tube feedings as needed. The patient will continue in individual, group and family therapy.

PLAN: As stated above.

The patient's prognosis at this time is guarded.

I still have trouble with eye contact. Looking directly into someone's eyes seems invasive. I look to the side instead. I have learned that people are uncomfortable with "I don't know" as a response, so I try to fill in the blanks, even though I don't always know the answers.

It is the last sentence of this treatment summary that sticks with me the most.

Guarded.

It means cautious, and having possible reservations. That is the official definition. When applied to medical conditions, it means serious and of uncertain outcome.

I use my journalism background to translate it into plain English: My doctors weren't confident I would make it.

Number 090 71 51
1986

After two weeks of being stuck in my bed in critical condition, and several more with not much moving around, I was itching to explore.

Of course, I didn't let the doctors know this, and I even sort of had trouble admitting it to myself. But it was there anyway. All the machines and tubes had managed to pump some energy back into me, and I no longer slept all the time. I was alive whether I wanted to be or not.

Not that all the machines and tubes were gone. They weren't. I heard Boss Nurse whispering plenty of times that my vital signs were unstable. I guess my heart would slow down and my blood pressure would drop. I didn't pay much attention to the details.

At first, I didn't pay much attention to the weekly meetings, either. But after a few weeks of hearing about them, I was curious, and I went to my first one—at least, the first one I was allowed to go to, without a fight. I was introduced to everyone in the Unit, or all the patients who were at the meeting.

That is when a strange thing happened. Being around other kids who wanted to die, I started to come alive—at least, a little bit. I was still closed off, but with some of the other kids, and with Dan and Sherri, I began to open up a bit.

The Unit was mostly teenage girls, but there were a couple of skinny diabetic boys who made a point of staying away from everyone else. After the boys, the group was split into the two blondes, a few other, older girls, Amanda and two girls with dark hair.

There was a sort of pecking order among the patients. The kids who had been there the longest were the coolest. Next came the cutters. The diabetic boys and eating disorder girls seemed to be of about the same rank, although the girls looked up to the boys, because the boys could eat anything and still stay skinny.

Lauren and Sandra seemed to be in a group all their own. They had short, dark, curly hair, were about sixteen, and were the only two to share a room by themselves. Lauren was tall and kind of slim, with a sweet, soft face. Sandra was shorter and tough-looking, with brightly colored nails, a look that said "Get lost," and a long history of running away. Lauren liked classical music and was always smiling. Sandra liked rock music and had a gruff, impatient voice. They were always together.

I don't remember everything that people talked about in the meeting. I think the blondes complained about not being able to shave their legs (they weren't allowed razors for obvious reasons). I spent the time looking around the room and pushing my cuticles back. Everyone seemed much older than me, and already very settled. I didn't say a word and longed for the security of my room. But being the newest kid, I was not to escape so easily.

At the end of the meeting Lauren was the first to make her way over to me.

"Who are your counselors?" she asked.

"Dan and Sherri," I said.

Now that Lauren was talking to me, I no longer wanted to escape to my room. She was one of the most popular girls at Roth.

"Sherri...I don't know who she is," Lauren said. "Dan's real nice, though, huh?"

I nodded my head in agreement.

"Sherri's the older lady with white hair," I said.

Lauren didn't seem to care.

"Do you want to see our room?" she asked.

Before I could answer she was moving toward the single room at the end of the hall that she shared with Sandra. As we entered, loud rock music filled our ears.

"That's Sandra. She has bad taste in music," Lauren joked. She pointed to Sandra, who was sitting on the bed by the window.

Sandra gave a quick smile and walked to the door.

"Where are you going?" Lauren asked.

Sandra shrugged, stepped around us, and left the room. I soon learned she wasn't much of a talker. That was fine with me.

"She's kind of funny, but you'll get used to her," Lauren said.

Because I was the youngest among a group of teenage girls, I ended up with a bunch of older sisters. I was Lauren's special pet, though, and it was soon known around the Unit that she was looking out for me.

Unlike most of the other anorexics, Lauren was energetic and outgoing. She didn't talk about food and calories; she talked about music and boys. I didn't have much to say about either, but I was a good listener, so she liked having me around.

It was Lauren who brought me out from behind the yellow curtains surrounding my bed. She was the one who showed me I could have a new family in the hospital. I could find a way to belong here.

But in doing so, I also became that much more removed from the outside world. I figured this out when Lauren talked me into going on my one and only outing.

I'd been in the hospital about a month or so when it happened.

"Hello there," Lauren shouted, peeking her head into our room. "Who's coming?"

"Coming where?" I asked.

"On the weekend outing," Lauren said as she came in and sat on my bed. "You haven't ever gone on any of the outings, have you?"

I shook my head and put down my book. "What's the outing?"

"We're going to a sushi parlor or something," Lauren said.

Seeing my disgusted face, she hurriedly continued. "What we do isn't really the fun part. It's just fun to get out of this place." Lauren gestured at the yellow curtains and white walls. "Sandra and I always go. We get to walk around and stuff. It's fun."

Sandra had just returned from running away, so I knew she wouldn't be allowed to go on this trip.

"Amanda, I bet you haven't ever been on a trip either," Lauren said. She got up and peeked around Amanda's curtain.

"Nope, and I'm definitely not going to a sushi parlor," Amanda said.

Lauren laughed and moved back toward my bed. "She's on medical bed rest, isn't she?" she whispered.

I nodded my head and we both smiled. Medical bed rest was a punishment for not gaining enough weight. If you missed your target weight, you were restricted to your bed. On most days at least two or three girls were restricted to their beds. Amanda was usually one of them.

"Lauren," I said, "if I go...I mean, if I go on the outing, will you stay by me? You know, not leave me?"

" 'Course I will. I'll be by your side the whole time," Lauren said, pulling me up off the bed.

"Grab a sweater, 'cause it gets cold."

Lauren pulled a sweater from the corner of my room and handed it to me. "Oh, and you don't have to eat any sushi," she added.

I followed Lauren outside and onto a small bus that was supposed to carry about fourteen people. The trip was only for our Unit; they made a point of keeping us separate from the others. A few of the boys from the unit came, along with the blondes and a girl in a wheelchair who talked a lot. There were almost as many counselors as patients. The counselors squeezed in the front and discussed directions while the rest of us whispered in the back, our eyes glued to the windows.

I sat next to Lauren.

The first place our bus stopped was at a cliff on the way to the sushi parlor. It was a lookout spot with a great view and a large drop-off.

We were supposed to get out and look at the view. We weren't allowed to get very close to the edge. Why they had taken us to such a place puzzled me slightly. I held Lauren's hand and followed her to a rock where we sat and looked out at the city lights below.

"Why do we go out at night?" I asked Lauren.

It was around seven p.m. when we left for our outing, already dark and hard to see.

"They always do that," Lauren said. She pointed to a small hill below. "Isn't that neat?"

I didn't answer. I was still waiting for her to answer my question.

She sighed. She didn't like to talk about sad stuff. Sandra was the doom-and-gloom twin.

"Sandra says it's 'cause they don't want people to see us," she said. "They want to hide us." Lauren was silent a minute before she went on. "I don't know, though. I think it's to protect us from all the people, all the noise of the day," she said.

Lauren was one of those people who always saw the good in things. That was strange to me, because it seemed like most of the kids at Roth saw the bad.

Or maybe she only did that for me.

"You'd be more scared during the day, wouldn't you?" she said.

I looked out at the dark sky and back at the other patients, whose dark bodies I could barely see. "Yeah, I guess I would."

"Let's get back on the bus. It's getting cold," Lauren said, pulling me toward the bus.

I scrambled inside, back to my seat by the window.

The other patients followed slowly. Chatty Girl in the wheelchair was last.

Lauren watched as her wheelchair was collapsed. "Poor thing," Lauren whispered in my ear. "They just got her out and now it's time to go."

I liked the drive best, looking out the window and watching everything whiz by. I had been allowed out on special status. I still wasn't eating on my own and hadn't gained much weight, but the staff thought being out might be good for me.

None of the patients talked. For a bus filled with mostly teenagers, we were a silent lot. Chatty Girl would pipe up with some kind of comment every once in a while, but her words would hang in the air only to be swallowed by silence.

"Final stop: the sushi parlor," the driver called as he parked the bus. "Everybody out," he said. "This is it."

He opened the bus door and counted us as we stumbled out.

I looked around. We were no longer in the outskirts hidden by rocky outcrops and scenic views. We were in a town filled with people.

A man and a woman passing by stared in our direction. I tried not to look at the woman, with her wispy hair and pursed lips, but she was hard to avoid. She had stopped walking and was tugging on the man's arm, pointing toward a counselor, who was helping Chatty Girl into her wheelchair.

The woman's sad face made me look at Chatty Girl again. She was skinny, like the rest of us, but other than that, she was just Chatty Girl. The same Chatty Girl who proudly told me about how she used to get by on a single diet soda a day, and who usually got around on a walker.

Then I saw it.

As Chatty Girl looked up at me and smiled, I saw the way her head bobbed on her neck a bit too much. I noticed how her arms and legs flopped out of the wheelchair.

She looked funny, not like a normal kid.

I turned away quickly and saw the woman's stare. She was looking at me the same way she had looked at Chatty Girl.

I moved away and grabbed Lauren's hand. Lauren held it tight and pulled me toward the shadows. "You okay?" she asked.

I nodded my head. We stood in the darkness, watching the others get out of the van. I tried not to see us as everyone else did. I tried not to see us at all.

When everyone was out, a counselor started to count the group. Lauren stepped forward. We were holding hands, so I followed. Together we walked back into the brightness of the streetlamp.

Lauren gave my hand a little squeeze. "Don't worry, I won't let go of you," she said.

And she didn't. As we walked up the sidewalk toward the sushi parlor, she held my hand tight, leading me around people, streetlights, and parking meters. She kept her body between me and the people, me and the cars, me and the world.

I stumbled along beside her. I wanted to shut out the noise, the people, and the lights, but there was no curtain to pull and no covers to hide under. I was completely exposed.

The happy prattle that came from people's mouths made me shiver. I didn't understand it. It sounded like fireworks exploding in a silent sky. It was as if they were talking in a different language, walking in a different way, and living in a different world. A world you could walk in and out of without getting permission, a world where you knew whether it was Tuesday or Thursday, and where that mattered.

I was still too skinny to feel safe. There was no layer of flesh to protect me from the chilly wind and questioning stares. I was used to living in a bubble with limited noise. I was used to shutting down, not opening up.

But the warmth from Lauren's hand kept me from going numb. I felt so proud to be her friend. I was the skinny little girl almost grown-up Lauren wanted to hang out with.

Lauren never let go of my hand, even when she decided to try a piece of sushi. I still didn't get why we were at a sushi place, even the kids who ate didn't like sushi. That Lauren ate it was even stranger. That was the only thing I didn't understand about Lauren. She ate. She seemed to like food. She didn't play with it; she just ate. It was almost as if she was normal.

Some of the girls on the Unit whispered that Lauren used to be chubby—maybe even fat.

I couldn't believe it. Lauren couldn't have been fat. Lauren was perfect.

Community Meeting Notes   *02 October 1986*
Patients Present: B (secretary), C (chairperson), F, G, H, I, J, K, L and M.
Staff Present: Dr. Kahan, Dan, Ann, and Janet
(medical student).

The meeting began on time. There were no staff announcements and few patient announcements. The meeting began with introductions for patient M who noted that he had previously been in community meetings. The community then began identifying considerable feelings of boredom, in particular patient C who in the last several sessions had been struggling with the issue of how to facilitate group discussion when "nobody has anything to talk about". In this meeting he appeared to take it somewhat less personally, although he was obviously still concerned about this.

In general, however, staff filled the vacuum by offering to have the patients play the "ungame." This was received enthusiastically by some people in the community, particularly patients F and H, and was somewhat resented by others, namely patient B. However, the community did decide to play the game. During this game most of the patients participated with a generally upbeat mood. However, patient M evidenced great difficulty in comprehending abstract questions. Patient G's participation was noteworthy for her rather humorous response to a question regarding "say something about TV". Patient K seemed quite defensive during the meeting and had great difficulty coming up with answers to her questions. The people who seemed the most spontaneous in their participation were B, C, F, H and I.

For each meeting write-up in my chart, one letter is circled. That is me: a letter. That is how patients are identified in the notes.

At the beginning of my stay, I am "G." Later I become "H," and then "I." Toward the end I am "C." At one point, both "G" and "H" are circled, as if I am somehow two people at once. Rarely is my letter mentioned beyond the beginning attendance list.

Which is why I want to remember my "rather humorous" response here. But it is gone.

INCREDIBLE SHRINKING KIDS
1986

"Come on, Mema. She doesn't want to see us," my sister said.

She picked up the stuffed polar bear and tugged at my grandmother's sleeve.

"I don't understand, Anya. Why doesn't she want to see us?"

"I don't know, Mema," my sister said, hugging the bear to her chest. It was a big white bear with a winter hat and a bell that jingled. Christmas had apparently come really early this year.

"Why won't she see us?"

"I don't know," my sister repeated.

I watched and listened from the safety of my room. They stood at the nurses' station, their backs to me. I heard the bell jingle as my sister walked away.

For three weeks I had refused to see anyone. I missed my mom. I missed Anya. I missed the Jingle Bear Anya was going to give me. But I needed to be away from them.

My mother sent cards. An aunt sent little packages. Each of the small presents my aunt sent came from a different place—a little ivory elephant from Africa, a shiny snail shell from South America, a glass cat from Europe. There was a story for each one. They were the only things I read.

I stayed in my room. For a while I didn't even talk to the other kids in the Unit. Not long after the sushi outing I shut them all out, even Lauren.

It was hard not to listen to Amanda. It was hard not to talk when curtains were all that kept us apart. Amanda was young, too, only a year or so older than me. But she was old in hospital ways. She had been in a lot of hospitals before this one. The nurses didn't really like her. Maybe they thought she was wasting their time.

Each patient was given two counselors who worked different shifts. There was another name for them, but I never bothered learning it. Because they dressed in normal clothes and didn't scold me, I'd come to like mine. It seemed like Dan and Sherri really liked me, too. They gave me hugs and never asked why I didn't eat. When Sherri showed me pictures of her granddaughter, I was jealous. I wanted to be the only kid she cared about. Still, I didn't fully trust Sherri and Dan. They were outsiders after all, not patients.

When it came down to it, I would choose Amanda over them. I knew she would do the same. We protected each other, even when it was my Dan we were up against.

The biggest battle was always the scale. That is when we were most scared. The rest of the time we could bundle in layers, hiding our bones. When we were weighed, we had to wear just our gowns.

I shivered in mine. The blue piece of cloth seemed more open than closed. Amanda and I stood with our backs against the wall in the hallway, waiting for the scale to be adjusted. Like me, Amanda was tall. Her hair was dark and cut boyishly short.

"Okay, Amanda, I'm ready for you," Dan said.

He motioned for her to step onto the scale.

I watched as Amanda walked slowly toward the scale. Even though her fate was about to be decided, she seemed less nervous than me. The numbers on the scale would either keep her stuck in her bed for the next couple of days, or free her to wander around the Unit.

All the girls except me had a chart outlining how much weight they were supposed to gain and how many days they were supposed to gain it in. If they weighed in under or over the given weight (it wasn't good to gain too much weight too fast) for a certain day, then they were restricted to their beds. They weren't allowed to get up except to go to the bathroom. They were stuck until they reached the right weight, which could mean several days or several weeks.

Because I was so young I wasn't put on medical bed rest. But I was still weighed every few days.

I held my breath as Dan adjusted the sliding weights.

Amanda was risking a lot. She had been on medical bed rest for almost two weeks now.

Before we left our room, she'd shown me a trick. Amanda was the master of tricks. She had hidden jars and containers all over her part of the room with food she didn't want to eat or food that was forced down her that she then barfed back up (which I learned later). It was gross, but impressive. More impressive was the fact that she rarely got caught.

This time I wasn't sure she would be that lucky. Stuffing batteries in the back of your underpants seemed pretty risky to me. They added weight, sure, but they were also bulky on a body that had no lumps.

How could the bulge be overlooked? How could Dan not suspect the added weight? How would she pass examination?

Amanda had smiled and reminded me it was only Dan weighing us and not Sherri or one of the others. Dan with his Hawaiian shirts and jeans, his laughter and his jokes. Dan was known as a softie on the Unit. If a patient was scared to talk to a doctor, Dan wouldn't make them. Instead, he would have them write a note and then deliver it to the doctor for them. He tried to figure out what we needed and give it to us.

Even so, when Dan congratulated Amanda on gaining weight and getting off medical bed rest, I had to look down, hoping my face wouldn't give her away.

After he weighed me, Dan adjusted the measuring stick at the top of the scale.

"Let's measure you guys," he said. "According to the charts it's been a while since you guys were last measured."

I stepped back onto the scale, eager to distract Dan from Amanda's weight.

"How tall am I?" I asked.

"Hold on a sec," Dan said. He fiddled with the stick. "Are you standing up straight?"

I nodded my head. Everyone in my family is tall—and proud of it. We don't slouch. One of my uncles got sent to military school for not standing up straight. It turned out he had scoliosis. I was starting to wonder if something similar was wrong with me. Dan kept looking at the stick and then looking at my chart. His head was going back and forth so much I was getting dizzy.

"That's strange," Dan said. He looked at me and then at my chart again. "According to this, you've shrunk an inch."

Shrunk? Having always been one of the tallest in my class, the idea of shrinking seemed impossible to me. "How could I shrink?"

"I'm not sure, but you definitely got shorter."

Amanda started to laugh. "We're young, Dan; aren't we supposed to be growing?"

Dan turned to look at me, his usual smile missing. He wasn't exactly frowning. It was more like his face had gone blank.

"Yeah, you're supposed to be," he said. He moved away from the scale and walked back toward our room.

"Aren't you going to measure me?" Amanda shouted after him.

Halfway down the hall he turned around and looked at us.

"No," he said. "Kids are supposed to grow. Kids are supposed to grow, not shrink."

It was Sherri, not Dan, who usually delivered the bad news. She had a gruff voice and a reputation for being tough, but the teddy bear sweatshirts she wore told a different story. Sherri was the one who told me about the talks. She did it gently one day, pushing my bangs out of my eyes as I sat on my bed.

"Now that you're out of critical condition, you need to go to the doctor sessions," she said.

I gave her my usual answer. "I don't want to."

I lay back on my bed and closed my eyes. Before I did, though, I noticed that Sherri had brought a wheelchair with her. She wasn't talking about going to the sessions someday—she was talking about today.

That was not going to happen. The sessions had been held without me so far. I didn't see why I should start attending one that day.

Amanda joined in from her bed across the room. "It's better if you go," she said.

"Honey, you on medical bed rest again?" Sherri asked.

Sherri pulled back my curtains so we could see Amanda, who nodded her head. A couple of days after Dan weighed us Amanda was weighed again, without the batteries. She ended up back on medical bed rest. She tried to pull herself up, but her skinny body sank back into the soft bed. Only her short black hair and skeleton-like face were visible above the mass of blankets and bedding.

I often wondered what Amanda was like before. I could picture Lauren's backstory, her life outside. It was different with Amanda. I didn't have to imagine her family, because I saw them. They were often around. Her home was in the big city, San Francisco. Their house was probably one of those pretty Victorians on a really steep street. What I had trouble with was picturing Amanda with them. I knew her backstory—a series of hospitals and eating disorder clinics. It had been a long time since she had been home. Amanda had been a patient so long I had trouble imagining her as anything else.

Sherri's voice brought me back, reminding me that right now, I wasn't all that different from Amanda.

"If you don't go to the meeting, they might put you on a program like the rest of the girls," said Sherri. "You might have to have medical bed rest."

I looked up at Sherri. Her eyes told me she wasn't joking. She was serious. They could change my program to include medical bed rest if I didn't go. Even though I'd never been on it, I knew medical bed rest was a torture treatment to be avoided at all costs. If that meant going to a meeting, I figured I better go.

"Will you go with me?" I asked Sherri.

"I'm not allowed," she said. She patted the wheelchair seat. "I'll wheel you there, though."

"I don't need that," I said. I kicked the wheelchair and stood up.

"They want you to have it."

I slid off my bed and walked out of the room.

Sherri pulled up behind me with the wheelchair. I hated the wheelchair, but I didn't want to start the meeting off wrong. I lowered myself to the edge of the chair and let Sherri wheel me into a big conference room with a long wooden table. She pushed the chair to the head of the table, patted my shoulder, and then left the room.

I looked up to see ten sets of eyes focused on me, eyes that belonged to men and women who sat around the large wooden table with stacks of notes in front of them.

The psychiatrist in charge of the Unit, Dr. Steiner, who I had only seen once, smiled and began to introduce everyone. He was tall, tan, and cheerful. The older girls whispered about him. They thought he was cute. I thought he tried too hard to be their friend. He pretended to listen to us, but I knew it was just a game. In the end he would do whatever he wanted. That was what adults did, especially doctors. They had the power to decide what happened to me, and it frightened me.

I looked quickly at the other adults in the room, careful not to stare at these doctors who sat so straight and stern in their chairs. I understood why they wanted me in the wheelchair. The chair set me apart. In the chair there was no confusing my role. I was a patient.

After introductions they started to talk about my case. I looked down at the floor. I picked at the skin around my nails as they talked about studies and vital statistics. A small man with a goofy grin, glasses, and dark hair asked why I wasn't on the medical bed rest program. He seemed familiar. I remembered him trying to talk to me a few times. I sat in the wheelchair, blood where I had been picking at my cuticles smeared on the tips of my fingers, my toes tapping with worry. They were talking about my case now, without so much as looking at me.

Finally, I looked up and glared at the geeky man who kept saying I should be put on a medical bed rest program. I had never answered any of his questions, yet he was sure he knew what was best for me.

I looked around the room, waiting for someone to rescue me.

A woman with short brown hair and a squeaky voice became my new hero when she said I was too young for that program. Besides, she added, Katya is progressing on the program she is on now.

Dr. Steiner seemed to agree with her.

I began to wiggle in my chair. The meeting must be over by now. I felt like a fake, sitting in a wheelchair I didn't need.

"What do you think, Katya?" Dr. Steiner asked.

He was at it again, trying to trick me into thinking I had power. His pen was poised above the paper in front of him, his chest bent over the table toward me. He didn't look as buttoned up as the other doctors; instead, he looked like he should be wearing a cowboy hat.

I looked up and shrugged my shoulders. With so many eyes suddenly on me, I didn't know what to do.

"Do you think we should put you on medical bed rest?" Dr. Steiner asked. "Is that what you would like?"

Tears began to form in my eyes, but still I could not speak. The words dried in my throat and stuck to the back of my teeth. My head wouldn't even shake. All I was able to do was shrug my shoulders.

"Is the program working for you?" Dr. Steiner asked.

He wasn't going to let me get away. He bent closer.

"Dr. Katz thinks you would do better on medical bed rest."

The geeky doctor nodded his head so hard it looked as if his glasses would fall off.

"Yes," I whispered. The words were uneven and half-choked.

"Yes, this program is working for you?" Dr. Steiner asked.

I nodded my head and tried again. "Can I go now?"

Dr. Steiner smiled and stood up. "Yes, I believe we'll let you go."

He walked to the door and called for Sherri to come wheel me out.

I was glad now to have the excuse of the wheelchair, as none of my muscles seemed able to move on their own.

LITTLE DIFFICULT ONE
2018

The hospital records I requested are incomplete. The small stack of papers includes far more community meeting notes than notes on my individual case. As far as my treatment goes, there is only my admission and discharge papers, plus a single-page follow-up. There is no detailed write-up on my treatment plan aside from a general summary. No regular updates on my weight gain, aside from initial observations and a note that I received nightly NG tube feedings for most of my stay and showed slow but steady weight gain. Medically, my vital signs were periodically unstable. Emotionally, I "remained clinically depressed," with a markedly low mood, with sad to irritable affect, poor eye contact, and psychomotor retardation.

There is no information about individual therapy sessions beyond the basics—they didn't work. There is nothing much on family therapy besides a similar conclusion. The results of the CAT scan I had on my head (brief mention of cerebral atrophy), the regular blood draws I was subjected to (general summary), the heart rate monitor

I used—it is all pretty much a mystery. The records raise as many questions as answers.

I wonder if there is more. Are they hiding something from me, or is that really all they had to say on my case? Four months of treatment, 120 days, summed up in eleven pages (if you don't count the community meeting notes, and I don't). The forms I signed authorizing the release of my health information numbered six.

I want more. They owe me more.

I try to find it in what I am left with, the daily community meeting notes. Even these are lacking. I have only been given a few days for each month and one meeting per day, although there were two daily meetings. To be fair, I remember attending just one meeting a day, and I may have missed more than I attended. In the notes staff members are listed by their first names: Pru, Scotty, Alger. The only complete name is that of the attending doctor and author of the notes: Bernard B. Kahan, MD. The same psychiatrist who ran a med-psych unit at Emory in Atlanta. The one who calls himself a "Steiner copycat."

I locate him in Atlanta, Georgia, where he has a private psychiatry practice. In e-mail and phone correspondence he is friendly, honest—and a bit surprised. Stanford was three decades ago, at the beginning of his career. He was there from 1984 to 1987, first as a resident, and then as a doctor. He doesn't remember writing the group notes, so I describe them to him as best I can. They are funny—a teenage patient blasting music in protest over a treatment decision. Honest and mundane—descriptions of staff and patients "straggling" into meetings, "giggling" and bickering. And heartbreaking—police supervising the sudden discharge of a six-year-old patient.

He worries he will find the notes "cringeworthy." Back when he wrote them, they were the standard form of medical documentation. Their intended readership was limited. In the 1980s medical records did not belong to patients. They also were not written for insurance providers, as they are now. Doctors wrote about their patients for themselves and their peers. No one else was ever expected to read them. The doctors had their own abbreviations. There was FLK for Funny-Looking Kid and LBK for Little Black Kid. Then there was mine: Little Difficult One. Kahan doesn't remember me at first, but as we continue talking, that is what comes to mind, the descriptive phrase.

The nickname came in part because of the difficulty of treating younger children like myself. The challenge is made clear in my records.

However, she continues to respond to direct questions with "I don't know", and is unable to engage with both peers and staff.

We were not just difficult to treat, but also difficult to diagnose, explains Kahan. With younger children you have to be careful about using a permanent label that will stigmatize them for life, especially when you don't know what they will be like in twenty years. When it comes to a sixteen-year-old with anorexia, Kahan knows roughly what to expect. Not so with a ten-year-old with eating disorder symptoms.

"I have no idea how things are going to play out," he says. "So why would I want to give you a diagnosis?"

It makes sense, only it isn't quite that simple. With psychiatry it never is.

To treat a patient, you need to diagnose them. In 1986 psychiatrists were using the third edition of the *Diagnostic and Statistical Manual of Mental Disorders*. The so-called "bible" of the profession organizes psychiatric disorders into different axes. Where I fall within these axes is listed on my discharge summary.

AXIS I Eating disorder secondary to underlying psychiatric disturbance, etiology unknown.
AXIS II Deferred.

AXIS III Vital sign instability secondary to number one, resolved.

Etiology unknown.

The younger a patient with an eating disorder is, the less likely they are to have a classic adolescent presentation, explains Kahan. In general, he adds, they tend to be more obsessive-compulsive and have more reactions to other issues. Their obsessions can make them aggressive. They also tend to be very hard to treat, oddly even worse than teenagers. Part of the problem, says Kahan, is that the incentives that work for an adolescent aren't necessarily relevant for a younger child with obsessive-compulsive disorder manifesting as eating disorder symptoms.

Today it seems they aren't even trying. According to Dr. Richard Shaw, a psychiatry and pediatrics professor at Stanford, few med-psych units still exist. With nowhere to go, these young patients often end up spending longer in the emergency room. While less restrictive, this system also means some patients are sent home before they are ready.

Another problem is that "home" may be what is causing the problem.

I wonder what would have happened had I just been sent home after a short stay in the emergency room. My medical needs would have been addressed, possibly, although it probably would have been more than a short stay in my case. As for my emotional needs, even at Roth they were a bit overlooked. I tell Dr. Kahan that therapy didn't work too well for me.

Individual psychotherapy was initiated. However, because of the patient's emotional state, she was unable and unwilling to cooperate.

I remember a few therapy sessions with Dr. Katz. He didn't seem to know what to do with me. That may in fact have been the case. The doctors assigned to the Roth Unit were young and inexperienced. That is how it was at Stanford. Therapy was conducted there not by seasoned experts, but by students, residents, and fellows training in medicine. That is the purpose of a teaching hospital, to teach young doctors.

It is what everyone does, says Kahan. "But nobody really thinks of the implications of it."

Those "implications" get more complex when it comes to child psychiatry. Having an experienced doctor watch over a less experienced doctor during surgery is one thing. Putting two psychiatrists in the same room with a ten-year-old is something else entirely. It doesn't work, says Kahan. The student must conduct unsupervised therapy sessions with a patient. The idea is that the less experienced psychiatrist can consult with the more experienced psychiatrist after they have seen the patient. In the meantime, they have to figure out how to deal with some of the most difficult cases by themselves, making mistakes that may make future therapy interventions more difficult.

As I listen to Dr. Kahan explain the clinical reasoning behind my therapy treatment, I realize none of it was about me—it was about them, the adults. Just like in joint custody cases, the children are the pawns, the players moved around at the whim of whoever is supposed to be helping them. The education of a doctor in this case is worth more than the recovery of a child. Maybe that is why I refused to see therapists in the hospital. I didn't want to be reminded how unimportant I was.

Kahan openly acknowledges the drawbacks of using residents in a med-psych unit in a 1991 paper. "The unpredictability in numbers and level of competence of trainees may compromise the stability of the unit's function," he writes.

I didn't think it could get worse, but it does. It is a former counselor, Tom McPherson, who tells me that patients were matched with residents not so much based on what the patient needed as what the adult needed. If a resident in psychiatry was skilled at treating teenage anorexics, they might be matched with a diabetic boy who was not taking care of himself. That way the resident could practice and improve on a type of patient they were less experienced with treating. It was like having a shot-put thrower compete in high jump at a track meet against a school from a different league. The outcome didn't matter. The learning experience did.

Only this wasn't a competition, it was a child's life. My life.

Dr. Stan Katz, the psychiatrist assigned to me, was doing a fellowship in administration. He was interested in learning how to run a unit, not in how to be a therapist. Tom knows because they are friends. He calls Dr. Katz a talker. Only he calls him Stan. It is a reference—both the name and the description—I find strange. That is because when I locate Dr. Katz in Sacramento, he does not want to talk to me. I have changed his name for this reason.

There is no clear contact information for him at the large health-care organization in the state capital where he works as a director of integrated care systems/mental health services. The company's media liaison is friendly and sees nothing wrong with my request to meet Dr. Katz in person. Only after the media flak calls back to tell me Dr. Katz is unavailable do I come to regret my request for a face-to-face interview. Meeting in person is always better, but from Dr. Katz's perspective, there must be some level of fear that a former mental health patient might become violent. I suggest a phone interview. The flak says she will ask again.

I never hear back.

I can't leave it at that. If I was assigned to him to help him learn, now it is his turn to help me learn. Dr. Katz was forced on me; now

I am forcing myself on him. I want to make him uncomfortable just as he once made me uncomfortable.

I dig up one of the few studies Dr. Katz published and track down his co-author. The man provides me with a direct e-mail address for Dr. Katz.

I send a brief and friendly e-mail. The reply that comes back is formal and curt.

I try again, and, when Dr. Katz does not reply, once again.

His reply is even shorter this time, and he stops answering my e-mails after that—just like he once stopped our therapy sessions.

Escape
1986

Maybe it was because of Sandra, or maybe it was just because. I don't know why.

What I do know is that it was the middle of the afternoon, a quiet time in the Unit. I didn't pack anything. I didn't need anything. I left my room and walked down the hall in the direction I knew Sandra always went before disappearing. I walked quietly, careful not to attract attention, even though everyone seemed to be busy. No one stopped me. No one followed me.

I kept on walking down the hallway, wondering where all the turns would lead. I didn't want to walk out the front door; I figured that would be too obvious. I decided that I would walk out a side door that led into the garden. I knew there must be such a door, because Sandra wouldn't have walked out the front door.

The problem was, I had no idea where the door was. In reality, I didn't even know where the *front* door was. I hadn't explored the hospital much at all. Just leaving Roth was an adventure. All the halls had the same empty look and seemed to end up in the same place.

I kept walking straight in the direction I had seen Sandra go. It wasn't too long before I saw a glass door on my right that led out toward some grass. I looked around the empty hallway, took a deep breath, and pushed the door handle.

The only sounds I heard were the swish of the door and my own heavy breathing. How could it be so easy to escape, to just walk out?

I let the door close behind me and started walking down a concrete path that led through the grass and trees. I walked slowly. With each step I took, a new experience hit me. The silence I had felt when opening the door was replaced by the noise of life. There were no longer walls on every side of me, protecting me from all the movements of the outdoors, all the noises of people. There were no curtains I could pull shut and hide behind. All the unfamiliar noises threw me off balance, and the light of the sun and the colors of the trees sent me spinning. I stopped suddenly to stand still and listen. I wanted to stop the colors from closing in on me and the noise from knocking me off balance.

There was so much noise—car horns, squeaking brakes, people laughing, people yelling, a gardener mowing the lawn, kids screaming. People made quick movements that made me jump. Everything was going so fast. I was in the outside world again, with cars racing down the street, children running over the grass, people walking along paths.

I turned around, dizzy from all the action, noise and colors. The bright green of the tree leaves, the shiny metal of the cars, the billboards filled with words. Everywhere I turned there was something— no peace, no quiet, and so many people.

I couldn't remember if this was how it had always been. Since I had been in the hospital, save my one-night excursion to the sushi parlor, the furthest I had ventured was down the hall. I had never gone outside my Unit, let alone outside hospital walls. Nothing looked familiar. I had never been to Stanford before the day I was admitted to the hospital.

I stared at the green freeway signs, looking for a place I might remember. OAKLAND, 50 MILES. Fifty miles to a city I knew, fifty miles away from anything in the outside world that was familiar to me. With only skinny legs for transport, the fifty miles might as well have been a thousand.

I stumbled toward a tree and leaned against its thick trunk. I wondered how Sandra had been able to stay out for so long. I bit my lip hard, trying to hold back the tears that were about to fall.

I pulled my arms tight around me as people passed by, staring at my pale body shivering in the sunshine. I scuffed my shoes, wondering if they could tell I was a patient; that I wasn't supposed to be out there. So many people, so many things to watch out for; how did people do it, I wondered. A woman passed close to my shoulder and I jumped, letting out a little cry.

I didn't understand how I had ever been able to live in this. I couldn't keep myself from crying any longer. I let my tears fall. When they reached my lips I used my tongue to stop them, the salty taste something familiar in a world that had become completely foreign. Although I hadn't been in the hospital that long, months, not years, I couldn't really remember what life had been like before.

Life was scary. The only way I knew how to deal with it was from inside the hospital walls. Everything moved so fast, colors, noises, and people. No one waited for you as the world closed in around, sucking away your breath and pulling at your skin.

I couldn't turn back. I knew the outside world would destroy me. Maybe that is why I had decided to run away. Slowly I started to walk forward, following the cement path to the sidewalk. I kept my eyes on the ground so I wouldn't have to see all the choices that were in front of me. I told myself, one step at a time. Once I was on the sidewalk I turned and looked at the hospital behind me. I had done it. I was off hospital grounds.

I took a deep breath and walked toward a traffic light, ready for my next move.

I decided the best plan of action was to cross the busy street. I stood leaning against the light post for support, waiting for the light across the street to turn green. All the cars whizzed by fast, creating breezes that chilled my already-cold body. I wondered how all the cars and people in them knew where they were going. The drivers must have understood those big green signs that listed numbers and places. The Oakland sign was across the street, so I decided I would cross the street. I had no idea what I'd do after that. Fifty miles seemed even farther away now that I was having so much trouble just crossing one street.

"Aren't you going to cross?" a small Asian woman asked me. She pointed at the light that was now green.

I shook my head and turned my eyes back to the cars. Many green lights must have passed while I was thinking, but I didn't quite have the courage to cross the street yet.

I watched the light change seven more times before a woman who looked about my mom's age started to cross the street. I walked with the woman, letting her walk between the cars and me. She walked too fast, just like my mom. I was left behind, watching as the light began to change.

I made it to the island in the middle just as the light turned red. I stood there waiting for another person to cross the street. Finally, an old woman crossed, walking slowly back toward the direction I had come. When she reached my island, I followed her back to the side I had come from.

Oakland was too far away, anyway.

Once safely on the other side, I decided the best thing to do was to go back to the hospital. Secretly I had hoped a cop, or someone, would come and get me. I wanted to believe that what happened to me mattered, that people cared. I wanted to have proof that I was important.

I walked slowly back through the grounds, imagining who might be looking for me—who had noticed I was missing.

I went in through the same side door and stumbled toward the familiar white walls of the Roth Unit. I looked around me, feeling the safety of the walls that kept the world away. I walked past the nurses' station and back toward my room. No one said anything.

I sat on my bed and waited for them to tell me how worried they had been, how scared and upset. No one said a word. No one had noticed.

It was afternoon, a week or so after my great escape, and I was in one of my rare talkative moods.

Noticing my good mood, Sherri had taken out her wallet and let me look through her pictures. I was sprawled on my bed. Sherri sat on a chair reading a card my mother had sent. Sherri liked to push me a bit, not bossy like the doctors, but she was good at strong hints. Reading the cards I ignored was Sherri's way of trying to get me to interact, especially with my family. She had her own family, a husband, an adult daughter, and at least one grandkid. She seemed like a made-for-TV grandmother, with her short white hair, teddy bear sweatshirts, and fake tough attitude.

My grandma wasn't like that; she didn't even go by "Grandma." Half the time people thought she was my mom instead of my grandmother. Sherri was more ordinary; not in a bad way, but in a comforting way. She was like the older women who worked at See's Candies, the ones who were always there. They let you taste the candies but only ever gave you one free sucker to take away with you—not a nugget or a truffle, just a sucker.

"Sherri?"

Sherri looked up, her smile encouraging me to continue. She was tougher on me than Dan, but it was the way a mother hen is tough with her chicks.

"Last night I got up to go pee and I thought I saw a baby wandering around the hall," I said.

Sherri didn't look surprised, so I kept on talking.

"It was really strange, this little baby in diapers just stumbling around, and some nurses and this woman running after it."

I waited for Sherri to tell me I was wrong, tell me I was dreaming. But she didn't. She took her wallet from me and put it back in her jacket pocket.

"They were in the hall last night?" she asked.

"Yeah," I said. "There aren't any babies on this unit, are there?"

I looked at her and whispered the next part. "I don't think I imagined it. I don't think I'm seeing things."

Sherri laughed. "No, honey, you're not seeing things," she said. "At least, not things that aren't really there." She put her hand on my shoulder. "Yesterday a baby *was* admitted, a little boy. He and his mother were both put into this unit."

"What's wrong with him?" I asked. "He's only a little baby."

Sherri sighed. "And you're only a little girl. Did you know my granddaughter isn't much younger than you?"

I nodded my head. I knew so much about her granddaughter, I felt as if she was one of my closest friends. She was the cute eight-year-old whose picture was in Sherri's wallet. She was a child model and always busy, running around from modeling shoots to friend's houses to sports practices. I hated hearing about her. I wondered if Sherri ever bragged about me to her granddaughter. I'm not sure what she would say—that she had a patient who could trick the doctors and knows how to avoid food?

"Well, even babies can have problems," Sherri said. "See, he was potty-trained and eating and all of that. Then suddenly he started wetting his pants again and he stopped eating."

"Suddenly, just like that?" I asked. I'd never heard of a baby who wouldn't eat.

"Just like that," she said.

"He didn't look really skinny, though."

"No, but he's supposed to be plump," said Sherri. "You know the expression, 'baby fat'? He needs to start eating, or it gets dangerous."

"Do they tube-feed him?" I asked. I shivered at the thought of a tube being forced up his little nose.

"No, he's too small for that. They just watch him and hope he starts to eat."

"That's it?"

"Yeah, basically that's all they can do. There are a few other tricks, but that's what it comes down to."

A baby who wouldn't eat. It must be hard for him. He could hear, see, and feel, but he couldn't speak. He was trapped by his own silence. The only way he could say anything was by hurting himself. It was like me, only worse, because I could talk; I just didn't know what to say. He didn't even have that option. I wondered what he was trying to say—what was so awful that it had made him stop eating. What had he seen, heard, or felt that hurt so much?

I wasn't sure I wanted to know.

Two days later the baby and his mom were gone. When I asked about him, everyone just changed the subject, unsure how to answer my questions, just as they had been unsure how to treat the baby. Whether that little boy died, lived, or remained trapped as a shadow, I never found out.

The doctor smoothed a suction cup to my chest and connected its wires.

"How many more?" I asked.

"Two," she said. She was younger than the nurses. Tall and thin, with long hair and quick hands.

Pretty Doctor stuck the suction cup she was holding to the side of my chest, where my ribs stuck out.

I winced. The cups were cold and uncomfortable, especially when they were stuck places that were already raw from where I had torn off past cups.

"It would be a lot less painful if you didn't keep ripping them off, you know," she said.

I tried hard not to wince again as she stuck the twelfth gooey suction cup to my chest.

"What are they for anyhow?" I asked.

"To monitor your heart."

She pulled out a small metal box that looked like a Walkman and connected it to all the cords hanging from the cups.

"See, when you carry this around, we can keep track of your heart rate," she said.

I looked at my goose-bump-covered chest and sighed. Twelve suction cups. These were going to take forever to rip off. And then there was the Walkman thing.

In order to fool the staff, I had to carry it around with me, even after I'd ripped off the cups and was no longer connected to it. This was not a problem, except when I forgot the darn thing and left it behind. When I did that, my game and the whole sticky process would have to start all over again.

"Okay. All done," she said. She wiped her hands together and nudged me off my bed. "Go on to school now."

Which shows just how clueless the doctors were.

If Pretty Doctor had come around more, she would've known that I had never attended school. Not once. A couple of times I had been forced to go, but I'd lost my nerve at the door and turned back.

I knew Pretty Doctor wasn't going to leave me alone right now, though. She was going to watch me to make sure I didn't rip off the cups again.

I slid off the bed and slowly made my way down the hall toward the other wing, where I thought the school was. I had pretended to go so few times, I couldn't even remember which way I was supposed to go. I had no intention of going this time, either. Instead, I stood in the hall outside our unit, waiting for the doctor to leave.

As soon as she was gone, I returned to my bed and pulled the yellow curtains shut.

I pulled off my sweatshirt and T-shirt, and shivering from the cold, started to work on my chest. Twelve. This was going to take a while.

I took a deep breath and began to loosen a cup at the top left side of my chest. Pretty Doctor had put a lot of goop on this one, and it wasn't loosening. I yanked as hard as I could and finally it came off. Underneath was a patch of red raw skin. It hurt, but if you have starved yourself, you're not really going to let pain stop you.

"Eleven more to go," I murmured as I chose the next one.

Whispers and what sounded like crying in the hall stopped me.

I quickly pulled my sweatshirt on and fixed the metal box.

I was relieved when I realized it was just Amanda coming back from being weighed. She must have weighed in under, and so would be restricted to her bed as punishment.

I knew better than to try to talk to her. Amanda was my roommate, the closest in age to me, and the closest thing I had to a friend besides Lauren, who was more like a big sister. But with Amanda there was always a distance. She could be touchy, just like my sister. It wasn't a good idea to surprise Amanda with comforting words when she wanted to be angry. When she was ready to talk, she would find me; until then, I kept to myself. Besides, I had work to do.

I took off my sweatshirt again and bit my lip as I began to work on the next cup. After I'd finished pulling all twelve off, I pulled my clothes back on over my raw chest. The entire front of my body was red and tender, and when my clothing touched my skin, it burned.

I tucked the suction cups under my sweatshirt and placed the Walkman thing in my right hand before opening my curtains.

I walked around with the Walkman thing all day, only leaving it behind once or twice. No one seemed to notice, either when I carried it or when I left it behind. Sherri was the only one who was a little suspicious, saying how it was nice I was cooperating and keeping the monitor on this time.

I thought her smile seemed a little funny when she said this, like she knew what I was doing. If she did, she didn't tell, which is weird, because Sherri doesn't let me get away with much.

Aside from Sherri's kind of fishy smile, everything went okay until evening. That was when Pretty Doctor came to check the readings on the Walkman.

She lifted up my shirt and gave a long sigh.

"Doesn't it hurt when you do that?" she asked. She placed a cool finger on my burning chest.

I shrugged my shoulders. Then I lowered my eyes so she wouldn't be able to see how wet they were.

She began to clean off the suction cups and put them in a little bag. I looked up.

"Aren't you going to put it back on?" I asked.

"No, there's no point," she said. "You'll just rip it off again."

She took the metal box from my shaky hand.

"But what about my heart? I thought you had to monitor it?"

"We haven't got a reading yet, have we?" She raised her eyebrows at me. "We'll just have to trust it's all right."

I watched as she rubbed her hands together to remove some of the sticky goop. Then she left my curtained room.

I had won. I had outlasted them.

As I pulled my sweatshirt back on, I looked at my chest. I was scared by what I had just done. I didn't understand why everyone gave up so easily. They were grown-ups. I thought they should try harder. But the doctors had stopped caring, just like my parents had. I wondered why no one stuck it out. I pushed people away because I wanted them to push back. Instead they walked away.

With Dad all it took was one embarrassing time when I hid from him in the bathroom and a few phone calls that went unanswered. That was it. After that I didn't hear from him again. Even Mom, who was more on top of things than Dad, had stopped coming when I told her I didn't want to see her. She came again when I told her she could, but when I said I didn't want to see her, she didn't fight me. She just stopped coming.

It was the same with the doctors and the medicine and machines. I fought everything because I wanted them to help me, to understand the pain I felt.

I wanted someone to show me why life was worth living, why *I* was worthwhile. I couldn't allow them to cure me, because I knew once I was better, they would turn me away. Let me go.

Filling my body with food wasn't enough. I needed more. That's what I wanted them to see. But they were already gone.

Antipsychotic
2019

...to date we still have not made significant progress in terms
of the final diagnosis.

That's what they wrote before they released me from Roth.

When I was discharged, I was on Thiothixene, an antipsychotic used to treat schizophrenia. It was noted that it might be the cause of a minor tremor I was experiencing. As far as I know, I was never diagnosed with schizophrenia or showed any signs of the disease. The reason for the medication is not listed in the charts I was given. I wonder if using it on me falls under the experimental subject's bill of rights. There is a form for that, which my parents signed. With no real diagnosis and not that many psychiatric drugs available at the time, maybe they just started trying things they thought might work. I can't think of another reason why I would have been put on an antipsychotic.

The charts note that I liked being on medication and even requested it, saying it made it easier for me to eat. My judgment at the time was more than a little flawed. As far as scientific education, I hadn't even learned my multiplication tables. A psychiatrist predicted I would need to remain on psychotropic drugs the rest of my life. I was ten.

Somewhere along the way I was switched to antidepressants. Zoloft came in high school. I have been on it pretty much ever since. The first time I tried to quit, I quit cold turkey. It didn't go very well. I was in my thirties, with a full-time job as a reporter, a long-term boyfriend, a dog, a cat, and a mortgage. I ended up having to take a leave of absence from work.

I was living in Kentucky, but went back to California for treatment. I saw the same psychiatrist I had seen as a child—not Rebeca, a real psychiatrist, a man who had seen me for a time when I was young. The same man who had said I would need to be on medication for life. I had a panic attack on the way to his office. He tried me on new drugs, a combination this time. The beta-blockers made my already low blood pressure too low and the new antidepressant didn't work. I worried I would never be able to work again. I saw myself on the streets, a crazy person without meds, or a mind, forever wandering.

I went back on Zoloft. I went back to Kentucky, to my life, to my work. I was skinnier and still had trouble making it through a conversation without crying, but on Zoloft I was able to eat and sort of function. I called it my mini breakdown.

Another one came a few years later. That one didn't require me going off Zoloft; it happened all on its own. When I started looking down the stairwell at work, imagining that falling down the center would be preferable to walking up to my office on the sixth floor, I knew I needed help. I quit my job—not because I had a better option, but because that was my only option. I was scared one day soon I would stop climbing the stairs.

I sold my share in the house to my boyfriend. He kept the cat. I took the dog, and headed to California. I started over back where I began. My mother and stepfather had convinced me to "come home" to the San Francisco Bay Area. My mom talked about unresolved issues, a favorite topic of hers. It all seemed pretty resolved to me. My parents had almost allowed me to die. I got sent to the hospital. I survived. End of story. Anger seemed pointless. I was sad, but Zoloft helped with that.

Until I decided to go off it again.

The second time I followed all the recommendations, cutting back slowly over a period of six months. It went even worse. Not at first, though. In the beginning all I noticed was a bit more bitterness, a bit less interest in the things I usually enjoyed. I chalked it up to middle-aged malaise. I was in my early forties, living in California's Central Coast, working as a writer and teacher. Working on this book. I functioned much the same as before—until suddenly I was slipping too fast to pull myself up.

I cried when I went to the drugstore, I cried at my desk, I cried in the shower. I could not stop crying. In the morning I hoped only for the end of the day, dreading every minute that would pass before then. I longed for the oblivion of sleep and yet anxiety ate at me, waking me up just a few hours after I went to sleep and keeping me on edge the rest of the night. I tried to eat, but there was a tightness inside me that made it difficult.

It was only after taking Zoloft again that I was able to force enough food down to keep from floating away. Back on the drug, I caught myself and kept myself from falling further. It saved me.

But in salvation I saw defeat. I had gone off Zoloft for the same reason I'd started looking into Roth. That they happened at the same time was not a coincidence. I wanted to know who I really was and what was wrong with me. I wanted to know if I needed the drug because I was born with a chemical imbalance in my brain, or if I needed it because of what had happened to me as a kid. I wondered if the trauma and the drugs had altered something inside me. Had my time in an institution as a child impacted my emotional development? I am not a scientist, so I started with what I could understand: writing; in this case, publications on juvenile med-psych units.

Roth was one example. Another was the unit at Emory that Steiner copycat Dr. Bernard Kahan ran from 1987 to 1993. In the first three years of its operation, the unit treated 237 patients, slightly more than half female, ranging in age from four months to eighteen years. The average stay was twenty-seven days, and almost all were discharged directly home. That was in the beginning, when doctors decided who could be treated on the unit. Over time, insurance companies became the ones to determine who could be treated, for how long, and how much their treatment should cost.

The model of care Kahan and his cohorts provided was not consistent with what insurance companies dictated. Part of the problem was that the patients did not fit into neat categories. They never had. These were the patients who were not treated successfully before med-psych units. Like at Roth, at Emory most patients received both medical and psychiatric diagnosis. Of the seventy-four different medical diagnoses, diabetes was the most common, at 12 percent, followed by obesity and renal disease/transplant, both at 6.6 percent. Next came abdominal pain, at 6.1 percent, followed by starvation state, at 5.6 percent. That there were more diabetics than anorexics surprised me. There were thirty-one different psychiatric disorders, such as somatoform disorder, one of a group of psychological disorders where a patient's physical symptoms cannot be fully explained by a medical or neurological condition.

Kahan remembers one such case of a little boy who lost the ability to walk. Doctors could offer no diagnosis. There was speculation he had picked up poison while the family home was being painted. His condition deteriorated and he became unable to attend school.

Eventually he was brought to the Atlanta unit. Physical therapy was initiated, one baby step at a time. Therapists also started digging. They discovered that the reason the house was being painted was because the boy's older brother was moving home. The older brother had been living elsewhere after it was discovered he had molested the boy's sister. After the family decided to move the older boy home, the younger boy lost the ability to walk.

When I ask what happens to patients like that boy today, Dr. Kahan has trouble answering.

"I'm not sure where those kids are anymore," he says.

He is thinking about hypothetical kids. I am thinking about the tall diabetic boy with blond hair who pretended to be annoyed with the teenage girls but was always nice to me. Cases like that have become invisible. The medical and psychiatric have been separated again, with psychiatric units only wanting to hospitalize pure psychiatric illnesses like depression and medical units only taking pure medical illnesses.

Dr. Shaw, the psychiatry and pediatrics professor at Stanford, explains that insurance companies often deny hospital claims for patients whose symptoms overlap. The companies might categorize a noncompliant diabetic as a psychiatric issue. But a purely psychiatric unit would not be able to deal with the medical side of the patient's treatment. The boy I knew didn't eat regularly. When you have childhood diabetes and you don't eat, you die. The medical problem seems pretty clear to me. It is a bit less obvious with patients who experience seizures, paralysis, and blindness, but lack a medical explanation for their disorder. They are left largely untreated, not just on the medical side, but the psychiatric side as well. Although they can be severely disabled, suffering seizures every time they attend school, there is no adequate way to serve these children, says Shaw. Because they are not suicidal, it is difficult to place them in psychiatric units. The best local option is outpatient therapy, but those programs are weekly, and most of these children need a much more comprehensive program of five days a week in order to get better.

Like Dr. Kahan, Dr. Shaw blames insurance companies for the demise of the med-psych units. Insurance covers medical necessity. Longer comprehensive psychiatric treatment is not cost-effective, and in the mind of insurance providers, not medically necessary once a patient is stabilized. The med-psych units that still exist today have severely cut back the length of stays from months and weeks to days, says Dr. Shaw. They provide stabilization, but not much more. The quality of inpatient treatment has degraded so much over the last decade that there really isn't very much psychiatric treatment going on at all, says Shaw.

While Stanford still has a shadow of a pediatric med-psych unit, it is diminished. Roth brought in just enough income that the hospital couldn't get rid of it, but not enough to take beds away from kids who needed more expensive treatment, like heart transplants. That is one former counselor's explanation, at least. It is probably not far from the truth. Research papers on med-psych units mention the fact that the hybrid units generate less income than purely medical units because the patients are less medically acute. The people they helped income-wise were the medical psychiatrists, who sometimes struggle to make budget in private practice.

What isn't as clear is if they helped the children. There are statistics on what happened to the children while they were being treated, but no comprehensive and comparative studies of what happened to those same children afterwards. The doctors I talk to assume longer-term care meant better care. I am not as convinced. It's true it helped in some ways. I was removed from a bad situation. But I was also removed from my home and placed in an institution. Was it worth it?

I am alive. But the hospital changed me. What I can't figure out is if that was for the better. As a journalist I am okay with ambiguity. As a human I want a clear-cut answer. I want to know the choices we should be making. Dr. Shaw seems confident in his decisions. When a pediatric patient needs inpatient med-psych treatment, he considers a facility in Rhode Island one of his best options. But that is a long way to send a patient from California, and there is a waiting list.

While he believes in the merit of med-psych units, Dr. Shaw also sees the advantage of some of the more individualized care that has replaced it. In intensive outpatient programs each disorder is now treated separately instead of grouped together. Shaw believes this specialization can lead to better treatment. It makes sense for those who have a clear diagnosis, yet much of our conversation was about those who do not have a single clear diagnosis, those with unknowns in their files. Those like me. The ones it is harder to see because we don't know how to look for them. Placed in med-psych units for long stays, they were safe, but hidden. Was that what was best for them, or just what was easiest for society?

Shaw believes it was best for them. But, he adds, "I don't know what the experience of a child was."

I do.

BLOODSUCKERS
1986

Lauren made me feel safe. Michelle got me to smile. She was the new girl in a wheelchair. The only other Roth kid in a wheelchair besides Chatty Girl, although Chatty Girl usually used a walker.

I don't remember what Michelle was in for. She liked to talk about her horses and was always smiling. She wasn't skinny. Besides the wheelchair, she seemed healthy. The others avoided her, probably because she smiled. That didn't seem to bother her. She just saved all her energy for me. She let me do anything, even zoom around in her wheelchair. I would climb onto her lap and she would take me for a ride. I worried I would hurt her injured legs, but she never said anything. Neither did any of the adults, which I thought was a little weird. But then, I already knew adults weren't so great at looking after kids.

Michelle even talked me into letting someone take a picture of us. I didn't do pictures, hadn't since I scratched myself out of the old family photos the summer before I was sent to Roth. But Michelle got me to take a picture with her.

She showed it to me later. We are both smiling and have matching brown bob haircuts with bangs. If I wasn't so skinny and she wasn't in a wheelchair, we'd almost look like normal kids, normal friends. Except that I was so much younger than Michelle. That was what the older girls liked about me—my age. I was the baby of the unit. The doctors even had a special program for me because they thought I was too young to be on the normal one.

I wasn't always the youngest in the ward, though. I had competition. A little girl, not much bigger than the Munchkins in *The Wizard of Oz*, would be admitted for the weekend every once in a while. She was sort of a regular, someone who was admitted about once a month because something had caused her asthma to act up. All I could get out of the counselors and nurses was that she often didn't drink enough liquids. Somehow this made her asthma worse and forced her to be admitted to the hospital for a short stay. Usually the weekend she was admitted was the same one she spent with her stepfather; at least, that's what the other girls whispered. I'm not sure if that was the truth or something they just made up.

She wasn't much younger than me, but her miniature form, curly hair, and roly-poly little body were a lot cuter than my hollow cheeks and wrinkled face. Because she was a frequent visitor, everyone knew her. Most people liked her. She was a happy change, and usually full of energy. She also liked puzzles. When I saw her and Michelle putting one together in the common room, I headed back to my room. I was Michelle's special friend. I was the kid she played with. There couldn't be two of us.

I hated the girl, which is why I made a point of talking to her. I wanted to show her that I wasn't jealous.

Her bed was near mine and we talked at night. It made me hate her less. It made me almost understand. When nurses brought her cups of water, she would grimace and I would look away, out of respect, and maybe sympathy. Still, I was happy when her bed was empty on the Monday mornings following her weekend stays. She had gone home and wouldn't be back for a while. Michelle was mine again.

Even among a ward of crazies, Chatty Girl was seen as strange.

While the rest of us dreaded having medical stuff done to us, Chatty Girl acted like it was fun.

When a staff member came up to us, she smiled. "Oh good, it's time to have our blood drawn," she said.

She used a walker or rode in a wheelchair, but no one knew exactly why. She was nice, but her endless talking, shaky movements, hunched back, loose limbs, and overall weirdness made me stay away.

"You like having your blood taken?" Amanda asked, wrinkling her bony nose.

Chatty Girl smiled at Amanda and nodded.

"I never used to mind," I said, touching my right arm. "But now that they take it so often, I hate it. Why do they have to take it so often anyhow?"

"I think it's 'cause of the pills we're on," Amanda said.

I leaned my head close to hers and whispered in her ear. "Do you always take yours? I usually just hold them in my mouth and then spit them out. But they're starting to figure it out. Last time they threatened to give me a shot instead."

Amanda smiled and nodded her head. Her smile told me all I needed to know. She took the pills even less often than I did.

I smiled back, realizing I should have known. After all, this wasn't Amanda's first stay in the hospital. She had been in three other hospitals before Stanford. Her parents kept trying different programs, hoping something would work. They seemed like a nice family, a gentle mom, a teasing dad, a pretty older sister, and an adoring little brother. I watched them walk through the unit every Wednesday on their way to family counseling.

My family never went to counseling.

I looked at Amanda's wasted body. In the time we had been in the hospital together, she had changed little. Although we were admitted on the same day, over two months ago, her short black hair still hung limply around her sunken face. Whenever she was weighed she would slip batteries into her underpants so she would weigh more. She would hide her food in the dresser drawers or under her covers. When the nurses started watching her eat, she would just wait until she could go to the bathroom and empty her stomach once again. Even when they put her on tube feedings and watched her in the bathroom, she still didn't gain weight. Unlike me she was an old hand at the trickery game. She had seen it all.

Her parents were running out of money and patience. Her next hospital stay was going to be back at the county hospital, where she said they left you alone with all the smelly old people. Her earlier stay in County added to her status on the ward. She was tough. At least, that's what we all thought.

I think Anya was the one who found out her family story. Amanda's older sister, the pretty one, had had a brain tumor. The sister was supposed to die, so the family spoiled her. By the time the sister was better, having miraculously survived, Amanda was starving to death. Forgotten while her sister lay sick in the hospital, Amanda had stopped eating to get attention. She must have figured that in her family, being sick was how you got noticed, so she got sick. The problem was, she never got well. The older sister was okay, but Amanda hadn't been for years.

I wondered about the little guy who always brought Amanda presents, the brother who wasn't sick. Would he be overlooked, like Amanda, and find his own way to get attention? Even if Amanda wanted to stop, I don't think she could. The game had gone on too long.

I was a beginner next to Amanda, and yet I had beat her on one thing: tube feedings. That was my specialty. So far I had rarely touched food, and instead was hooked up every night to a machine, through which they would pour chocolate, vanilla, or strawberry Ensure.

"What shall it be tonight?" Sherri asked cheerily. "Chocolate or strawberry?"

I shrugged my shoulders as she rolled the hanger into my room. When you eat through a tube in your nose, flavor doesn't really matter.

"Chocolate it is then," Sherri said.

She opened a can and poured it into the plastic bag that hung from the hanger. She looked at my face and the place where the tube was supposed to hang out of my nose. There was nothing there.

"Why did you pull your tube out again, honey?" she asked. "It must hurt, having to always put it in."

It did. I didn't tell her that, though.

Sherri pulled a fresh tube from a bag and began to grease the end.

"This one's a little smaller than the others, so it should go down easier," she said. "You want to put it in tonight?"

I couldn't get the words out. I took the tube instead. Then I took a deep breath. I began to push the tube up my right nostril. I worked slowly. Speed would have made it easier. But you couldn't go too fast or you would end up feeding the tube wrong. First you had to go up. Then you had to go down.

I started with the up. I winced as it tore at the raw skin inside my nose. I had pushed it too far up. I pulled it out a little, trying not to gag as I did so. I tried again, pushing it down toward my stomach. Once

I had it in position, I slowly pushed the tube further down until it was in my stomach. It was a creepy feeling, an uncomfortable feeling.

It was also familiar. This is how my days ended—with a tube stuck up my nose.

The end of the tube that wasn't in my stomach extended a foot or two out of my nostril. Sherri took that end and connected it to another tube that hung from the bag of Ensure, which itself hung from the hanger.

With a flip of a switch the brown liquid slowly began to ooze into the first and then the second tube, and then up toward my nose.

Her mission complete, Sherri leaned over and kissed my head. "I'm off for the weekend," she said. "I'll see you on Monday." She closed the curtain around my bed.

As soon as I heard her footsteps fade away, I turned off the machine. It was going too fast. The brown liquid was speeding through the tube and filling my stomach so quickly it felt like a roller coaster. I didn't like roller coasters. Now that only a few leftover drips were passing through the tube I could breathe easy again.

I shut my eyes and tried to sleep. I was just drifting off when one of the night nurses making the rounds came to check on me. She glanced at the full bag and the empty tube.

"The machine isn't even on—did you know that?" she asked.

She didn't wait for a reply. She wasn't really expecting one. She flipped the switch back on and left.

As soon as she was gone I turned the machine down so the liquid would flow more slowly. I knew she would be back to check again, so turning it off wasn't a good idea. Making it go slower was.

She was back before long. I don't think she trusted me. When she saw that the bag was still more full than empty, she left and returned with a chair. She pulled the chair up to my bedside and sat down.

"I'm just gonna have to watch you until it's done," she said.

She switched the lever that allowed the Ensure to flow at full speed. If there was anything worse than food filling my stomach, it was being watched while it happened. With the nurse sitting there I couldn't turn the lever again.

Luckily the place where the tubes connected was under the covers. I pulled them apart, and the Ensure flowed onto my sheets. After a few minutes it was damp enough that I squirmed away.

The nurse looked more closely at the tube hanging from my nose.

"Doesn't seem to be a lot of Ensure going into that nose tube, does there?" she said. She moved her bulky body closer to the bed and pulled back the covers. "Now why did you do that?" she asked, knowing I wouldn't answer. "Now we're just gonna have to start all over."

Start over? I hadn't thought about that. I figured she would connect the tubes again but I would just have to finish that can. I didn't think she would open a new one. That would be more food—the Ensure that had already come from the first can, plus a second can. That was too much. I had just wanted to slow it down. Now I had not only failed at that, but I was also getting more.

The nurse opened a new can of Ensure. It was strawberry. She didn't seem to care. She poured the pink liquid into the brown mess.

Tears formed in my eyes as I watched the bag expand. It was going to be a long night for both of us.

In the morning the first thing I did was pull the tube from my nose. When you are on regular tube feedings, you are supposed to just leave the tube in, sort of like when you have regular IVs. That would have been a sign of acceptance, though, and once I figured out that I could pull it out, that's what I did. I was not about to accept food that easily.

I sat on the side of my bed and began to slowly ease the long tube out of my stomach. As I pulled, the tube would become slimy with mucous and stomach acid. When I got toward the end, I would take a deep breath, trying to ignore the taste of the acidic pulpy mixture that had filled the tube. The more I pulled the tube out, the more it hurt every time they put it down again.

Some nights I fought harder than others. With Sherri I put the tube down myself. The nurses wanted to do it for me. I didn't like that.

One night when Boss Nurse tried to get near me with the tube, I pushed back. I wasn't strong, but putting a tube down someone's nose is hard. With me pushing her, Boss Nurse wasn't able to safely put the tube down my nose. She turned her head toward the hall.

"Hey, give me some help in here, will ya?" she called.

A young man hurried into my room.

"Hold her hands down while I put the tube in," Boss Nurse directed him.

He reached for my hands, but I kicked the air in front of him. He took a step back and shook his head.

"Come on," said Boss Nurse. "I've got to hook her up to this machine."

He stepped in again, but I kicked my legs at him. This time he managed to grab one wrist, but I was still too jerky for the head nurse to push a tube down. Another nurse joined them.

"We're gonna have to tie her down," Boss Nurse said.

The new nurse ran off, returning with a few scraps of cloth. It looked like pieces of a torn sheet. She handed them to Boss Nurse. The man raised the railings on my bed. As I kicked and hit they slowly grabbed my arms and legs and secured them. They used the cloths to tie my ankles and wrists to the railings. I pulled my arms, trying to yank them free, but the ties were too tight. I couldn't move. I couldn't fight. I lay there helpless as the head nurse pushed the tube down my nose. It hurt more than when I did it myself. That might have been because I knew how to guide it better. Or it might have been because I was in control. Now I had lost everything.

The machine was turned on. The liquid dripped from the bag into the tube. I watched each drip. So did Boss Nurse. The fight had exhausted me.

The steady drip must have lulled me to sleep, because the next thing I remember is waking in the middle of the night. Boss Nurse was sitting in the corner of my room, her eyes focused on my bed.

I vaguely remember seeing my mother that night. I don't know if it was in a dream or if she really came and watched in fear as they tied me down. Whether in dream or reality, my mother left long before it was over. Boss Nurse was the only one to wait out the storm. I secretly liked her for that.

A bell rang out. It was a handheld copper thing, and it made a loud and strange noise in the halls of the hospital.

"Time for school," a counselor called as he walked up and down the main hall of Roth. "Everyone up and out," his voice boomed. "Time to go study."

The bell stopped for a minute as he entered our room. He looked at all the empty beds and then at me, still on my bed. I was awake and fully dressed. I could make my way to school as easily as the others could, but I lay on my bed instead, listening to the bell call the others to school.

"Aren't you going to school?" he asked. He moved his large body so he could sit on the edge of my bed.

I shook my head and stared at his bearded face and blue overalls. He looked like he belonged on a farm and not in a hospital.

I heard a sigh and then a rustle as he changed his position. I knew I was in for it now. Farmer Counselor was the one who called everyone to school and made them attend classes. He wasn't going to let me off with just a shake of the head.

I looked across the room for Amanda's help. For once she was not on her bed. She had escaped the restrictions of medical bed rest and was at school.

Farmer Counselor sighed.

I sensed a lecture was coming.

"You know," he started. "I had a brother who didn't go to school. He would cut class and just hang out and stuff." Farmer Counselor pulled at his overall straps. "You know what he does now?" He looked at me as if he actually expected me to answer.

I shook my head, and he continued.

"Nothing," he said. "He can't get a job. He started trying to go back to school now, but it's hard."

I waited for the clincher, the shock that was supposed to send me running to school. It didn't come. Farmer Counselor just sat there looking at me, hoping I would learn from his brother's story.

"You don't want to end up like my brother, with no options," he said. "Stuck in the life you chose as a kid."

A small smile crossed my face. If this speech was supposed to inspire me to go to school, it had failed.

Maybe Farmer Counselor cared about his brother, but I didn't know the man. I did know I would never be like him. I wasn't planning to last that long.

My future was something I never thought about. While other kids were dreaming about being firefighters and astronauts, I thought only of today. I didn't consider the long-term effects of not going to school, just as I never thought about the long-term effects of anything I did.

Even with the regular Ensure feedings my weight gain was slow; it had to be. Too much weight gain, too fast, was dangerous. But being as skinny as I was also was dangerous. My heart was being taxed either way. There was always the chance it would just give up.

I wasn't playing this game for the long term. In my head I only thought about the next move, never about the next game. Life held possibilities for others. For me it held a dead end I knew would come before any dreams could be realized. I lived in a world of spirits, transitory beings that were neither here nor there, alive nor dead, shadows of what were once bodies. I wasn't a part of Farmer Counselor's world, the world where school and the future mattered. None of us were. Even those who got out came back or were locked up at a different place. We didn't make it in the real world. We only survived in the shadows. We existed in a realm that was neither alive nor dead.

Farmer Counselor didn't understand this. What he understood was that school was good.

Every day he made his rounds, shouting "Time for school!" He rang his bell as he went from room to room.

It had been a few days since Farmer Counselor had given me his speech. After his talk the last time, I'd decided it would be safest to pretend I was still in bed. So far he had left me alone, mainly because I'd made a point of avoiding him.

When I heard his bell down the hall this time, I quickly jumped under the covers and pulled them over my head. Just as I pulled the covers tight over my head I heard his heavy footstep and gruff voice.

"Time for school," he said. "You remember the story about my brother?"

Under the sheets I couldn't help smiling. If that had been a story, Farmer Counselor had a lot to learn about plot and characters. I waited a minute until I heard him go over to Amanda's bed, and then I popped my head out.

"Caught you," Farmer Counselor said, whirling around to face me. "Have you ever gone to school here?"

"No."

He motioned me to get out of bed. "If you're quick, the older girls will direct you toward the younger school—they're about to leave."

I slowly slithered out of bed, deciding that at least if I went to school today, maybe Farmer Counselor would leave me alone. I was already dressed. And I was a bit curious.

I felt a nudge as Farmer Counselor pushed me toward the others waiting in the hall.

I slowly made my way over.

"Are any of you going to the younger kids' school?" I asked.

"No," said Chatty Girl. She began to push her walker down the hall. "You're lucky you get to go there. I've heard the teachers are a lot nicer."

I walked slowly, to keep pace with Chatty Girl's jolting pace.

"Which way do I go?" I asked.

"It's right down the hall that way," she said, stopping to motion with her arm. "See the big door on the right?"

I nodded and made my way toward the door.

"Have fun," Chatty Girl giggled as she pushed past me.

I walked toward where she had pointed and stood outside. I looked at the shut door and thought about turning back and spending the day in the safety of my room. I touched the tube that hung out of my nose, reaching for security from its smooth feel. I had left it in that morning. It wasn't because I wanted to make it easier on myself, or the nurses. It was because I had figured out that the tube hanging from my nose made people squirm. I liked making people squirm.

I stood still and listened at the door. I wished some of the girls from my unit went to this school. I heard another young voice inside. I was glad it wouldn't just be the teachers and me. And then I remembered. I was from Roth. How would this other kid treat me? Would they ignore me? Make fun of me? Pity me? I leaned back on my heels and turned around just as the door swung open.

Too late. I was trapped.

"Well, hello," a cheerful teacher voice said to me. "Look, we have another student."

A pair of plump arms pushed me through the door and toward another teacher and the other kid. The cheerful teacher seemed to change her mind about going out and followed me back into the room.

The room was about half the size of any classroom I had ever been in before. Instead of desks there were four large wooden tables and a bunch of chairs. On the walls of the room were books and maps and other school things. The long tables were empty, looking more like craft tables than desks.

The second teacher who seemed to be in charge pushed her chair back and stood up to introduce herself. She was a small woman with short hair and rather impatient eyes. Although she was nice, she seemed less cuddly than Cheerful Teacher, who was curvy and had a thick brown braid that stretched down her back and a soft voice that lulled you closer.

Head Teacher moved toward me. Cheerful Teacher gave me a small nudge from behind.

"We're lucky, today we have two students," said Head Teacher. She smiled at me and pointed toward a girl with short tufts of hair sitting in a wheelchair at the end of the table.

"That's Monica, and she was just telling us what color she wants her hair to grow back in as," said Head Teacher.

I looked over at Monica. She looked about eleven or twelve. Her face was pale and thin, but her smile stretched across her face, inviting me to come closer. She tugged gently at a wisp of brown hair.

"I was just saying I hope my hair will come back in red," said Monica.

If she had said blonde I might have been able to resist. Red was different. That was the color Anne had in *Anne of Green Gables*. Red was the color I probably would have chosen if I had a choice.

The teachers laughed and sat down by Monica. Then they gestured for me to do the same.

I pulled up a chair across from Monica and studied the few short stubs of hair on her otherwise bald head.

"Well, actually I want it to come back in a sort of strawberry blonde, you know," she said.

Cheerful Teacher smiled and stroked her own braid. "Strawberry blonde—now, that would be pretty on you, with your pale skin."

"Yeah," said Monica. "The doctors say there's a chance it will come back that color. Black would be neat, too, but I don't think it changes that much."

Monica smiled at me. Strawberry blonde was less impressive; black, on the other hand, seemed cool. Still, she had a really nice smile.

"It's kinda neat not knowing, though," she said. "It will just surprise me. I won't know what color my hair will be until it all starts growing back in."

She seemed genuinely excited by this surprise. Her cheerfulness and large smile were contagious.

I smiled back. The fact that she was as skinny as a rod, in a wheelchair, and almost fully bald didn't seem to bother her.

"What's your name and which unit are you from?" Monica asked.

The teachers got up and went to the other side of the room. They said something about needing to set up the day's lesson.

"Katya," I said.

I looked at her expectant face. I was just starting to like her. Telling her I was from Roth would ruin everything.

I looked down and mumbled "From Roth."

I wasn't surprised by the silence that followed. Eventually I would have to look up. I figured I would find Monica turned away from me, doing some school task. Instead, when I glanced up, she was beaming at me.

"It's nice to have another kid at school," she said.

That was it. She didn't mention Roth. Didn't say I wasn't really sick. Didn't ask if I was crazy. Instead she leaned closer so the teachers wouldn't hear.

"They're nice and all," she said. "But it's kinda weird when you're the only kid, you know."

I looked to the other end of the room where Head Teacher and Cheerful Teacher were pretending to arrange books but were really watching us to see if we would get along.

I smiled and nodded my head. I understood exactly what she meant.

"No talking in class," Cheerful Teacher called. She moved toward our table, a large smile on her round face.

Monica and I looked at each other and giggled. Because there were two of us, Cheerful Teacher let us get out the plastic bowling balls and pins and play. She called it PE. I didn't like bowling, but Monica loved it. She would bounce in her chair with excitement whenever she knocked any of the pins down. Monica's excitement pulled me in, and by the end of the school day I was even having fun with the math problems Head Teacher had given us.

The next day I pushed open the school door and rushed in. I had been waiting in the hall even before Farmer Counselor came around with his bell. As the door closed behind me my eyes searched the room. At the far end sat Head Teacher and Cheerful Teacher, mugs of coffee steaming in front of them. My eyes looked over the room again. Nope. No one else was there.

"Hello, Katya," said Cheerful Teacher.

She took a sip of her coffee. "Good to see you back."

I stood by the door, not coming in any further.

"Where's Monica?" I asked.

"She started treatment again today," said Cheerful Teacher. "She won't be in for quite a while." She smiled and patted a chair by her side. "Come sit down."

I slowly made my way toward the chair.

Cheerful Teacher continued, her soft voice pulling me closer.

"None of them ever get to come that regular, too much treatment and stuff," she said. "Actually, we were surprised to see Monica yesterday. We thought she might be resting, but she wanted to come to school."

"Do you think her hair will come back strawberry blonde?" I asked.

"There's really no telling. It could. I hope it does."

"Me too."

After that I stopped going to school, only stepping through the door when I could think of nothing else to do. Farmer Counselor stopped bothering me, only sometimes reminding me about his brother. After a while he even stopped doing that; maybe he found a new patient to pick on. Or maybe he had just given up on me like all the others.

THE STORYTELLER
2018

Michelle eventually walked again, while at Roth, although I didn't see it.

The Michelle I knew was always in a wheelchair. She was a friendly and cheerful teenager who seemed genuinely happy with herself and her looks, a rarity not just on the Unit, but for teenage girls in general. Her outfits appeared to be chosen more for comfort and practicality than style, and her hair was cut in a practical bob with bangs. She didn't hang out with the other girls her age. Instead, she would work on a puzzle with me, or chat with one of the boys. I remember the adults saying something about Michelle having been injured in a horse-riding accident. They said she should have been able to walk—except she hadn't yet.

Until one day she did.

Tom McPherson was her counselor, and he witnessed her first steps toward recovery. He is the first person from Roth to talk to me about kids, not patients. They have personalities, not symptoms.

177

Dr. Steiner and Dr. Litt talk about Roth in general terms. Tom talks about how it was, day in and day out. If Roth did any good, I am starting to think it is probably because of people like Tom.

Yet Tom's motivations are different than I imagined. I don't learn that right away. First, I learn about the kids. About Michelle. He tells me her story without revealing her name or that of any other patients.

Michelle was with another teenager on the unit, a diabetic boy who had a crush on her. They were in the grass field behind the hospital, a spot chosen for its privacy. Michelle told Tom she wanted to show him something. Then Michelle got out of her chair and walked into Tom's arms.

"For years that was one of my big crowning moments—something I've done in life," says Tom.

We are seated at an outside table close to where the old hospital used to be, and where a new hospital has since been built. Tom still works for the hospital, only at a different location. He is no longer a counselor—he is in IT now—but he keeps in touch with many of his former Roth colleagues.

He was there when I was, although we don't remember each other. He spent his time mainly with the boys, who tended to be more difficult, in his opinion. He ended up at Roth a few years after he left Pennsylvania for California in search of adventure.

After working as a whitewater river guide and in a youth home, he was hired as a relief counselor at Roth in 1984, and then as a staff counselor, working the second shift from 3:00 p.m. to 11:30 p.m. He was young then, not long out of college. Now he's in his sixties. His hair is gray, and just a little longer than the professional standard. He has the lean body of a lifelong athlete who still does yoga, and the memory of a storyteller.

We talk about the people we both remember and the place that neither of us can forget. For both of us the story starts with the children.

Michelle is first.

She wasn't physically paralyzed. Yet when she took those first steps in the field, it was intense. Tom wondered if she was playing up to him a bit, showing him what he had made possible. It happened, especially between teenage girls and the young male staff.

All of this comes as a surprise to me. If Michelle walked while she was in the hospital, she never told me about it. I never even knew there was a grassy field behind the hospital where the other patients hung out, or that one of the boys had had a crush on Michelle. I knew some of the older girls flirted with Dr. Steiner, but I didn't know they flirted with the counselors as well.

In Tom's telling, Roth sounds like summer camp. Not the sleep-away summer camp I attended when I was nine, where the older girls peed in our sleeping bags. My dad chose the camp for the trees, not the campers, some of whom had been in or were headed to juvenile detention facilities. The summer camp I think of when Tom talks is the classic, made-for-television one with saccharine teenage crushes, innocent food fights, and mundane pranks. In other words, normal.

At Roth, that is what Tom tried to be—normal. He made an effort to be someone the kids could hang out with, be alive with, and not worry about "a bunch of deep psychological analysis or anything like that." He wanted to demonstrate what it meant to be a happy, healthy, and interesting person. It wasn't anything he was taught, just what he'd figured out on his own, what he had learned by working on the unit. He was good at what he did, and not just with Michelle.

Still, eventually, with or without his help, Michelle would have walked.

"Having behavioral problems like that, it's really hard to maintain them," he says. "It takes a lot of stamina if it's not really a super deep disorder."

Later he digs up his old diary and sends me an e-mail. Working with Michelle was an important relationship in his life and career. In his diary entry from the day she walked, he mentions the sense of awe and honor he felt, and the intensity of the moment. He also wrote: "There was much more than just the horse-riding injury."

On Roth there was always more to the story.

The mainstays on the Unit were children with eating disorders, diabetes, and asthma. While asthma isn't caused by emotions, getting anxious exacerbates it, so children would learn techniques at Roth to help them combat their anxiety. The diabetics worked on their diet.

Then there were what Tom calls the truly psychosomatic cases. The boy with a heart transplant so obsessed with drinking water that he flooded himself and put himself into heart failure. These were the children no one else would take. At Roth they were able to help them, and to "save a lot of kids that wouldn't have been saved any other way."

Not just save them. Some of the children went on to become extremely successful once they learned to shift the energy they were focusing on anorexia or another disorder into something more productive. Their single-mindedness could be put toward greatness. That is what the staff at Roth told themselves. It is the same thing Dr. Steiner told me earlier.

Sometimes it worked. Those are the patients Tom hears from. A woman who credits him with transforming her life sends him holiday greetings each year. The idea of sending holiday greetings to any adult at Roth—or sending holiday greetings to anyone at all, actually—is hard for me to imagine. What Tom says next seems even stranger: He has walked a former Roth patient down the aisle. Tom changed their lives—and Roth changed his.

It changed mine as well, only in a different way. Roth was one of the worst times of my life. For Tom, it was one of the best. He was in his twenties and felt part of something bigger, something special. It was an extraordinary time, a hopeful time. Many of the staff members were also in their twenties. They had come of age in the late 1960s. They were psychology majors who believed psychology was going to be the new religion. They were going to make everyone whole and healthy.

Helping them implement this new world order were the "magical" Hans Steiner and Iris Litt. Even now the doctors will always be doctors to me; it is only the counselors and patients I can call by their first names. There is a distance with the doctors.

Not with Tom. To him they were just Iris and Hans; he worshipped them both, and still does, to some extent.

Ideas flowed from Dr. Steiner, while Dr. Litt was the perfect doctor. They were geniuses and fun to work with, creative leaders who allowed their staff freedom. If you had an idea, you could try it. Whether you were a doctor or a counselor, it didn't matter. It was as if the staff had been given "toys to play with," says Tom.

I realize he's referring to the patients. I wonder if he knows how his words sound to me.

I don't think he does, because he keeps going, talking about how back then, administrative procedures didn't dominate the field like they do today; there was time to establish long-term therapeutic relationships with patients. There were outings. (Those would be impossible today. If you are well enough to go out, you are well enough to be discharged.) Tom and his colleagues saw themselves as rebels who were helping a new generation of rebellious teenagers find themselves.

"It was lucky," he says of that period of time. "Whether it worked or not, I don't know."

What he does know is that they never lost a patient. They came close, but it never happened. He also knows it could have been worse. That it was worse, in some of the group homes where he worked, before he worked at Roth. At these homes there were people on staff who were there for the wrong reasons, people who did things they weren't supposed to.

That didn't happen at Roth, at least not according to Tom. His Roth was an open fifteen-bed unit in a modest, one-story, sixty-bed pediatric hospital located in a quiet neighborhood with a creek and plenty of oak trees.

Like many of the other counselors, Roth was an early job for Tom. When they weren't working to make the patients happy, the counselors were hanging out, making themselves happy. A core crew of counselors and staff went bowling and out to eat together. A few remained apart, like Farmer Counselor, who tried to get me to go to school. According to Tom, Farmer Counselor "wasn't having as much fun as we were." He did his job, he lived his life, but he didn't hang out with the rest of the crew outside of work.

The same was true of Sherri. But that had more to do with her age and background than her interests. She had been a nursing assistant on another unit. That made her an outsider. It happened sometimes. If the outsiders fit, they could stay. Sherri fit.

Tom's Roth wasn't my Roth. But then, I wasn't a teenager—and I wasn't rebelling. I was trying to survive. I never saw the creek. The only oak trees I knew were the ones I could see from the window.

I listen to Tom because I believe of all the people at Roth, it was the counselors who made the biggest difference. I am not the only one who feels this way. It was the counselors in many respects who ended up providing much of the therapy, says Steiner copycat Dr. Kahan. That wasn't their exact title, but it was their basic role, a kind of mental health assistant who shadowed the patient. According to Kahan, most of them were college-educated and were there to get clinical practice. Some went on to get master's degrees in counseling. Others stayed at Roth. Overall, they tended to spend more time on the unit and got to know the patients better than the residents. They also tended to be easier to talk to than psychiatrists.

Each child was assigned a day and a night counselor to care for them. They also had a pediatrician and psychiatrist on their "team."

Patients were assigned a level of care: A, B, or C, with A requiring the most care, and C, the least. An A-level of care could be intense. Because the unit wasn't locked, looking after an actively suicidal A-level patient required a one-to-one counselor-to-patient ratio.

In most cases, staff were assigned two children, both of them B-level. C-level was reserved for those children about to be discharged. If a counselor had only C-level patients, then they might have three or four of them at a time.

The head nurse made assignments based on the counselors' talents and their availability. Maybe that is why patients liked them better than the residents assigned to them, based on the residents' needs. The counselors were actually chosen based on the *kids'* needs and the counselors' abilities.

Tom explains that Sherri was probably assigned to me because she was a mothering type who did well with younger children. I like that better than the alternative he suggests—that I was given to her because she had an opening after one of her patients was discharged. The patients—those are the people we both knew. Sandra. Lauren. Like me, Tom remembers the two teenage girls with short, curly dark hair as best friends. He also remembers their fights. One day they were friends, the next day they were not. I never noticed that part.

To me, Lauren was the tall anorexic who gave me a teddy bear. To Tom, she was the patient he accidentally insulted by using an abbreviation of her name that had a double meaning, implying heaviness. To me, Sandra was the tough bulimic who liked loud music. To Tom, she was a teenager with social skills who related well to people. Both girls were in and out of the hospital for quite a long time. Sandra turned out really well. He hasn't heard from her in years, but what he heard a while back was very good, although he doesn't offer details.

I try to find Sandra. Her name is too common, my memory too distant. Tom doesn't know anything about Lauren, and I can't locate her. There are others he doesn't want to find, cases that scarred him for life. I know before he says it that at least one of those cases will involve Munchausen syndrome by proxy. Those are some of the hardest cases, when parents make a child deliberately ill to get attention and medical care.

"It's honest to God like living with the devil," says Tom.

As a teenager I described my time living with my dad as hell. He did not have Munchausen syndrome by proxy, and yet he enjoyed the attention my sickness granted him. He liked the way people felt sorry for him because of his sick daughter. And he didn't make me eat. He never made me eat. If he had, I always said I would have stopped starving myself.

I am not sure if that is true. What I know is he didn't do anything to help me get better. Maybe because he wanted me sick, and wouldn't have minded if I had died, because it would have made him even more sympathetic.

I don't say any of this to Tom. Instead, I let him keep talking about his own memories.

There was one case in particular, he says. He tells me it is a terrible story that he doesn't want to talk about. Then he goes on.

THOSE WHO HAUNT THE MIRROR
1986

You didn't ever talk about why you were in the hospital; that wasn't something that was discussed. Most of the girls were in for anorexia or bulimia, and most were teenagers. No one was quite sure about the two blondes; they weren't skinny like anorexics, and they didn't seem to have weird food fixations like bulimics. I never got a good look, but I think they had scars on their wrists. The other girls seemed to respect them, as if their quicker, bloodier method of suicide was more daring. Me, I was scared of them. But then I was scared of most of the kids. They were all so much older than me—and tougher.

Except Lauren. She was gentle. She made me feel safe. It was Lauren who pulled the curtains away from my bed and held my hand when I was frightened. She was a teenager, but she wasn't like the others, who laughed at me for not knowing the names of bands or the trendy kind of jeans. I imagined Lauren at high school, a popular girl who wore tight Guess jeans and pastel sweatshirts but still smiled at the nerdy kid who was wearing corduroys and a button-down shirt. After school and on weekends Lauren probably babysat and held the hands of the kids she watched, like she held mine. She would have taken them places, like she took me on the hospital outing, explaining things to them and staying close, treating them like her friends and not just kids she had to watch.

Lauren was a dancer. She took ballet classes because she liked classical music. Her friends called her when they broke up with their boyfriends or got in fights with their parents. Lauren was a good listener and always knew what to say. I was pretty sure she had a boyfriend; she was perfect, after all. But I wasn't really into boys, so I tried not to think about that.

The only thing I couldn't picture was her family—not because I didn't want to, like with her boyfriend; they just wouldn't appear. I could picture Lauren's friends. I could picture her at school. I could picture her babysitting. But I couldn't picture Lauren at home with her family.

For a long time I didn't have to. Then, one day, without any warning, Lauren announced she was going home to visit her grandparents for the long weekend. She didn't tell me first. I heard the news at the same time as everyone else, during a meeting. The counselors acted happy, like Lauren had done something right. They seemed eager for her to go, excited almost. I stopped listening halfway through. I sank into my beanbag chair and waited for it all to finish.

I had sunk so deep that I didn't hear everyone leave and Lauren make her way to my side. She was biting her bottom lip.

"I didn't want to tell you because I knew you would be upset," Lauren said. She sat down next to me and touched my hand. "I wasn't sure I was going until recently, and I thought it would be better to let you know this way."

I looked up. I wanted to tell her something, but I didn't know what.

"I'm sorry," Lauren said.

I watched her for a minute. I took a deep breath before asking the question neither of us wanted to hear.

"Are you coming back?"

"I'm not sure, sweetie," Lauren said.

She leaned closer and looked into my eyes. When she saw the tears, she tried again.

"I'll probably be back by the end of the weekend," she said. "And if I'm not, I'll come visit."

She wrapped her arms around me and then pulled me out of the beanbag. I wondered if it would be the last time that she would pick me up.

That weekend was my worst since I had arrived. I became a ghost around the Unit, walking the halls for no reason and haunting the nurses. I couldn't stand not knowing whether Lauren would be back or not. I didn't want to be alone in my room, but I didn't know whom to talk to, or how. Lauren had been the one to draw me out; without her I wasn't sure how to act.

I walked up and down the hall pretending I had a place to go.

On Sunday morning I found Sandra painting her nails at the far end of the ward.

"Hey," she said as I passed by. "Want your nails painted?"

I looked down at Sandra and the bottle of black nail polish beside her. I had never liked painted nails. I thought they looked stupid and were for prissy girls. I also thought they got in the way. My sister always wanted to mess with my nails, and I never let her.

But Sandra wasn't my sister. Sandra had never talked to me before. As far as I knew, she had never talked to anyone besides Lauren.

If Lauren was the popular girl at school, Sandra was the cool outcast the popular kids secretly envied. Sandra did what she wanted. She cut class, she stayed out late, she wore jeans because they looked good on her, not because they were the same kind everyone else was wearing. She sat in the back of the class and drew pictures to go on the cover of her favorite bands' albums. Sandra didn't have a boyfriend, but she had a lot of boys that were friends. They all secretly wanted to date her; they were just too scared to ask. Sandra knew how they felt but she didn't care. She wasn't into boys the same way Lauren was. Sandra didn't really care what they—or anyone else—thought about her.

I wasn't as tough as that. I cared what people thought, especially Lauren's closest friend.

So I sat down next to Sandra and held out my hands. I wondered if it was even allowed, to paint our nails in the hallway. I wondered if it mattered.

Sandra started on my right hand. She held each finger gently and painted the nails with more care than I thought they needed.

"You run away a lot?" I asked.

I already knew the answer.

"Yeah," she said.

She began to work on my left hand.

"Where do you go?"

"I don't know, just around," she said.

She kept her eyes on my nails. "You ever had your nails done before?"

I shook my head no.

"They're going to look gooood," Sandra said. She still didn't look at my face.

"Lauren is supposed to get back in a day or so, maybe," I said. "Are you gonna run away before then?"

Sandra shrugged her shoulders.

I decided she probably would.

Later that night I whispered the news to Amanda and two other girls who had never been lucky enough to have Sandra paint their nails and talk about running away.

She did run away, and they found her and brought her back the next day. I never asked her where she went. I just smiled and let her look at my nails.

Lauren came back on Monday. I knew I was supposed to be sad, because this meant things hadn't gone well, but I wasn't. I was just glad to have her back. In the meeting she almost started to cry when she pulled a little stuffed bear out and gave it to me. I was the only one who got a present. The bear was brown and tied down in a little red box. He was supposed to be packaged like a chocolate. I didn't care if he was meant to be food. He was from Lauren, and that was all that mattered.

She didn't say why she was back. She didn't need to.

During group she let us know as much as she could. "One night, it was late, and I was sleeping. My door just opened." That's all Lauren ever told us about going home, besides something about creaking doors, strange grandparents, shadows that followed her, and ghosts. I didn't ask why she hadn't stayed or if she was going to be sent home again. The answers weren't important. She was back.

It wasn't for long, though. Soon she was gone again. All I had left was the bear. I think they sent her back to her grandparents, but I don't know because no one told me. She never wrote. She didn't visit either. I don't know what went on in that ghost house, but I know it wasn't good for Lauren.

After Lauren left, Sandra ran away more and more. Then one day I never saw her again. Everyone wondered why she had been here. She was bulimic, I know that much, but I think it also had something to do with her running away. She might have had scars on her wrists, too. I just know one day she was gone, and I knew I would never see her again. She never said good-bye.

I did learn while I was in the hospital. I learned from all the older patients, from all of my sisters.

I wasn't anorexic when I entered Stanford, but I was when I left. For a while I was also sort of bulimic. Amanda was my tutor on that.

"Don't you hate that feeling after they tube-feed you a lot?" I said. I squished up my face before continuing. "You know, that fullness that sits in your body."

Amanda nodded. "That's why I throw up."

I looked at her, unsure of how to answer. I had always thought you were either bulimic or anorexic. I didn't know you could be both.

"How do you...?"

"It's really pretty easy. I only do it when they force me to eat too much."

"Do you use your finger?"

Amanda laughed. "No, not usually. I just lean over and kinda gag and it usually starts to come up."

After tube-feeding that night, I tried Amanda's method. I leaned over the bathroom sink and started to gag. I coughed for a while until finally a small clump of something came out of my mouth. I rinsed the sink and my mouth and went back to my room. I soon found out Amanda and I weren't the only ones who used this little trick. In fact, most of the girls on Roth could be found leaning over a sink or toilet at one time or another. Of course, being new at it, I was discovered. But it wasn't the nurses who found me out.

My mom bounced into my room.

"You get to have your braces off," she said.

"I don't want them off." I moved to the corner of the room, waiting for my mom to leave.

"Well, too bad, they're coming off," she said. "If you had brushed your teeth, maybe things would be different." My mom grabbed my arm. "You aren't brushing regularly, so they have to come off before your teeth start rotting," she said.

I never brushed my teeth. I hardly ever combed my hair, and I rarely washed. My nails were dirty and uncut, my hair rumpled, and my teeth rotting. I had never liked my braces, but I didn't want to get them off. I was used to them. But more than being used to them, I didn't want to leave the hospital.

I was scared. I could tell my mom's excitement was fake and that she was really in a bad mood. The cheeriness and bounce to her step did not come with a smile—at least, not a real one. Her anger probably had something to do with the amount of money she'd had to pay for the braces and the fact that they were now coming off before my teeth were fixed. Or maybe it upset her that my survival had become so uncertain that having nice teeth no longer seemed important. No one comments on a corpse's smile.

She was not gentle that day. She pulled me to the parking lot and prodded me into the car.

I shut my eyes for most of the ride. I figured the less my senses were active, the less things would change, and the less I would have to deal with. I sat silently in the orthodontist's chair, my eyes half closed and my body limp.

"All done."

After my braces were off, I was taken to my dentist. He was going to clean my teeth.

I never understood why people hated the dentist. I liked seeing mine. I had never had a cavity. He usually ran his tools over my teeth, smiled, said nothing was wrong, and let me go. Sometimes he would tease me about needing to eat more candy and drink more soda so he wouldn't go out of business.

This time when he ran his metal tool across the back of my teeth, I heard it catch. Then I heard him sigh.

He nudged me toward the waiting room and turned to face my mom. His usual smile had fallen away. His touch had been extremely gentle. It was as if he was scared I would crumble away. He had been my dentist for as long as I could remember. He had served in the military. He told stories about Vietnam, living in the jungle. I looked back over my shoulder to see what he was saying to my mom.

He caught my stare and forced a smile. "Now look at that," he said. "What a beautiful, braces-free smile." He tried to laugh. The office staff giggled nervously, unsure what to do.

There was no smile on my face; hadn't been for months. And my face and teeth were far from beautiful. My gums were dark and swollen. My teeth were yellow. My skin was so pale it almost glowed. My lips were chapped and cracking, my hair thin and patchy.

It was my dentist who informed Mom about my bulimia. Bulimia is less visible than anorexia. It leaves its mark on the teeth, the heart, and the electrolytes. All it got in my case were my teeth.

Back at Roth, my doctors didn't want to believe that I was throwing up. But my mother must have convinced them, because it wasn't long before I was being watched in the bathroom. I discovered the toilet served just as well as the sink. Soon all privacy was gone, the stall door kept open with a nurse staring at me while I went to the bathroom. I felt like a convict, and promised not to throw up again if they would let me pee in peace. They didn't believe me. I was forced to pee without privacy and devise sneaky ways to throw up. I threw up now to spite them more than to relieve the heaviness in my body.

I knew many of the girls threw up in their drawers or sheets or clothes, anywhere they could. I was scared to throw up in anything that would smell afterwards, so I wasn't very good at it. Soon after they trusted me enough to go pee by myself, I cut back on my throwing up. I only puked when I couldn't figure out any other way to get rid of the trapped feeling inside me.

The outing to the orthodontist and dentist took most of the day. After, my mom drove me back to the hospital.

Back in the security of my room, ready to flop onto my bed, I stopped short. There was a large stuffed animal on my pillow.

"What's this?" I asked, tugging at the stuffed gray-and-white dog on my bed.

"I don't know," my mom said.

She grabbed the stuffed animal to see if there was a card or any identification.

"Looks like a gift someone left you," she said.

I grabbed the dog back from my mom, already possessive of my new gift.

"They left you balloons, too," my mom said.

I followed her gaze to the side of the bed where a few balloons were tied to the bedpost. She walked over to the balloons and looked to see if there was a card or note.

"No card here either," she said. "I'm going to ask around and see if any of the nurses know who left you this stuff."

She let the balloon strings glide through her fingers.

I hugged the dog to my chest and then held it back to inspect it. Its fur was so soft it felt like it had been made out of the soft fur on the belly of a real puppy. Its gray ears flopped and its tummy was snowy white, while its back and face were covered with gray and black splotches. I pet its head and wondered who had given me such a posh gift. The dog was definitely not a cheap stuffed animal; it was a carefully chosen, huggable creation.

My mother walked back into the room.

"The nurses say some people from your class dropped it off," she said.

I looked up. I tried to imagine kids from my class here in the hospital. I held the dog back and looked at it closely. Its large black eyes stared back at me.

"Wasn't that nice of them," my mom continued. "I guess they came while we were at the orthodontist. It's a very pretty dog."

I pushed the dog further away. "I don't want it."

"What? It looked to me as if you loved the thing."

"I don't want it," I said again.

I turned my back on my mother and the dog I wanted to hug so much.

"Is it because of who it's from?" my mom asked.

She waited a minute for me to answer. My back offered her no response.

"Okay, I'm putting it away," she said. "I'll just leave it in this corner until I leave."

I heard rustling as my mother moved the dog to the corner. I turned around only when I was sure the dog was out of sight. The soft furry friend was too tempting if it was in my view.

If only the kids in my class had given me the dog, I would have accepted it. But I knew such a nice dog was sure to have been paid for by their parents. And it was these adults who had not helped me. So, I would not allow them to win me over with a stuffed dog. I was glad my mother hadn't taken the dog away, though. I still hoped to hug it again someday.

BY PROXY
2018

Bingeing and purging, or stuffing yourself and then throwing up, causes the body's electrolytes to undergo extreme dips and rises. The heart has trouble keeping up, and stomach juices chip at the enamel on your teeth. Even though I only flirted with bulimia briefly, it left its mark on my body. The enamel on the back of my teeth started to erode.

Bulimics die when their electrolytes go haywire. Anorexics die when their hearts stop beating. Both usually go to sleep and never wake up. I don't think I knew this when I was at Roth, but I did by the time I was in college. That was my first relapse—and the first time I feared falling asleep.

It wasn't the last. Never waking is my recurring nightmare.

Tom has another one. Eating disorders might have been the most common disorders on the Unit, but it was Munchausen syndrome by proxy cases that seemed to fascinate the staff. The syndrome is named for Baron von Munchausen, an eighteenth-century German soldier and politician who also happened to tell tall tales. The Munchausen name was first associated with adults who appeared to be faking illness. The "by proxy" was added in 1977 to describe cases where parents were making their children sick. According to an article Steiner copycat Dr. Kahan co-wrote on the topic, the child abuser in these cases is almost always a mother. The most common types of fabricated illnesses that Kahan lists in his article are seizures, allergies, blood in the urine, and vomiting. Mortality is reported at around 10 percent; and the frequency, impossible to know for sure.

At Roth Kahan remembers a Munchausen syndrome by proxy case that shaped his career. The patient seemed to have allergies to everything. Her case was believed to be terminal. The Make-A-Wish Foundation built her a life-size playhouse with electricity and running water. A local newspaper covered her story.

The neurologist treating her became concerned that the girl's mother was enjoying the publicity a little too much. That is how Kahan got involved. He doesn't tell me what happened, just that Munchausen syndrome by proxy cases are "really hard to treat."

Tom is more blunt.

"If you ever want to know what evil is, just watch this perfect mother who you know is murdering their child," he says.

The girl he is talking about was at Roth when I was there. I know she was young, like me, and small. I know she shared a room with me for a while. What I don't know is who exactly she was. My memory of her is blurred, a sort of composite of several different girls. She could be the girl with short curly hair all the older girls thought was adorable. Another option is the girl whose mother was always visiting and bringing gifts. A part of me suspects the girl who had the bed next to me for a while, and whose parents wanted her in a ward with the "real sick kids." Then there is the girl who used to get around on a walker, or sometimes a wheelchair, Chatty Girl.

With all of them there was a bit of a mystery around their diagnosis, not unusual on our unit. I could be describing almost any of them when I tell Tom I never knew what was wrong with her.

That's because there wasn't anything wrong with her, says Tom. "Except she was being poisoned every day by her mother."

The girl was in and out when I was there. The next year she was in for almost a full year straight. Tom spent virtually every day with her. He was her counselor. His job was to keep her alive.

"I was one-on-one with her and her mother, who was trying to poison her," he says. "My job was to stop that for, like, a year of my life."

One night the girl went into cardiac arrest. It was around 10:30 p.m., and Tom was helping to administer aid, along with a nurse. They gave her an EpiPen. Administered CPR. Everything they did, they documented in written form, as is required.

When they were done, they discovered their notes were gone. Tom suspects the mother stole them. Later the mother sued them for not having documentation. It is one of numerous court cases, lawsuits, and custody battles involving this patient. The hospital was trying to build a case against the mother, but it was hard, because the mother was extremely devious and hard to catch, says Tom. She had also made the girl almost completely dependent on her, to the extent that the girl could not survive without her. In the end, the mother died. The girl survived.

The psychiatrist who treated the girl was the same one who treated me—Dr. Katz.

"That's probably one of the reasons he didn't want to talk to you," says Tom. "He doesn't want to come back to that."

Dr. Katz had been treating us both at roughly the same time. I wonder if he mixed us up or just lumped us under the same bad memory. I wonder why Dr. Katz, of all people, a man who wanted to work in administration, was given two of the more difficult cases.

Tom tells me he has only scratched the surface of the Munchausen syndrome by proxy case. "Check your imagination and triple it," he says.

Although he doesn't want to relive it or know too much, he did look the girl up on Facebook. He was happily surprised to see she was doing okay. He didn't reach out.

"I'm not sure I want to go back there again," he says. "I'll take it for what it is. She's still around and writing decent Facebook posts, which is more than I expected."

Later, I too find her on Facebook. Her profile picture features a middle-aged man and woman. I assume it is her and her partner. She has marked that she is in a relationship. She is short in comparison to the man, with curly hair—and a smile. Her posts feature food, beer, funny quotes, and occasional statements about faith and hugs. Aside from her profile picture, there are no other photos of her or her friends and family (although she has hundreds of friends), and nothing personal—just reposts of humorous and cute things related to her interests. She lists a job in child care and another at a college, the same college she lists as having attended. Under movies there is just one—*Maleficent*, the 2014 Disney movie about a villain. There are more television shows, mostly about the same thing, including *General Hospital*. I find both entries fitting.

We have no friends or interests in common, so I am surprised when I see a post about an out-of-the-way tavern that I e-mailed to a friend the week before. A coincidence, but weird to see that our worlds still intersect. I message her and ask if she wants to talk. She doesn't answer. I ask if she wants to meet. She says she does, but not tonight, maybe tomorrow. The next day I tell her I am there.

I never hear from her again.

A year later my friend request remains pending. I am secretly relieved. There is only so deep I can go and still manage to resurface.

A ROCK FEELS NO PAIN
1986

"Katya," my mother said. She touched my hand. "Katya, have you heard anything I said?"

I looked up at her face, a face I had looked at so many times. What had she been saying? I looked down at the pale hand resting on my own. I knew her hand was touching mine, but I knew this only because I saw it, not because I felt it. I studied the wrinkles on her face, the angle of her mouth, the tilt of her chin. I watched as her hazel eyes started to blink more rapidly, tears forming in the corners. I watched her face become wet, listened to her voice begin to crack. I heard the tone of her voice, but I didn't hear the words. I saw the tears, but I didn't feel the frustration. I saw the arms that reached toward me, but I never felt the hug.

I shut my eyes and pulled myself further back against my bed, creating even more distance between us. No thoughts filled my head; it was empty, as empty as my stomach. I looked down to see my mother place a blanket on my legs—legs so cold they were covered with goose bumps. I looked up at the clock. Visiting hours were almost over. Soon my mother would leave for the day, go back home.

"Your sister misses you a lot," my mother continued.

I leaned my head against the wall and looked past my mother to the yellow curtains she had pulled shut. Missing someone was not something I could do. I am not sure why, but my feelings kept flip-flopping. I had been in the hospital around two and a half months and was more confused than ever. I wanted people to notice me and I wanted to be left alone. What I felt at any time depended on which emotion was winning at the time.

"It's like talking to a rock," my mother said, bringing her hands to her damp face. "Do you hear anything I say? Do you understand that I love you?" My mother took her hands from her face and placed them on my forehead. "Where are you?"

I turned my eyes upward, trying to see the hands that reached for me. Love. I didn't understand the word. Why did she tell me she loved me? Why did she waste so much energy on me, so many tears? Why didn't she let me go? Why did people have to keep trying to bring me back?

There was a time when I had seen her tears and had wanted to be able to cry, to be able to feel her pain.

Not anymore. I didn't want to be a part of that world, a world that hurt so much. I was safe in emptiness. Like a bear hibernating for the winter, I had shut myself off from the world and I no longer knew how to wake up.

"It's like there's a veil between us," my mother said. She shook her head at me. Her hands were no longer on my face. "Is anybody there?" she asked.

My teeth began to rattle. It was so cold.

I focused on my mother. Her arms were grabbing my shoulders, shaking me back and forth.

"Is anybody there?"

Most of the time, there wasn't.

———

Dan placed the lunch tray on my lap. He moved toward the corner of my room to sit down and wait.

I looked at the tray in front of me: a burnt hamburger, a pile of peas, soggy mashed potatoes, a roll, and a carton of milk.

I adjusted the tray on my lap and leaned back against the wall behind me.

I was still refusing to actually put food into my mouth and allow it to fill my stomach. The only way calories entered me was through the tube hanging out of my nose. The variety of my diet consisted of chocolate, vanilla, or strawberry—not that I actually tasted any of those flavors. It was more a different color for me to watch as it trickled down the tube.

Bringing me food was a new thing. The doctors thought if I had to sit with a tray of food in front of me for an hour, I would eventually eat an apple, or, better yet, a hamburger. Geniuses, really. On most starved people this theory would have worked—even with too-white potatoes and burnt burgers. But being forced to bond with my food only made me mad.

At first when Dan started to bring the lunch trays I sat patiently and stared at the food until Dan figured it had been long enough and took the tray away. It was a few days before I decided to do something new. Sick of watching the food on my lap grow cold, I decided to have some fun. Instead of wishing the food away, I started to play with it. I pushed the peas under the potatoes and stirred. It looked like a ski slope with grass shooting through.

I put down the fork and examined the food on my tray. The hamburger, carton of milk, and roll were untouched. I picked up the roll and tore it into little pieces. Then I dropped the little pieces on top of my ski slope. After I had mixed in the bread I started on the hamburger, cutting it into chunks before smashing the chunks into the mashed potatoes.

I looked at my creation. It still lacked something. The hamburger and bread had dried up the mashed potatoes. I shook the carton of milk and carefully poured it over my food, watching the food turn to mush. I stirred everything once more. Then I sat back to enjoy my handiwork. My lunch plate had been transformed into a plate of mashed madness.

"You going to eat it now?" Dan asked.

He watched as I picked up the spoon and started stirring the ingredients again.

I let out a little giggle. I pushed the tray toward the edge of my bed.

"You like it?" I asked.

"Great," he said. "Although I think it could use a little ketchup. That would add some color."

I looked at the creamy creation in front of me and imagined it with ketchup. Dan was right, it could use some color.

"Yeah, but no one brought me any ketchup," I said.

Dan looked at his watch and then at my tray.

"I guess it's safe to say you're not going to eat any of that," he said.

I nodded and Dan got up to take the tray away.

Dan was the definition of easygoing. He played along with whatever I did. When I messed up my food, he laughed. He didn't scold me or talk about the waste. I knew many of the other counselors would have been harder on me. Sherri would have definitely lectured me. Not Dan. He always enjoyed a joke, and would rather laugh with me than upset me. I guess he figured I was already upset enough as it was. Out of all the males on the Unit—doctors, nurses, and counselors—Dan was the only one I let near me. Maybe that is why Dan was the only one I ever tried to hurt.

"Lunchtime," Dan called. He pushed my yellow curtain back.

"Go away," I shouted.

I was in a bad mood, and the last thing I wanted was cheery Dan and a plate full of food. Dan was my buddy, but by bringing the tray he had crossed a sort of line in my book. On good days this didn't bother me too much. Today was not a good day.

"I don't want that," I said. "Go away."

I knew he wouldn't.

As the anger built up, I tried to think of how to stop him from making it worse. I looked for something to throw at him. I grabbed a small stuffed animal and aimed it at his legs. The animal landed on the floor in front of him, a foot away from its target. Dan stood just inside of the curtain. He was unsure how to deal with my new rage. He held the food tray in both hands in front of him and watched me closely to see what my next move would be.

I looked at his face, which was more amused than scared. He didn't laugh, though. He knew better than to make fun of my feeble attempts at anger.

"I hate you," I screamed. "Why don't you just get out of here? I want you out of here."

"I have to bring your lunch," Dan said, holding up the tray.

"No, you don't," I screamed back.

His laid-back attitude was suddenly annoying me.

"Just 'cause they said you have to bring it doesn't mean you have to," I said. "You don't have to listen to them instead of me."

I stopped to catch my breath. It was true. He didn't have to do it. He could fight back for once. He could fight for me.

"You know I'm not going to eat it," I added.

The words didn't seem to bother Dan. Which made me even madder.

He calmly walked closer to my bed. As he neared the edge I hissed and yelled. Nothing seemed to affect his cool. I resorted to what I thought might work.

"Get out of here, you jerk!" I yelled. "I can't stand you!"

Dan placed the tray on the chair in the corner and turned to look at me. His face showed no hurt, only surprise.

"I'm leaving," he said.

He moved back toward the curtain.

"Good. I hate you," I said.

I watched him pull back the curtain. Then I spat out my finale: "Fuck you, Dan."

At this, he finally left the room.

Normally, I didn't swear; I didn't yell. That wasn't me. I wasn't sure where that had come from, and as soon as I had gotten rid of Dan, I missed him. Sitting alone with the tray was even worse than when Dan was there. Food was intimidating. Playing with it in front of Dan made it feel safer. He might not have helped with the actual stirring and mushing of the food, but his comments and laughter made me feel less alone with the thing I feared most: food. Life.

Yet for the rest of the week when Dan brought me my lunch tray, I yelled at him. I swore at him. I planned my words for hours beforehand. Once I even managed to hit him with a stuffed animal, although it just bounced off his leg.

In the afternoon when Dan would come back, he would joke with me, like usual. He never mentioned my earlier outbursts. When he didn't have the tray, I didn't attack him. I treated him the way I usually did, as my friend. I think he put up with my outbursts because the spark of life was better than endless "I don't knows." He took my insults and listened to my tantrums because they were the first sign that I had not completely given up, a sign that I was still able to feel.

Once when I stumbled over a swear word, I think I even saw a smile on his face. Not a laugh, just a smile.

He could laugh with me, but not at me. Dan didn't care what it took to bring me back; if it was anger, he would take it.

Even after the anger was gone, I'd still remember the way Dan took my outbursts in silence, and I would feel a sense of warmth. Unlike the other adults, he didn't give up. He didn't leave me alone. He kept coming back. I could yell at him because I knew he would return.

I wasn't so sure about my parents.

It wasn't Dan I hated, it wasn't Dan I was mad at, but it was Dan who would let me swear and yell at him and then act as if nothing had happened. I needed that. I needed to know that I could say those things to him and he would still come back. He wouldn't give up. I think in a way I told him what I couldn't tell all the others, especially my dad.

I couldn't be angry with my parents. I didn't feel safe enough to yell at them. So I took my anger out on the people who had nothing to do with hurting me. I was angry with happy kids for having what I didn't. I was angry with nice guys like Dan because they weren't my dad. I was angry at Dan because I knew it hurt him; I knew he cared. I wasn't so sure about my dad.

After a couple days of yelling, my energy began to go, along with my voice. The doctors realized their new idea wasn't working, so I was no longer forced to commune with my food. I went back to being a rock.

EVERYBODY LOVES DAN
2018-2019

Hey Katya this is Dan. My goodness, time flies. I'm fine with
us getting together for a meeting...

The text surprises me. He isn't excited or happy to meet me, he is
"fine," as if I'm an ex-girlfriend whose memory disturbs him. It wasn't
the reaction I was expecting. Of all the people from Roth, I thought
Dan genuinely liked me, cared about me, would want to know what
happened to me. Instead he has disappointed me, the same way the
rest of the adult world disappointed me when I was a child.

The text comes a day or two after I leave him a voicemail, as if
he needs time to process my request. The voicemail in turn was left
after weeks of trying to find him via those who know him. It turns
out I wasn't the only one who liked Dan. Everyone liked him. Steiner
copycat Dr. Kahan liked him so much he took him with him when
he left Roth to start a similar unit in Atlanta.

On Dan's last day at Roth, the mood was dreary. Yet Dan wasn't sad or nostalgic. He was funny. He walked in with two fistfuls of ballpoint pens and announced: "I stole these." That is how he returned the pens he had taken home accidentally over the years, making everyone laugh.

It was a classic Dan move—to make people smile when they felt like crying. He did it with patients as well. He was one of the rare staff members who could work with almost any patient, including the girls, something not all of his male cohorts could handle. He was versatile and skilled, but he was also just plain good with kids. It probably helped that he had five younger siblings.

He came to Roth in 1980, just a year after it opened. It is easy to see how he ended up there. He was a local guy in his late twenties, a sociology major who had trained as a nurse. In a way it was his dream job, talking and hanging out with kids. He tells me this when we meet at the tasting room of the Napa winery where he works. The only other former counselor I have been in touch with, Tom, has tracked Dan down for me.

I arrive early to our meeting, before the winery is even open, and sit in my truck, waiting. I am wearing boots with a bit of a heel and a leather jacket I inherited from my sister, who in turn inherited it from a former boyfriend. I want to look nice. I want him to see me as successful, beautiful, and strong. I am not sure why this is important. I liked the old Dan because I could be myself with him; I could be scared, sad, mad, whatever I needed to be, and he would stay by me.

But his text unnerved me a bit. He is "fine" with meeting me. As if I am a leper people are afraid to get near. I am reminded of Dr. Katz and how he was not fine with meeting me. He wanted nothing to do with me. But Dan is different. Dan is my buddy.

Only now I am starting to wonder if I had it wrong, if he was my friend simply because that was his job. The only way to find out is to get out of my truck and walk the hundred or so feet to the winery entrance.

I worry I won't recognize him. It is early in the day, though, and hardly anyone is at the tasting room, which consists of both an indoor and outdoor seating area. Near the entrance, before I even make it inside, an older man greets me. He is several inches shorter than me. That's the first thing we both comment on, that I'm taller than he remembers. He is shorter than I remember. As if we both expected I'd still be the same height I was at ten years old.

He offers me a seat and a drink. I ask for water, not because I am thirsty, but because it gives me a minute to take things in while he goes to get it.

I sit down outside and wait. When he returns, Dan tells a joke. He used to work with children, he says. Now he works with adults acting like children. He is still the Dan I remember. He is trying to make me comfortable. The thing is, I can tell by the practiced way he delivers the joke that he uses it often. I imagine him telling it to customers he serves at the winery. It is a joke for strangers, not friends.

It is a joke, nonetheless, and I do remember him being a jokester. Other things are similar as well. He dresses the same way, in khaki pants, hiking shoes, and sunglasses held around his neck with a strap. Dan is sixty-seven now. His hair is white, his face slightly weather-worn, his midsection rounder than I remember.

After we get through the surface-level updates, he tells me I am the first former patient to find him. He spent almost a quarter of a century working with patients, yet I am the only one who went looking for him. He wants to know why. He is curious—and wary.

The wariness surprises me. I always thought of Dan as someone I could trust and someone who trusted me. Now I suddenly wonder if it was all an act.

That he has not connected with other former patients surprises me. If any counselor should have been asked to walk a former patient down the aisle, it should have been Dan. We all loved him. He was the equivalent of a big teddy bear: soft, cuddly, and comforting.

I am not sure how to answer his question. I thought he would be happy to see me, not suspicious.

I tell him I am a writer, hoping that will serve as enough of an explanation. Then I give him a copy of my first book, which is about baseball.

He already knows I'm a writer, I find out. Tom told him I had an author website, but he hadn't looked at it. He wanted to wait, he says.

I understand. He needed to know I turned out okay before going further. He was protecting himself without fully closing the door.

It was Dan's idea that we meet at the winery, a public setting. Soon after we greet each other, another employee about Dan's age joins us. Dan tells his colleague that we go way back. He doesn't tell him where to. He is careful about protecting privacy, both of ours.

I wonder if he had asked the man to stop by and check on us beforehand. Did they agree on a certain signal to use in case I turned out to be crazy? I did that once when I was meeting a sex offender for a story. The photographer and I agreed on a signal I could use if it got too weird. It got weird, but I never used the signal.

It doesn't upset me that Dan might view me the same way I viewed the sex offender. It disappoints me.

What he says next crushes me.

He talks about maintaining a "post-professional relationship."

It is a strange phrase to use, considering the close relationships Dan and the other counselors had with patients. Before I left Roth, Dan took me to a toy store and let me choose a stuffed animal. I chose a bulldog, because it seemed both tough and gentle, like Dan.

Even now he is the only one I really feel comfortable enough with to talk about the straitjacket.

He tells me that wasn't something they liked to use. That is all he says about my experience, other than acknowledging that it must have been traumatic, and that it was probably initiated by the medical staff, not the psychiatric staff.

He breaks the staff into categories I never considered, and tells me how they, like the patients at Roth, were treated differently. Staff on the other units would complain that the Roth crew had it easy. They would see them watching TV with a kid and think that was all they were doing. But Dan was never just watching TV. He was watching the kid, because the kid might lash out at any minute. And when the kid did, you let them.

Dan and the other counselors recognized that anger was good, and that the children needed to know Roth was a safe place to be angry. If they were yelling and screaming it meant they had a spark, and a spark meant there was hope—they might get better. The fighters... those are the patients Dan remembers.

I wasn't one of them; not really. I threw a stuffed animal at Dan and yelled at him for a few days, but that was it. Most of the time I was passive. Notes describe me as curling up in the fetal position and repeating a regular mantra of "I don't know" rather than "Fuck you." The passive patients were harder.

I wonder if that is why Dan doesn't remember me. He tells me he is trying, but aside from the fact that I was young, no other memory comes to mind. I wonder if it was a protection mechanism to forget the ones that he didn't think would make it.

I ask again, certain he has to remember me. I recall him so well, I have a hard time comprehending how he could forget me.

"I can't," he says. "I've been trying."

He can picture me being younger, but it is "kind of diffuse." It's not callous, he explains, but you move on.

"If it is nothing earth-shattering, you just move on to the next."

My story wasn't earth-shattering—not like the Munchausen by proxy cases. In a freak show I wasn't the freakiest, so I was forgotten.

THE PRETENDERS
1986

I woke up to the sound of a bell, much louder than the one Farmer Counselor used to call us to school. It was more like a siren.

Rubbing my eyes, I crawled out of bed. I stuck my head out into the hallway and watched as nurses scrambled around the nurses' station.

"I'll go, you stay on here," said one of the nurses. She tossed down a chart and began to jog out of the Unit.

The other nurse got up and walked toward the hall, her eyes following the first nurse's movements.

Amanda got out of bed and joined me in the doorway.

"What's going on?" she asked.

I shook my head and ventured out into the hall. "Some emergency or something," I said.

Michelle wheeled her chair toward us and stopped.

I still hadn't figured out why Michelle was in our unit. She always had a smile, and her skin was as shiny as metal in the sun. I liked Michelle, but her bear hugs and upbeat attitude were sometimes

213

hard to deal with. The teenage girls, the ones closer to her age, didn't like her. I think they were suspicious because she didn't talk about them the way they talked about her. I wondered if it had anything to do with her slight lisp. Maybe she was just used to being the one people talked about and knew what that was like, so decided not to talk about other people the same way. Instead she talked to the adults, which meant she usually knew what was going on.

As she parked herself outside our door, Amanda and I looked to her for answers.

"What's going on?" we asked.

"It's an emergency in the cancer ward," Michelle said. "Something about a kid needing more blood or something."

I waited for her to make a joke or change the subject to something more cheerful. That's what she usually did. She never lied; she always told things like they were, but she did not like people to be down, especially younger kids like Amanda and me. She was protective of us and tried to keep us innocent, which I found a little funny, because there was nothing innocent about Amanda anymore, and not a lot left in me either.

Now, however, Michelle just sat in her chair, staring straight ahead.

Amanda nodded and turned back toward her part of the room. She was an old hand at hospital goings-on and had probably experienced something like this before.

Not me. I stood in the doorway, wondering if the kid would live. I sort of wished I would die instead of him. I didn't understand it. Kids so full of life and loved by so many died, while the rest of us, those who were already half dead, were forced to stumble through life, dreading each new day.

I went back behind my curtain and got dressed.

Later that day I went to the community room where everyone seemed to be gathered.

Amanda was talking as I approached.

"Who was it?" she asked.

One of the blondes answered. "Gabriel," she said. "Remember, he came to school a couple times?"

"Yeah," said Michelle. "He was a real joker in class, made it fun."

Amanda nodded. Like the others, she went to the older kids' school, when she went at all.

"He was only there once when I was there, but I remember he was always cracking jokes," Amanda said. "He was about thirteen, right?"

Michelle nodded. "I don't understand why they couldn't save him," she said. "Why they couldn't get him enough blood."

"He died?" I asked.

All the girls looked at me.

Up until now I had been left out of the conversation. I never knew Gabriel, because I went to the younger kids' school.

"Yeah, he died this morning," Michelle said.

She backed up her wheelchair and pushed it toward her room. It was strange for her to leave when I was there; she wasn't much for being alone, and I was one of her favorite sidekicks. I think she liked the younger kids because we didn't ask questions and she could be nurturing with us. Only now, when I needed reassuring, she was leaving me.

"All the nurses were rushing around," I said.

I looked at the blonde girl who I thought always had the answers.

"Didn't they do anything?" I asked. "Couldn't they get him some blood?"

"I guess they weren't fast enough," Amanda said.

I looked toward the blonde girl again. She shook her head and walked away. In a hospital with so many machines, doctors, and nurses, it seemed strange to me that a boy so funny and nice could die because no one had gotten to him in time.

I didn't really understand the details. Gabriel's situation probably involved more than a need for blood, but to me his death seemed a sad reminder of how little adults were able to control the world. Gabriel's death was further evidence of how adults stood helplessly by while children suffered. This told me all I needed to know about the world—and God. If there was a God, I wondered why he would allow Gabriel to die and me to live. The one he took was full of life. The one he left behind had never understood it. I figured he must be a cruel man who wanted us all to suffer—Gabriel through death, me through life.

I knew it would have been better if I had died instead of Gabriel. I knew this and wished this. At the same time, a small part of me was relieved. I wanted to die, yet there was a little something inside of me that was happy it was Gabriel and not me who had died. I felt bad for this happiness, especially because I felt I didn't deserve it. It didn't seem fair that someone like me, who only brought tears and anger to people's lives, should live, while someone who could make people smile had died.

The only part of death I feared was its finality. I had always had trouble making decisions, and I knew there was no turning back with death.

The afternoon after Gabriel died, I decided to explore the hospital a little more. I wanted to go to the cancer unit, because all the children I had met with cancer had been so full of life. I wanted to look at these children and try to understand what they saw in the world that I did not. What did they have that I was missing?

I walked down the hall and ran into a boy in a wheelchair. With his bald head and smile, I figured he was probably from the cancer unit. I slowed my pace and followed him into the game room. Inside he wheeled around in search of something to do. Nothing seemed to interest him, and after a few minutes he wheeled himself back in the direction he had come from.

I followed close behind him, my hand trailing against the wall.

Toward the end of the hall he turned right and disappeared into what I hoped was the cancer unit.

When I reached his turning point, I also turned right and entered the unit I expected would have the answers. Nurses rushed around, none of them sitting at the station looking bored, like in our unit. All the beds were taken and all the curtains, open.

Most of the kids were in their beds, small heads peeking up from beneath mounds of blankets, machines, and tubes, surrounded by relatives. Every bed seemed to have a parent, nurse, or guest huddled around the patient. There weren't many kids out of bed, and those that were almost all were in wheelchairs.

I passed beds with kids who seemed barely bigger than the pillows, and beds with kids whose legs reached the end. Everywhere it was the same. Almost all the kids smiled at me, curious. All the parents, guests, relatives, and nurses eyed me suspiciously, scaring me off with their glares. I felt like a vulture that the people wanted to keep away from the kids, a germ that was going to contaminate them.

I wanted to talk to the kids, visit with them, but the grown-ups had built a wall between us. Feeling unwanted and out of place, I made my way out of the unit and back down the hallway.

My visit offered me no answers, no real clues. The smiles of the kids and the glares of the adults made me jealous. Watching the adults crowd around those kids to keep the dangers away made me wonder why no one did that for me. While their bodies were dying, my emotions were already dead. I wanted to be those kids, whose eyes still believed in this world, in this life. I wanted to see things as they saw them. I wanted to see each day as a blessing. I wanted their strength to face the world. I wanted to see things without fear. I wanted to look at the world through their eyes. I wanted to be able to feel things as they did, to be a part of this world.

But then, because I couldn't, I simply wanted to die and let all the pain go away.

217

DEDICATION
2019

My outreach to Sherri stops before it even starts. She was from Pennsylvania and had a daughter and husband, but those leads don't go anywhere. She was older than the other counselors, so I know it may be too late. Tom hasn't been able to locate her, either. He has tracked down or is still in touch with many of the others. Some of the former staff members talk weekly. Others meet up annually.

Dan isn't one of them. He has put all of that behind him.

Which is why when I am going to be in his area for a signing for my most recent book, this one about Ukraine, I am at first reluctant to reach out. But this is me, the author, not me, the former patient, so I e-mail him.

Hey Katya, wonderful to hear from you. Exciting news as well...
A Book release!! I put you down in my calendar...

His tone surprises me. Gone is the hesitation of his first message. Now suddenly I am his friend again. I wonder about the "post-professional relationship."

I am confused. This is what I wanted from him, but it's almost as if it has come too late. I can't erase from my mind his hesitation, his distance, his fear at our first reunion. Maybe it reminds me of how we used to be treated at Roth.

I remember Dan telling me the staff was treated the same way. He knows, then; and yet he still acted afraid.

Then I remember how I acted when I tried to reach out to the former patient I found on Facebook, the one whose mother had Munchausen by proxy. I was relieved when I didn't hear back. Because I was afraid of who she might have become.

Dan knows that not everyone gets better. He didn't give up, but sometimes he got tired of fighting. He knew about the cheating. He saw kids sneak batteries into their underpants before being weighed. Sometimes he let it slide. It just meant they were going to be there longer. The key was to keep coming back. The goal was to be there for the kids in a way that other adults in their lives hadn't been. Dan did the best he could. Then, at the end of his eight-hour shift, he walked away.

"You do a good job and hope it works out," he told me during our initial meeting.

Except, it was more than that, because the next day, he always came back.

It wasn't easy. Everyone at Roth knew this, and they supported each other. Sometimes they were outspoken. There were plenty of psychiatrists among them, after all. They were also individuals when it came to how they dealt with cases. It could be exasperating for those working on the other units and challenging for those working on Roth, but they never felt alone. Nevertheless, the issues they were dealing with were sometimes hard to process.

It is during that first meeting that he tells me what most of the others avoid saying: how lifelong it is. He didn't mean eating disorders or any other disorder in particular. He was talking about how, in general, there was no "one-stop fix" for what was ailing the kids he worked with. What the children had was not something that went away. His job wasn't to offer a cure, but rather to try to provide the tools that would help the kids deal with their issues.

It is not just me that Roth changed. I ask Dan if he ever had children. He was such a natural with kids, the rare man who wasn't afraid to interact with them and had the ability to see things from their level. But he tells me working at Roth skewed things for him. He got accustomed to seeing sick kids, and started thinking they were all like that.

I decided long ago I wouldn't have children. I don't want to risk doing to them what my dad did to me. I don't want to pull them down with me when the depression takes over.

And it does take over—has continued to do so in the years and decades that followed my hospitalization. Medication helps, but it isn't always enough. I couldn't, wouldn't, put a child through that. The only one I let in is my mom. I figure she owes me. If she had been there when I needed her as a child, maybe I wouldn't need her now. Maybe I would have escaped.

My mom is at the book signing, and Dan says hi to her before introducing himself to my stepfather. Like at our first meeting, he is not alone; he has brought a friend.

When there is a pause in the discussion, Dan asks an easy question, keeping the conversation going. When he brings me a book to sign, I write what I know he has always wanted to hear. I tell him he made a difference.

GET WELL SOON
1986

"Read my card, Woofys," Anya said.

She sifted through the large manila envelope to find the card she had made me.

"It has a dog on it," she said.

"Mine does too," Emma added.

Emma was Anya's best friend. Mom had brought both of them there that afternoon so they could hand-deliver the cards their class had made for me. Unlike most of my other visitors, shy Emma didn't back away from me. She treated me as she always had, as her best friend's little sister. When she saw the tube hanging from my nose, she only stared for a minute.

"Here they are," Anya said.

She pulled out two cards and handed them to me. On the front of my sister's card was a cute sleeping dog cut out from the comic strips in the newspaper. Inside she had written that the dog was waiting until I came home to get up. Emma's dog was a hand-drawn cartoon holding purple balloons that spelled out my name.

I stroked the dog pictures, trying to ignore what Emma had written inside in large letters.

Get Well Soon.

The words made me angry. They made it sound like I had a choice, that I could just flip a switch and I would be well. I was pretty sure the cancer kids didn't get told to "get well soon." It was understood it wasn't up to them. But for us, we were the ones to blame. That's what I felt like those cards were saying.

Anya didn't understand this, but she knew never to give me a card that said "Get well soon" on it. The one time she did, she was careful to cross out the evil words and write that she only got the card because the cartoon mice were so cute.

"Do you like it?" Anya asked, pointing at her card with its carefully rounded edges.

"Yeah," I said, nodding my head for emphasis. "I like them both. The dogs are real cool."

"I cut mine out of the Sunday newspaper," Anya said. "I liked mine, 'cause he's half asleep, and Emma's is real cute, too."

I placed the cards next to me on the bed and picked up the book Emma had brought me. I hated to read.

"I know you don't really like books, but it's a funny one," Emma said. She pointed to the title: *The Cat Who Sniffed Glue.* "It's about a cat detective," she said.

I nodded and ran my hand over the shiny cover. It felt slippery to the touch.

"Let's see what the boys said in their cards," Anya said.

She turned the large envelope upside down and shook it over my bed. "I want to see what Zach wrote on his," she said.

I picked out a few cards that had fallen out of the envelope with misshapen corners and "Katya" written across them. No doubt the messier ones were the work of seventh-grade boys.

I opened them and saw the usual words scrawled across the page. The only difference was the handwriting and the color of pen. Inside they all said the same thing: "Get Well Soon."

The words had lost all meaning for me. They hurt more than helped because they reminded me that my sickness was incurable. How could I get well soon when I didn't even know what was wrong with me? How could I get better when nothing in my world seemed to be under my control?

I snatched the large envelope and started to stuff the crude cards back inside.

My sister pushed a card toward me. "This one is better," she said. "John made it."

The card was covered with bright swirls and inside was a picture of a dog and some other animals I couldn't make out. The words were the same as the others, but the feeling was different. Instead of simply scrawling the message, taking the easy way out, John had added his own touch, personalizing the impersonal phrase with his bright colors and weird animals.

"Hey, Emma, look at what Rhonda wrote," Anya said. She passed a neatly folded card to Emma and sifted through the rest of the stack.

"I don't want to read any more," I said. I pushed John's card back in the envelope and slid off the bed.

Anya raised her head and dropped the card she was reading. "Not all of them say 'Get Well Soon,' " she said.

"I know. I just don't want to read any more."

"Okay. Come on, Emma. Let's put the cards back in the envelope."

Anya slowly pushed her classmates' cards into the envelope.

"I'll leave mine and Emma's at the top."

Anya waited for me to nod my head.

I nodded.

"A lot of the kids, they didn't know about the 'Get Well Soon' thing," she said. "Even Emma forgot."

I nodded again. I picked up my new book to let her know I didn't want to talk about it anymore.

"You liked ours, though, right?" Anya asked. "It was hard cutting the dog out so neat."

"Yeah, I liked those ones. Your dogs were real cute," I said. "Thanks."

I stared at the cover of the book, hoping my sister would drop the subject.

My mom poked her head around the door. She had been waiting outside my room. She liked to let us kids have time alone together.

"We should get back on the road before traffic gets bad," she said. "You girls have school tomorrow, and I promised Emma's mom I wouldn't have her back too late."

Anya placed the envelope gently in the corner of my room and moved closer to give me a hug. Emma got up and walked toward the door, pulling at her pink sweatshirt.

I followed Anya to the doorway where my mother and Emma stood.

"In church the other day they said a prayer for you," Emma said. "Sister Kathryn was saying the prayers for everyone, and—"

My sister nudged Emma.

"Church is as boring as ever," Anya said. "You're lucky they don't make you go here."

My mom gave me a quick hug and pulled the girls away, hurrying them down the hall and out to the parking lot.

I remembered the church prayers. While the sisters were asking us to pray for someone, I would whisper to my friends.

It was strange. Two years ago, I never would have thought I would be the one they were praying for. I wondered if the kids I used to play with thought the same of me as I had thought of the people in the prayers back then. I had wanted them to hurry up and either get better or die, so we could stop praying for them.

READING BETWEEN THE LINES
2018

In my hospital file—not the one where I put the few copied pages the hospital gave me, but the one my mother kept—there is a single business card. Although the card is for Dr. Katz, there are numerous other names scrawled on it, front and back. I recognize two of them—Hans Steiner, and Iris Litt—but others are blanks in my memory. There is a Dr. Olga Fisher, a Julie Hooper and a Mary Nackers. After several of the names my mother has written phone extensions. That is how she was able to reach them.

To reach me she used the pay phone, the number of which is scrawled on both the front and back of the card. It is the same way I now reach prisoners for stories I am writing, via a pay phone. The tedious communication method is one of many barriers between the outside world and those inside.

The only other thing I find in the file aside from bills is a card from the principal of my grade school, Sister Allen. It is not to me but to my mother.

Dear Karla,

I just wanted you to know how much the entire faculty is praying for Katya — and all of you. I feel so helpless as you and Denny must. But know of our support. Not a day goes by that one of the teachers does not make a comment — wondering how all of you are doing. If you see that Anya needs more support — or a different kind, please let us know! Sister Allen

Extracurricular Activities
1986

The new medical student had short hair and dressed in jeans and T-shirts. "Want to do the weekend activity?" she asked.

At first, New Student had just been around the diabetic boys, but one day in early December she started to follow me around. Because she was young and asked me only easy questions, I didn't bother to push her away. Unlike the others, she didn't let her curiosity show too much. Instead of asking stupid things, she watched me and talked to me like she would to anyone else.

It seemed like Amanda was on medical bed rest more than she was off these days, so I rarely got to do anything with her. Michelle actually went to school, so she had homework and other things to do. This helps explain why I didn't push New Student away like I did the real doctors and nurses. Where once I'd always wanted to be alone, now I often wanted to be around other people.

"What's the activity?" I asked.

We were walking down the hall toward the large community room, which had a kitchen, tables, couches, and a TV.

"Baking cookies," she said. She licked her lips as she bounced toward the room.

I stopped and stared. What kind of idiotic hospital was this, that it had an afternoon activity of baking cookies in a unit filled with patients with eating disorders?

New Student's bouncing slowed and then stopped. She turned around and looked at me, her eyebrows raised in confusion.

"What's wrong? Don't you want to make cookies?" she asked.

I just looked at her.

She looked back. She seemed confused. Then she let out a long "Ohhhh," followed by "Oh my God." She started to giggle as she began to understand.

"I wonder who came up with such a dumb activity?" she said. She waited for my body to loosen up before continuing. "You want to go in there anyway and see what else is going on?" she asked.

I slowly started walking again. We made our way to the community room together.

It was dinnertime. The diabetic boys were hunched over the tables, their faces hidden by mounds of food. One girl was actually at the counter making cookies, attracting stares and questioning eyes.

Only three girls sat at the tables eating, the two blondes and a new girl I hadn't met yet. The new girl had long brown hair that was always in her face and a sneer that kept all the other patients away. Unlike the soft voices of the anorexics or the gruff voices of the bulimics, this girl had a hysterical voice. She used it to accuse. The girl had been in our unit such a short time that I still didn't know her name.

I sat down by New Student and the others and watched them eat. It was funny watching the boys pile the food onto their plates while the girls, except the three at the table, avoided the table and the food.

I watched the girl with the long brown hair inspect her food, turning over the vegetables and pressing on the rolls.

"They've done it again," she shouted. She got up and took her tray to the sink. Turning on the water she picked up the piece of chicken from her tray and placed it under the faucet. She held the chicken with one hand and scrubbed it with the other.

I leaned in close to New Student so I could whisper in her ear. Like pretty much all the patients in our unit, the brown-haired girl was older and bigger than me. I was scared of the noise she was making.

"Doesn't she like the sauce?" I asked.

New Student shook her head. "She thinks they're trying to poison her," she whispered back. "She washes all her food."

A counselor got up and slowly moved toward the sink.

"That's enough," the counselor said. "You've washed everything off by now."

"Get away," the girl spat, taking a wet hand out of the water and shaking it at the counselor. "It still needs washing," she continued. "You're probably in on this, aren't you? You're all trying to poison me."

She dropped the chicken back on her plate and fingered through the rest of her food. "None of this is safe. I can't eat any of it." And with that she left the room.

With a long sigh the counselor got up and followed her out.

"Does she eat anything?" I asked New Student. I was trying to ignore the wet chicken and smashed bread that sat on the counter.

"I'm not sure," said New Student. "She washes everything that is cooked or not wrapped, and smells and prods all the other stuff."

New Student got up to turn off the still-running faucet.

I followed her to the sink so I could look at the ruined dinner on the counter.

"Why does she think everyone wants to poison her?" I asked. "Has someone tried to poison her before?"

"I don't know. I don't think anyone knows. She's only been here a few days, and she won't let anyone near her."

The girl who washed her chicken was gone before the end of the week. No one ever mentioned her again.

Book III
AFTER

The Comprehensive Care Unit
2019

In the brief moment the heavy hospital unit doors swing open, I see a small, bright balcony and a long, empty hallway. There are no people in the scene: no patients, no doctors, no nurses, and no visitors. Just a hall, the edge of a nurses' station, and windows looking out on a balcony. That is all I am allowed to view.

Then the doors swing shut, closing my window onto the world where I once walked.

I am no longer allowed entrance into the Roth Unit, or what it has now become.

It is ironic. The place I once desperately wanted to escape now will not let me inside.

Since leaving the hospital I have often wanted to go back. Not as a patient, but as a former patient. I wanted to help the kids in a way I felt outsiders and adults had never helped me. I wanted to let them know that they hadn't been forgotten and cast aside. Seeing their pain distracted me from my own and gave me a purpose.

Because the pain never fully left.

I have never been cured. I've just found a way to live with it—and that's always included trying to help others. At least, that is what I wanted to do. But I've never again been granted access to children's psych wards.

It was easier, in fact, to volunteer at youth detention facilities and to gain access to a Cambodian-American community devastated by repeated trauma. So that is what I did. I volunteered at a detention facility, and wrote articles and then a book about the Cambodian refugee community. In all those years, I had never tried to visit Roth again. I had tried unsuccessfully to volunteer at other units in other hospitals, but never at Roth.

I had been back, though.

A few weeks after I was released from the hospital in 1986, I was required to return to be weighed. I wanted to say hi to my old friends, but I was told no one I knew was still there. The patients had all changed.

I asked about the counselors. Sherri wasn't there, but Dan was. I still had the stuffed bulldog he had given me. He said hi in a hurried way and then went back to what he was doing, to the kids he was now looking after.

I wasn't one of them. I had left that world behind.

Now I am back, trying to see what it has become. The woman who permitted me a glimpse tries to describe what I cannot see.

Mary Sanders and I are seated near the main hospital lobby. The fifteen-bed unit Sanders helps run several floors above us forms a sort of square, with the nurses' station and balcony on one side. On the other sides are two consulting rooms for meeting with parents and patients; a "super cozy" meeting room, with art supplies and whatever decorations du jour the nurses have chosen; a school room; a dining room; and a kitchen. In the center are the patient rooms, singles and doubles, each with their own bathroom.

Roth is no longer Roth. It is now called the Comprehensive Care Unit. Although it is still part of Stanford, the unit is not physically connected to the children's hospital. It isn't even in Stanford. It is in nearby Mountain View, on the fourth floor of the El Camino Hospital.

The move didn't happen immediately after the old Children's Hospital at Stanford was torn down and replaced by the Lucile Packard Children's Hospital in 1991. It happened slowly, as the hospital's mission changed.

It all started in 1919 with the Stanford Home for Convalescent Children, known as the Con Home, which cared for children with chronic illnesses. The Con Home was replaced by Stanford Children's Hospital in 1969, a decade after Stanford University Medical Center was founded. The new children's hospital cost $5 million and had sixty beds. It was shaped in a sort of square with four wards—units, or pods. In later years those pods were general medicine, cystic fibrosis, cancer, and psychosomatic. There was also a cafeteria, recreation room, a school system, and therapy rooms.

According to Tom, the counselor, the original children's hospital didn't really have access to high-tech medical intervention, beyond the basics of some X-ray machines. It was more of a community hospital, which meant it did not have surgery suites, making it difficult to care for complex cases. When a child needed heart surgery, they had to be shuttled back and forth between the main adult hospital and the children's hospital.

That is why Lucile Packard Children's Hospital was built in the early 1990s, and physically attached to the main hospital. It was named after David and Lucile Packard, who donated $40 million toward the hospital's construction. The Roth Unit relocated to this new hospital, but most flu seasons, it moved to the adult hospital in order to free up space at the children's hospital.

Over the years the children's hospital gained recognition for organ transplants, heart surgeries, and the separating of conjoined twins.

In time it also began to outgrow its space, which is why a new $1.1 billion, 521,000-square-foot addition was added in late 2017. The extra space included six surgical suites, bringing the total to thirteen. The modest hospital that once suffered from a lack of technology had become one of the largest in Northern California in terms of children's operating rooms.

In addition to the surgical treatment center, the hospital now has a cancer center, acute-care and intensive-care units, and 3.5 acres of surrounding "healing green space" and gardens. It has 149 more beds, bringing the total number of beds to 361.

What it doesn't have is psychiatric care. None of the new—or old—beds are dedicated to psychiatric patients.

The ostracism I felt as a child is now complete. Exile is no longer metaphorical; it is also physical. The hospital is top-rate, too good, in fact, for any of the germs of the Roth Unit. They have been moved to El Camino Hospital, which was undergoing its own reconstruction when the Comprehensive Care Unit got kicked out.

During the construction period Sanders remembers the floors shaking. The constant moving added another element of instability.

"I had a dream once we were a traveling circus and Hans [Dr. Steiner] was driving, which was hilarious, if you've ever ridden with him," says Sanders.

I haven't.

Sometimes the staff members forget. I was never their colleague; I was their patient.

I arrived at Roth just a month before Sanders arrived in October 1986 to begin her first job as a licensed psychologist. The daughter of a traveling audiology and speech pathology professor, she can't offer a single answer as to where she grew up. Where she was educated is easier; that happened mostly in Tennessee. In college she changed her major four times. It was while studying fashion design that she discovered an interest in human physiology, and switched to psychology.

She came to California for an internship and was hired at Stanford to teach and practice family therapy. Her work centers around getting the family to understand that everyone is on the same side, and they are all trying to do the same thing: fight the illness.

"It's basically recognizing that the problem's a problem, and the problem is separate from the person," she says.

Sanders is warm and friendly, punctuating both pleasant and frustrating recollections with a short laugh. She explains that food is a key part of all treatment. That is because the kids on the Comprehensive Care Unit (CCU) now are there for one reason only—malnutrition. What is behind the malnutrition is what varies. It could be depression; it could be trauma; or it could be psychosis.

A newer diagnosis is avoidant/restrictive food intake disorder (ARFID): when someone avoids food due to lack of appetite, taste-sensitive issues, or fear of adverse consequences, like choking or vomiting. A noncompliant diabetic might occasionally still land in the CCU, but only if they are suffering from malnutrition.

Whatever the underlying cause, the treatment is the same.

"We've got to get the food in," says Sanders.

It sounds simple. It isn't. Although there is more information on eating disorders than there was in the 1980s, most people continue to be baffled by them. Why don't they just eat? It is a question for which Sanders knows there is not one answer. There are many.

And none.

It is her job to try to find something. A slight, intense woman with short blonde hair and stylishly large glasses, Sanders wakes at 3:45 a.m. most days in order to beat the traffic. Her home near the ocean is farther from work, but close to what she finds calming: the water. She needs to be unflappable when dealing with her patients and their families.

Part of family-based therapy is teaching the parents their role in helping their children get the food they need and in supporting their children before, during, and after meals. When that doesn't work, family therapy is abandoned in favor of adolescent-focused therapy. The idea is to help the adolescent fight the disease and encourage them to find someone to support them in this. The concept has evolved, but basically it is the same as when Sanders started at Roth.

The same cannot be said of some other practices.

When Sanders was first hired, kids were weighed every morning. They were given books with possible selections and a calorie count and told to choose their foods from these books. The result was daily hysterics.

"Do you remember that at all?" she asks.

I try to think back. I have a vague memory of a book you could flip through to choose meals. I don't remember ever making a selection from it, however.

"I didn't eat," I tell her. "I was mostly tube-fed."

"That's rare for us now," she says. It sounds like an apology—or an explanation. It is neither. It is information.

More follows.

These days food is chosen by the staff, although each patient gets to list two foods they never want to eat. ARFID patients are allowed more leeway. They group foods from comfortable to challenging, so the staff can help them work from one end of the spectrum to the other. For everyone else, the hospital staff chooses the menus the same way the children's parents would, helping to mimic what will happen outside the hospital in a family setting.

The goal is to normalize food intake. Eating through a tube is not normal. Neither is living in a hospital, which is why they try to get the kids out as quickly as possible.

At least that is the explanation Sanders gives.

The children are only in the CCU while they are medically unstable, one measurement of which is if they fall below 75 percent of the median body mass index for age and sex. That means they are usually there for at least three to four days, and more often, for one to two weeks. Occasionally they are there for months, although that is rare.

Returning is not. Because they are just barely medically stable when they are released, they often end up coming back for another short stay.

"It's like a little flurry," says Sanders. They are admitted, released, admitted again.

Unlike Roth, the CCU is not a med-psych unit. It is a medical unit with a strong psych presence, which means there is still a stigma attached.

The topic comes up in group therapy. The children discuss what they will tell their friends when they return to school. They don't have to worry about the other kids in the hospital, because they are not allowed off the CCU, except on very rare occasions, and then, never alone. Their hospital stay is restricted to the CCU. All they need—treatment, school, activities—is behind the doors I wasn't allowed to pass through. The unit is unlocked—and yet closed off.

Visits from famous athletes and celebrities are rare. Young children are also rare. Although they officially take children as young as five, the majority of the patients are teenagers between the ages of thirteen and seventeen. There are also a few young adults. The decision to extend the age range to twenty-five was made "basically to make sure these kids survive," says Sanders.

That is also one reason why the unit became solely about malnutrition. "These kids are high risk for mortality; this can be deadly," she says.

Maybe that is why eating disorders now have some of the most robust outpatient treatment options, each with their own acronyms, from partial-day intensive outpatient (IOP) to full-day partial hospitalization programs (PHP). There are even one-month-long and several-months-long residential programs that help with food and offer group and family therapy. There are hard parts, says Sanders, but "for the most part, they get well."

They recover, fully. "And they do wonderful things with their lives," she adds. They become doctors and nurses. They have careers and kids and lead full, healthy lives. They don't die, at least not on the CCU.

But there are others, ones they have lost after they were discharged. It usually happens later, when they are adults and are able to choose whether they want to receive treatment or not, and can sign themselves out against medical advice.

"Sometimes folks just aren't ready to get well," says Sanders.

That was the case with a young woman they treated as a child and again as a young adult. The woman had moved away and was struggling. Her family was trying to get her back to Stanford. The Comprehensive Care Unit was trying to accept her, trying to help bring her back.

"She didn't make it."

That isn't the story Sanders wants to tell.

She writes juvenile fiction in her spare time, and is writing a middle-grade historical novel about growing up in the South in the late 1960s. It is semiautobiographical.

The rest of her story is harder to talk about. She had a son. He was sixteen when he was struck by a car and killed.

SCARED STRAIGHT
1986

I didn't know what the pills were for. Sometimes I took them. Sometimes I pretended to take them. And then one time I refused them. That happened when I had energy because of the Ensure I was being force-fed.

When I wasn't eating I was cold, tired, and numb.

Food made me feel things. Most of what I felt was anger.

I was still nice to the other patients and to most of the female nurses and counselors, and of course, Dan—so long as they didn't ask too many questions. But when people tried to make me do something instead of asking me to do something, I got mad. It was a game: patients against staff. I wanted to play my part, so I started to put on a show.

When Pill Guy walked around with his little plastic containers of pills, I shook my head and pressed my lips together. When he got closer, I ran—weaving in and out of the hallways and dashing through the rooms. Pill Guy stumbled after me and waited around corners. He was bigger and stronger than me, but I was thin and slippery. With one last spurt of energy I dashed between the wall and the built-in wood cupboard in my room. My hiding place was too small for anyone to reach me. I was left alone while they waited for me to come out.

A couple of hours later, after everyone had gone to sleep, I ventured from my hiding place. As quietly as I could, I crawled into bed. I pulled the covers tight around me and began to drift off. I was happy with my victory.

"She's out," a gruff male voice said. "You hold her down while I give her the shot."

I sat up, pushing my back against the wall behind me. Two night nurses I didn't recognize stood above me. They were smiling at their success. I struggled as they nudged me.

After hours of hiding I had little energy. They turned me over and pushed a needle into my butt. I squirmed but couldn't stop the needle.

From then on whenever I didn't want to take my pills, I went back to pretending to take them and then spitting them out. When I thought about refusing the pills I remembered the sting in my butt. It was hard to sit down for days afterwards.

Fighting took a lot of energy, and I didn't always have it. It is hard to wage a war when you know ahead of time that either way, you lose. After a while I even stopped fighting when they came to put a tube down my nose.

That isn't quite true. I stopped after the straitjacket.

It happened after they used the torn pieces of bedsheets to tie me down. That worked one night. But they must have run out of fabric—or patience.

The next time I fought them they brought the jacket out. The anger had overtaken me. I needed to let it out. Instead they strapped me in the jacket, almost suffocating me in the overpowering emotion.

I had never seen a straitjacket before. When they brought it out, I didn't know what it was. It was evening, time for tube-feeding. I was struggling. They forced my body into the jacket. But it wasn't me they strapped into the jacket. I couldn't be there.

So I wasn't.

I saw the girl in the straitjacket from above. I don't know when it happened, but I had learned how to float out of my body. I didn't do it often. But when I couldn't handle it anymore, I left. Watching from above was easier. I didn't feel pain the same way. I didn't feel anything. And when it was all over, I didn't remember what had happened.

I couldn't control it and couldn't do it all the time. I never got used to watching the Ensure go down the tube and feeling its coldness travel into my stomach. But I couldn't always escape it like I escaped the straitjacket. To keep calm I would turn my face away from the machine, lying nervously in my bed until it was done. I did the same with blood draws, as if somehow by not looking, I could pretend it wasn't happening.

I was hiding from something else as well. I knew the Ensure was entering me; I knew I was not controlling what was being done to my body. I knew life was being forced into me—and secretly, I was starting to admit to myself that I was a little bit glad.

And that was the scariest part of all.

The way Sherri brushed my bangs out of my face, the way Dan had silently taken my insults, and the way my sister hugged me so tight I could hardly breathe. These were things I liked. They were what I needed even more than the Ensure. The thing is, not everyone was like Dan, Sherri, and Anya. In fact, most of them weren't. That is what I discovered as I got better and started leaving my room more often.

A lot of people didn't really seem to want me around.

Farmer Counselor walked up and down the hall, calling out as loud as he could. "Who wants to go see the clown?"

I listened to see what he would say next.

"If you want to see the clown, come gather by the sofa."

I slid off my bed, I had skipped the Halloween party and had never attended any of the other events, but I was sick of sitting on my bed. I made my way to the couch and waited for other people to show up.

"You gonna come?" Farmer Counselor asked.

He had entered the community room from the opposite hallway.

I nodded my head. So far there were only three other people going.

"How about you?" Farmer Counselor asked one of the diabetic boys. "You coming?"

The boy was tall and skinny with short brown hair and acne. Like most of the diabetic boys, he spent a lot of time in the community room, and so was often talked into attending outings and shows.

"Where are our seats?" the boy asked. He barely glanced up from the magazine he was flipping through at the table.

"I don't know," Farmer Counselor said. "What's the difference?"

The boy stopped flipping and looked up. "What's the difference?" he asked, staring directly at Farmer Counselor as he repeated the question. "The difference is, they always give us the worst seats. Last time I went to a show I had to stand up the whole time, and I still couldn't see what was going on. What's the point of seeing a clown if you aren't going to be able to *see* him?"

I wasn't sure if the boy was just being a teenager or if he had a point.

I waited for Farmer Counselor to clear things up, but he did the grown-up thing of trying to have it both ways. He seemed to agree with the boy while also assuring him it would be different this time.

We all knew the units without the psych part in their name were different, more important.

"The other units get priority," Farmer Counselor said. "But I'm sure we'll be able to see."

We weren't. The boy was right.

Our seats were in the very back, on benches instead of chairs. A large pillar blocked any chance I might have had of actually seeing the clown. I knew he must be good because everyone was laughing and clapping. I waited until the end, thinking I could go up and get a good look at him. But when the show was over we were pushed to the back of the line. We were told it would be better just to leave. The wait to see the clown would be very long.

When I saw the smiling face of the nurse, the one who told us it would be better if we left, my anger came back.

I didn't do anything. I didn't even say anything. But the feeling boiled inside me. Hatred, not love, was what broke through my numbness. Sherri and Dan had produced cracks, but the nurse and her warning brought about an earthquake. She made me hate a world that wanted me to disappear. I hated the fear hidden behind her words. She was scared of us because she didn't understand us. And for some reason, that made me want to live. I wanted to scare her. I wanted to do what she didn't want me to do—be seen.

The problem is, hate doesn't get you very far. The energy my hate gave me was short-lived. By the time I got back to our unit, all I wanted to do was climb into my bed and disappear.

One day, after best friends Lauren and Sandra were gone, their small private room was filled again. None of us ever saw the girl inside.

She wasn't allowed to leave. The door remained locked, and the only ones to ever enter were nurses with trays of food. The nurses always went in with gloves, face masks, and long blue gowns. The window on the door was covered with paper.

"What's wrong with her?" I asked Amanda.

We were standing outside the room, watching a nurse wheel in a lunch tray.

"I don't think they know," said Amanda. "I wonder how she pees, though."

"They leave her one of those bedpan things," I said.

Then the room was empty again and the nurses were busy cleaning any lingering sickness from its white walls.

Besides being the unit where the unknown was explored, ours was the one with the most space. When the other units became overcrowded, children would temporarily be placed in ours.

During the first three months of my stay, the bed next to mine had remained empty, so when I discovered the curtain around the bed next to mine had been drawn, I was eager to meet my neighbor. I took off my shoes and softly curled onto my bed, listening to the new sounds and unfamiliar voices.

"I can't believe this, putting her in this unit," a woman said. "There must be space in the cancer unit. This is just ridiculous—as if things weren't bad enough."

"Come on, I'm sure they are doing all they can," a male voice said. "I know it isn't great, but hysterics aren't going to help."

From the *hmmph* the woman made in reply, I was pretty sure she didn't agree with him.

"I'm going to go talk with the doctors now," the male voice said.

I heard the sound of his footsteps as he walked out of the room.

"In with a bunch of crazies..." the woman said.

She kept talking, as if to herself. No one else said anything. I tuned some of it out.

"What kind of place is this," the woman continued. "Can't they put you with the other kids?"

She didn't say it; she didn't have to. I knew what she meant. The "normal kids." Not the freaks. I saw the way people visiting other units hurried past ours.

"Mom, it's not that bad," a kid's voice said. "I don't really mind."

Mean Mom didn't answer. I heard her footsteps as she left the room.

It was quiet for a minute. Then I heard rustling from the other side of the curtain. A pale hand drew back the curtain and a friendly face smiled at me.

"Can I open these?" the voice asked.

"Yeah, sure," I said.

I looked at the small form hidden by machines on the high bed.

"Aren't you supposed to be at the Unit meeting?" the girl asked.

"Yeah," I said. "They don't make me go, though."

"My name's Bess. What's yours?"

"Katya."

"That's really pretty. How long have you been here?"

"About three months."

I pulled the curtain all the way open and stood up, leaning over her bed.

"Have you been in the hospital before?" I asked.

"Yeah, not this one—another one, a couple months ago," said Bess. "I got to live at home for the last two months, though. It was cool, hanging out with all my friends and stuff."

I looked at the girl whose small body was being destroyed, probably by cancer, I thought. Her brown hair was thick and shiny. I knew in a matter of days it would probably become thin and patchy. Her cheeks were red, and her eyes looked at me, and didn't look away, her face breaking into a smile instead of a grimace.

During the week or so Bess was in our unit we became close friends, laughing over what color we thought her hair would change to after treatment, and talking about her many friends. Bess could always cheer me up. In the morning when she woke up or at night when she couldn't sleep, she would pull back the curtain and tell me stories about the outside world. It was nice having her so close. I liked being able to say good night to someone again. Amanda wasn't big on greetings, and anyhow, she was across the room, not right next to me.

Bess liked to talk about the first thing she was going to do when she got out. It was always different. With a distant look and a smile, she would begin: "I'll have ice cream—hospital food sucks," and she would talk about the local ice-cream parlor for an hour. The next day it would be "Go over to Shane's," and then she would describe Shane and all her other friends in detail.

I started looking forward to the mornings. I couldn't wait to get up and hear Bess's excited voice. I was afraid Bess would think I was strange, so I even tried to eat solid food occasionally. I tried not to think about any of my actions. I told myself I was forcing food down my throat so Bess wouldn't take her friendship away. I told myself that I was doing it for Bess. I ate slowly, agonizing over every bite I took. I ate so little that I still had to take most of my food through the tube.

Now I pulled the tube out in the morning so Bess wouldn't see it, not because I wanted to fight treatment. I asked the nurse to hook me up only after she had pulled the curtains closed for the night. I didn't want Bess to see me with the tube down my nose and the machine on.

While Bess was in the bed next to me, our curtain was hardly ever closed during the day. I would pull it shut at night before I was fed and tug it open in the morning after I had pulled the tube out of my nose. I kept the curtain open because Bess didn't like to be alone. I told myself I was helping her, keeping her cheerful, but it was really Bess who was helping me.

There was only one other time, besides at night, when the curtain was closed. When Bess's parents were there I would sit on my bed and watch as her mother would quickly yank the curtain shut, scowling all the while.

After they moved Bess to the cancer unit, I never went to visit. I stuck to my own kind. I didn't want to infect the cancer kids with my misery. Although I really wanted to befriend kids like Bess, I knew that wasn't something you were supposed to do. The hospital was organized into neat little units, and you stayed within your own. Intermixing would have thrown the tidy little universe into disarray.

Community Meeting Note   13 November 1986
    Patients Present: A (chair), B (secretary), C, D, F, G, I, K and L. Patient H refused to come to the meeting. Patient D left the meeting early because of illness. Patient C was the only patient actually there on time and given that the rest of the community was so slow in coming to the meeting, she became angry and decided to leave before the meeting got under way.
    Staff Present: Dr. Kahan, Scotty and a medical student.
    As noted, the meeting began late with both staff and patients straggling into the meeting. The first issue was introductions for Patient L who asked several questions about the Level system. There was brief discussion of an issue of how one is made to feel welcome on this unit with Patients C and G being identified as very supportive to new patients. The first issue was a request for a room change by Patient I who presented in her usual fashion of wanting a change "just because I want it". She was not able to elaborate on the reasons behind wanting the change and instead simply perseverated with her saying she wanted it because she wanted it. Patients A and K seemed to have as their agenda also wanting her to make the room change out of their room

and so they were prompting her with suggested approaches to staff as to how to answer their questions.

The following issue regarded the abrupt discharge of a 6-year-old girl from the unit without an opportunity to say goodbye to her in the meeting. This seemed to engender a number of strong feelings on the part of patients, particularly Patient G who said that she felt very close to the little girl. There was talk of the rather frightening way in which the discharge happened in terms of police coming to the unit. The unstated but more likely equally frightening theme in the discharge was the fact that patients knew that this girl had been removed by police from the custody of her parent. This seemed to strike a resonant note in many of the kids. The community as a whole decided that they would attempt to do a goodbye project for this little girl and get it to her at the Children's Shelter.

The last issue was raised by Patient K who wanted feedback as to their earlier request for an eating disorder group. Details of this group were discussed in brief.

I wonder if the girl who got removed was the one whose mother had Munchausen's syndrome by proxy. It's possible Dr. Kahan got her age wrong in the meeting notes. It is also possible it was just another sick kid whose parents were the real problem.

TALK THERAPY
1986

There was something wrong with us. The problem was, nobody seemed to know exactly what. It was the doctors' job to find out. Every day the patients on our unit would be locked in a room with any number of psychiatrists or wannabe psychiatrists from the college. I hated their notepads and questions and tried to scare them. They never reacted. Their indifference bothered me. So, I copied them. I muttered, "I don't know" and sat without moving the whole hour. It wasn't easy. It was a bit like with Rebecca the witch, only worse.

First, I was forced to see Dr. Katz, a little man with black hair and squeaky shoes. We met in the same room once a week. I never said a word, but he filled plenty of pages in his notebook with his thoughts on me.

I think they finally figured out I did better with women. It probably should have been obvious. In my experience, men were scary and untrustworthy. Dad had been willing to let me die, a teenage boy had molested me, and none of my mom's boyfriends had ever stuck around long enough to matter. I trusted women—not men. Yet they assigned me a male psychiatrist.

I put up with him for a few weeks, then I opened my mouth and didn't shut it. I screamed. I made strange noises. We were never put in a room together again.

That's when I got the college girls, or maybe they were in medical school. It doesn't matter.

During a session with one of the students, I picked up a pink-covered book and started turning its pages, looking at the bright pictures.

"Why did you choose that book?" asked the woman, who wore big glasses and had a very serious look on her face. Her pen was carefully balanced on her yellow notebook. "Is it because the girl on the front is smiling and happy? Do you want to be that girl?" Serious Student asked.

I had to smile. Her questions were even more basic than Rebecca's. I had only picked up the book because it was the closest one on the table.

"Leave me alone," I shouted.

It was time to wake this girl up, show her what a really crazy kid acted like. I jumped from the couch and threw myself at the locked door.

"I hate you," I shouted. "You don't know anything."

"This is good," she said. "Show more anger—yell at me."

Her calmness further annoyed me, and I began to shout at the door. I felt trapped inside that room. I shouted and hit the door for the rest of the half-hour.

When they finally let me out, I saw Serious Student pull at her ears. She whispered to the nurse that she thought I was improving.

It was what they always said. Just like Rebecca had reported. If I was so much better, I wondered why I was still in the hospital.

After that day I wasn't locked in the room with the psychiatrists anymore. I guess they were right. I *was* getting better. I was getting better at getting rid of them.

"Her voice must really hurt," Amanda said.

We stood in the hallway together, looking toward the counseling room where the ceaseless screaming was coming from.

"Who is it, anyhow?" I asked. I was curious as to who had perfected their method to be better than mine.

"I think it's that new girl. She hasn't stopped screaming for the whole hour. Bet they never make her go again."

That was the new girl's first and last time with the psychiatrist. I wonder if they decided she was also improving.

Laughter and loud voices filled the Unit, sounds as foreign to my ears as French.

I pulled my arms around my legs and rocked softly on my bed, trying to hide from all the living going on.

"You'll regret it later, Katya," my mom said. "I know you will." She pulled at my sweater.

I looked up, trying to remember what her last words had been, what she wanted me to do.

"You don't have to stay out there," she continued. "You can just go out for a minute and I'll stay right by your side."

I shut my eyes and tried again. It was no use. Even the bed vibrated with the energy of the laughter. I opened my eyes and looked at my mother, her face flushed and excited. What was everyone so excited about? I pulled my sweatshirt tighter around my chest. Something about football players.

Now I remembered. Dan had peeked his head into the room a while back, announcing that the San Francisco 49ers had come to visit. My mom wanted me to go out there and get their autographs. She thought I would regret it later if I didn't.

What later? I didn't even know the names of the players, except Joe Montana. Everyone knew the famous quarterback.

"Come on," my mother said.

She dragged my limp body off the bed.

I let her pull me toward the community room, my eyes on the floor, my feet dragging down the hall. I wondered if the football players had ever seen a kid so reluctant to meet them.

My mom approached a man who was handing out 49ers' T-shirts.

"Can I get one for her?" my mom asked. She nodded her head in my direction. The man smiled at me and handed my mom a T-shirt and pen.

I looked up at him and then around the room. There were so many people, big people: men larger than giants and more stable than trees.

I pulled my mom back toward the hallway, my legs shaking. Everywhere there were huge men with booming voices and big smiles.

Suddenly Sherri was at my side.

"Over by the wall is Joe Montana," she said, pointing toward a giant signing a shirt in the corner.

"I want to go back, Mom," I said. I tugged at her hand.

"Come on, let's at least get Joe Montana's autograph," Sherri said. She pulled me toward the other side of the room.

My shoes squeaked on the ground as she dragged me toward the corner. By the time we reached Joe Montana, he was done with the shirt he had been signing. I looked straight ahead, focusing on his stomach. It was solid, large, and blocked my view of anything else.

"Would you sign this for her, please," Sherri asked.

She handed him my 49ers' T-shirt.

"Of course. What's your name?" he asked. He bent down to look at me.

I took a step backwards.

"Katya." I looked at his face when I said it, a face that didn't look at me with fear or annoyance, only interest. I stood in front of him, hoping he would say more, but words didn't seem to be coming from either of our mouths. Sherri asked him a few questions and then pulled me back toward my mother. My mother and I headed over to another player.

I liked this player even better, but I didn't recognize his name—Ronnie Lott. He talked about his finger, which he said he might have to have cut off or something, so he could still play. He joked that his signature was pretty bad, 'cause his finger was all messed up and missing the tip. He wouldn't sign in the center of my T-shirt; he wanted to leave that space for the "more important" guys.

I stared at him, listening to his stories. He treated me like a regular kid and not a freak. He asked my name and how to spell it.

"That's a real pretty name," he said. "If I ever have a little girl, I might just name her Katya."

My mom took me to a few other players. With all of them it was the same; they treated me like a kid, ignoring the wrinkles on my face and my absent stare. None of them asked me what was wrong with me, told me to get well soon, or looked nervously at their watches.

I didn't stay until they were gone. My neck was getting sore from walking around among a forest of giants.

I went back to my room and wondered about the guy's finger. I didn't want him to lose another part of himself. He seemed so complete.

MEMENTOS

2021

I still have my 49ers T-shirt. After I got out of the hospital, I used to wear it all the time. I never cared about football, but having Joe Montana's signature made me feel special. When people asked how I got it, I explained that the team had visited the children's hospital where I had been a patient. They didn't ask why I was in the hospital, and I didn't tell them. I wasn't sure I wanted them to know that part. That I had been in the hospital was enough. It made me different. I liked that. I hated that.

Then one day a boy was impressed not by the autographs but by the fact I was wearing the shirt, that I had even washed it. It was too valuable, he explained; Joe Montana's signature would fade. I put the shirt in the bottom drawer of my dresser after that. It has remained there ever since, moving over the years to different dressers in different homes, but always staying safely tucked away.

I dig it out now and find the autographs have faded. But not entirely. I can still make out Joe Montana's. Today's children probably wouldn't recognize it. They have a new set of heroes. Montana isn't a football star anymore. He is a grandfather.

As for the others, Ronnie Lott, the humble young safety with the injured finger, made it to the Pro Football Hall of Fame in 2000. He named his two daughters Hailey and Chloe. After football Lott worked in business, and now he is a podcaster. The name of his show is *Mind Games*, and the subject is mindfulness and sport. Lott's partner in the project is his daughter Hailey.

Lott has another partner when talking primarily about mental health, a former 49er famous for being one of the greatest pass-rushers in football history—and having a legendary temper. Charles Haley was just a kid, twelve or thirteen, when he attempted suicide. Much later he was diagnosed with bipolar disorder. Now the two former NFL stars are raising awareness about mental illness in youth, as well as raising money to bring psychiatrists to schools. They aren't bringing the psychiatrists in to educate the kids, but rather to educate the teachers about what the kids are going through. Lott gets it; he always has.

I write him an e-mail through his podcast. I don't expect him to write back; I just want him to know he is doing the right thing. I tell him about this book. I like to think it is my attempt to do the right thing.

I never forgot his words, but until I dug out the T-shirt, I had forgotten his name. Even then I had trouble making it out. His autograph is unclear, maybe because of his hurt finger. Or maybe because he never wanted it to be about him.

I have to ask my mom if she remembers his name. She does.

That isn't the only thing she reminds me about.

COUNTDOWN
1986

I pointed to the binder in the nurses' station.

"Wow, look at this, Amanda," I said. "It shows how long we've been here."

"Who has been here longer?" she asked.

"We were admitted on the same day, remember?"

"I know but I left for a few days," she said. "See, you've been here 102 days and I've only been here 98."

"Why were you gone for a while?"

" 'Cause the insurance wasn't going to pay or something. You know it's a lot of money to be here."

"It is?"

Amanda nodded.

I looked again at the binder. One hundred and two days. How was my mom paying for it? Was our insurance covering it? I knew we didn't have a lot of money to start with.

I looked at Sweet Nurse, the nurse on duty.

"How much is it for us to stay here?" I asked.

"It's a lot of money, but don't you worry about it," said Sweet Nurse. She took the binder back from us and shut it.

This isn't what I had planned at all. I had stopped eating to save money, not to use it up. Dad obviously couldn't be paying for my stay, and Mom was having enough trouble paying the bills as it was.

I tried to think of who else could be paying, but my mind was blank. Mom had talked about running out of money and sending me to the free county hospital, where they put you with old people and pretty much left you to die. But I thought those were just threats.

I looked at Sweet Nurse again. She was bent over the counter, waiting for us to leave.

"What if your parents don't have the money to pay?" I asked.

Sweet Nurse looked up. "Don't worry about it."

That was all right for her; her mom wasn't about to lose her job because she took too much time off to visit her daughter in the hospital.

I looked at Amanda to see how she was handling the news. Amanda had spent much more time in hospitals than me, and I figured if anyone knew about this money thing, it would be her.

"The insurance will pay for it," Amanda said. She turned away from Sweet Nurse and started back toward our room. When Amanda realized I was still standing at the nurses' station, she turned back around.

"It's your first time here," she said. "That means the insurance will pay for most of it."

I must have looked unconvinced because she walked back toward me. "Trust me, I know about these things. Okay?"

I nodded and followed Amanda back into our room.

I wasn't sure if she was right, but I didn't know what else to think. I didn't know where the money was coming from, but someone was paying, or I would have been kicked out.

I never thought about the money much after that; it was one of the things I couldn't deal with. After all, money was part of the outside world—one of the parts I'd refused to participate in. I hadn't asked to be sent here. I wasn't the one who'd chosen to come to a hospital and rack up huge bills. Any worries about money went to the back of my head and stayed there. I had already spent enough time trying to figure out my father's money problems; I wasn't about to take on any more.

PRICELESS
2018

It may not have been my choice, but Stanford became my burden. Growing up I often heard how much the hospital cost. Figures were never mentioned, but the implication was clear. It was enough that my sister got modeling lessons and I didn't. Enough that ice-skating lessons ended not long after they began. Enough that my college money was mostly gone. My stepfather paid instead. It is only three decades later that I discover my Mom got a lot of the money back. They lost the house, yes, but it wasn't because of the hospital.

This is how it happened.

Initially my mom's insurance paid my hospital bills. My dad didn't have insurance because he didn't have a job. But after a few months my mom's insurance stopped paying. They said I was using the hospital to hide from my father. The hospital in turn threatened to call Child Protective Services if I was removed against their recommendation.

Stanford suggested that my parents give custody of me to the State; that was their suggested solution, for how to pay the bills.

265

My mom didn't want to lose custody of me, so she kept me in the hospital and used money from the house sale to pay the hospital bills. The house had belonged to both of my parents, but my father kept it when they split up, and when he didn't pay my mother for her half—or the property taxes—she foreclosed on him before the tax authorities did. After spending most of the money from the house sale, my dad qualified for Medi-Cal, which paid most of the rest of my bills. He didn't get the money from the house back, and he never spoke of the hospital again.

It was my mother who held the cost against me, even though she later sued her insurance company—and won.

If I had been in a different unit, I wonder if she would have said anything about it.

GIVING UP
1986

My mother sat on the edge of my hospital bed. "I can't take this anymore," she said.

Her words didn't surprise me; her tragic tone, the helplessness of the situation, and her threats were nothing new to me. Out of desperation she seemed to make the same speeches over and over again. Maybe she figured if she repeated them enough, I might actually listen.

"It's not fair to me, it's not fair to your sister, and it's not fair to your grandmother." Her voice began to quaver. "We can't all just sit around waiting for you to get well." Her eyes moved to my face. "I've still got one healthy child, and if this is how you want it to be, that's how it will be. If you don't start making an effort to get better, I'll have to put you in the county hospital. I won't visit you there very often. It's too hard on me and not fair to your sister."

Her hands pulled my chin up so she could look in my eyes.

"Katya, I'm serious. Things have to change, or we're just going to have to forget about you."

I pulled my head away and looked out the window. I knew one thing: I didn't want to end up at the county hospital. Amanda had been there and it didn't sound good. You went there to die. The doctors and nurses were overworked and didn't have time for head cases; if you didn't eat, they put a tube down your nose. If you pulled it out, they let you. Amanda hadn't gained any weight when she was in County. Actually, she'd lost some. In County, Mom said there wouldn't be curtains for privacy, just rows of beds with cranky old men mixed in with anorexic girls. She made it sound like a dumping ground where you left people and never picked them up.

I wasn't ready to be quite that forgotten.

The last part of her speech was new. Either that, or it was the first time I had heard it. My mom couldn't lie well. But had she really had enough—could she really leave me and move on? Could I be forgotten that easily, pushed to the back of her memory?

My sickness had aged her. There were lines under her eyes that didn't seem to go away, and her voice always sounded tired.

She began to cry.

I slid off the bed.

I knew there were other choices. Dr. Steiner had talked about youth homes and even old people's homes, once I was ready to leave. They didn't want me to go home. Family counseling had failed, and they knew I wasn't talking to my dad. They were scared of what would happen if they sent me home, demonstrated in this letter I found in my file:

> To Whom it May Concern:
> ...The parents and the Children's Hospital at Stanford staff fully support residential treatment for Katya and feel an immediate placement is indicated. As Dr.Katz' note describes, Katya is a youngster who has eluded diagnosis, but has

symptomatology indicating an affective disorder and an Atypical Eating Disorder. She has recently been able to eat food and drink liquids without supervision and we feel this progress came as she learned she would not be returning to her home...Katya is a disturbed and fragile youngster who requires a structured, therapeutic setting to progress. Thus, we are hoping for expedient placement. . . I realize many cases take precedence over voluntary placements, but I do believe this case is also of an emergent nature.

The Warmth of a Ghost
1986

Sometimes when I felt lonely at night, I would look to the side of my bed and see the stuffed bear Lauren had given me, and would feel a little less alone. When that didn't work, I would call to the other girls in my room. I would help Amanda out of bed and we would go to the back of the room, by the other girls, and sit down. We would talk about the other patients in the unit and play guessing games as to their sicknesses and their chances of survival. We talked about whatever we wanted and laughed as loud as possible. Our unwritten rules: We never mentioned each other's cases, and no one but me ever called these little meetings. I would have been happy if one of the other girls had decided to hold a meeting, but the only voice that ever came in the night was my own. We never met during the day. It was as if the matters we had to discuss could only be approached in darkness.

At first the nurses put up with our gatherings because they thought they were good for us. They were happy that we were showing an interest in something besides how to get out of eating our next meal. After a while, though, they began to get annoyed with the way we ignored the lights-out and bedtime rules. Privileges were taken away if we spent too long talking during the night. In time the gatherings stopped making me feel better. Watching Amanda's skeletal face and listening to the others' rasping laughs made my loneliness worse.

I was the leader of a group of ghosts. It was as if they had chosen me to speak for them, to organize for them, to live for them. Maybe I knew it all along. Maybe I knew it when Amanda told me about her previous hospital stays. Maybe I knew it when I learned I was the only girl in the unit who wasn't on the medical bed rest program. Maybe I knew it when I slowly started to force food down my throat. I don't remember when I figured it out, but one day I knew I couldn't spend the rest of my life in hospitals. I knew I wouldn't die the same way some of the other girls would die. I knew some of us would have to live, and I would be one of them.

The meetings ended because I stopped calling out in the night.

I started to wonder how Amanda could look the same while my cheeks were slowly becoming fuller. I knew the difference wasn't in the way we were fed—it was inside us somewhere. The more I thought about this, the more I knew I would survive.

And that scared me.

Dan slid the scale back to zero. "Sixty-eight," he said. "Before you know it they'll be sending you home." Dan raised his hand for a high five.

I stepped off the scale and started walking down the hall.

I was gaining weight and there was nothing I could do about it. Even though I didn't eat much, I was slowly coming back. I still shivered under the blankets at night, but Dan didn't treat me the same as he used to. Sherri no longer touched my face as if I might break if she pressed her fingers too hard. Dan no longer looked so worried every time I became upset. The nurses no longer seemed to care when I unplugged the bed-warming machine.

"I didn't mean to upset you, Katya," Dan said. He had followed me down the hall and into my room. "I just wanted to let you know I was proud of you," he said, "happy you've gained some weight."

"But I didn't want to gain weight," I said, wheeling the tube-feeding hanger away from my bed.

Dan stood in the doorway, blocking my way.

"What are you doing?" he asked.

"I don't want it in here," I said. I pushed the hanger into Dan.

Dan stepped aside, and I pushed the hanger into the hallway.

Dan laughed. "Don't worry," he said. "You still have quite a ways to go."

I walked back into my room. I tried to hide the relief I felt when I heard Dan's last words. As I got better, people paid less attention to me. I was scared to get too healthy. I was scared that if that happened, no one would notice me anymore. I worried that no one would care.

A woman carried an oversized brown bear toward the room at the end of the hall.

"Another stuffed bear?" I asked.

Amanda scooted to the other end of the couch so she could get a better look.

273

"Yeah," she said. "They certainly bring that new girl a lot of toys."

We were sitting on the big central couch in the community room, a great location to watch the goings-on around us and to catch up on the news of the Unit.

"Who is she?" I asked.

I leaned my head toward the hallway, hoping to catch a glimpse when the woman opened the door to the girl's room.

"Someone whose parents are pretty rich," Amanda said. "Have you seen her yet?"

I shook my head. I didn't want to admit I was jealous of all the stuffed animals. Her room had been filled with visitors early last week, and ever since then, at all hours of the day we would see the girl's parents, or at least her mom, trudging down the hall, arms filled with yet more toys and gifts.

Seeing the visitors' confused eyes and fumbling steps, I envied the girl her family. I was jealous of the attention. I even missed the hot blankets that used to crush me when I was first admitted.

"They look pretty stupid, bringing her all those presents," Amanda said. She pulled at the threads of the old couch.

"Yeah, what's she gonna do with all of those stuffed animals when she can't even get out of bed?" I laughed nervously and looked at Amanda. She was also laughing.

Our laughter covered the missing question: What would they do with all the stuffed animals if she died?

Stuffed Animal Girl had long blonde hair that wasn't thinned from starvation. I think she was anorexic, but she was pretty new at it, because she wasn't that skinny, and her face was wrinkle-free. She smiled more than everyone but Michelle, and she didn't pull away when someone got close to her. Her mom, the one who had brought most of the gifts, had discovered her daughter's condition early on. She had saved her before she left them, before she was pulled under, sucked down beneath the surface.

Or so we thought.

As soon as we saw that she could get out of bed, Amanda and I went to visit Stuffed Animal Girl. She had her own room at the end of the hall, and I was eager to see how she had fit all of her gifts inside.

I also wanted to see what special power she had that I lacked. What did she do to make her mom love her so much?

"This your first time in the hospital?" Amanda asked.

The girl pulled at a flower on the table. "Yeah," she said, smiling.

I noticed that her face was pale.

"That's Gruff," she said, pointing to the stuffed dog I was stroking.

"He's real cute," I said. I placed him carefully back on the table by her bed.

"Yeah, I love stuffed animals," she said. "My mom is always bringing me more."

"Yeah, we noticed," Amanda said. Her eyes were already focused on the door.

Just then it opened and a woman stepped through. "Hi there," a very happy voice said.

"We better go," I said.

I remembered when my mom used to come see me, every visiting hour. That time had passed, but Stuffed Animal Girl's had just begun. There was no point in letting her know what I had learned. Maybe it would be different for her; maybe her mom would keep coming right on time, every visiting hour, a new stuffed animal clutched to her chest.

My mom didn't come as often anymore. I was out of the real danger zone. I had been in the hospital long enough to be better. I had gained weight, but I was still too skinny. Almost all of my food came through my nose. Everyone had been patient. They were tired of waiting. They wanted me to choose. My mom wasn't going to force life at me forever; either I started to live and eat, or...

"You know that if you don't get better," my mom said, taking a deep breath, "you know I'll have to give up."

She sat on the side of my bed, crossing and uncrossing her thin fingers. "I'm serious about the county hospital. I really will send you there."

She kept looking at the blankets on my bed, never looking up at my face. This was different. Last time this came up a week or so ago, she'd made me look at her. Now she wanted to look away.

"Life goes on, Katya, whether you're here or not," she said. "I'll visit you in County, of course, but not often."

"Will I be in with old people?" I asked. I pictured myself in a bed next to a toothless, shriveled old woman.

"I don't know," she said. "I don't think there's a separate children's wing at County. They don't care about you there. If you give them trouble, they'll strap you down or put you in a straitjacket again."

I lowered my head so my mom wouldn't be able to tell that she was winning.

It was working. She was scaring me.

I knew I didn't want to die; I didn't want people to stop forcing me to live. I didn't want them to stop paying attention, either. With each pound I gained, I felt myself losing power. My mother had trapped me, though; either way, I was losing control.

"I still have one child," she said. "I still have Anya, and if you aren't going to try to get better, then I'm just going to have to learn how to live without you." She stood and picked up her purse from the chair.

I closed my eyes. I couldn't watch her leave.

I knew she meant it. I knew she would go on without me, and it scared me. Life, her life, would go on whether I lived or not.

The threat had worked. I was scared enough that I wanted to get better.

But only well enough to stay out of County.

FLOWERS ON YOUR GRAVE
1994-1997

Threats, antidepressants, and an obsessive exercise program kept me eating in middle school and high school. I didn't go to County or a group home, I went back to my mother's condo and then to her boyfriend's house. When I was twelve my mother married her boyfriend and I was threatened with being sent away if I ruined things for them. This was their chance at happiness. Not mine. Where I would be sent was never quite clear. I had been away before.

I went away again for college in 1994 when I was 18, far away, as far as I could go and still pay in-state tuition: the University of California at San Diego. I needed to escape the ongoing threats, and my role in the family. I had become the scapegoat, the sick one, the excuse. Everyone else was fine; it was Katya who had a problem. Although once in a while, Anya also got some of the blame (my stepdad's out-of-control temper was because we were such "difficult kids").

Something happened when I left home for college. All the anger that had been holding me together during my teen years melted away.

277

The freshman 15 became the freshman 25. Only, instead of gaining the weight, I lost it. By Thanksgiving I was sleeping under a comforter and three blankets—and I was still cold. I worried that if I shut my eyes at night, I might never open them again.

The student trainee at the college health center who took my temperature laughed at the reading. "You should be dead with this temperature," he said, figuring it had to be a mistake.

I knew it wasn't.

He took my pulse. When he discovered it was irregular, he turned me over to the doctor. An EKG was ordered in late 1994. My heart rate was too low. I was dying, again. In hunger and emptiness I had found power, and I wasn't ready to give it up. It was the first slip since Roth.

Even after I started eating again in college, I did it almost in secret, like a closeted alcoholic, eating hardly anything during the day and then feasting alone in my room at night. I was anxious, and thought if I ate while the sun was up, I wouldn't be able to stop. At night there was an end time: sleep. I chose friends who didn't ask questions and boyfriends who didn't dig too deep.

When Anya hugged me, she would feel for my ribs. My sister always hated to leave me. It was as if she feared next time she came to visit, I would no longer be there.

A year or two later in 1995 or 1996 there was another EKG. Hushed whispers. Sideways glances. My body was eating my heart this time.

My mother advised me to write a will.

"I'm serious," she said. "You have some money saved up, and half will automatically go to your father and half to me. It would be better if your father's half went to your sister."

I counted the swirls on her rug. She had a house I could visit now.

After I went to college, my mother and stepfather sold their house and moved to England. Then they moved to a remote California ranch located on a dirt road that washed out in the rain. The distance was too great from their world to mine. I didn't belong with them anymore. It was as if I had been erased from their lives.

Now that I was in danger, they were forced to see me again. They had moved to a city with paved streets and sidewalks in Sonoma County.

"We might as well talk about it," my mother continued. "You never planned on growing up, did you? That's why you had all those crazy plans. You didn't think you'd be around to see them through."

I kept silent. It was true; when I was younger, I had planned to play professional basketball in Europe—a bit of a stretch, considering I only picked the sport back up again my sophomore year in high school.

But I had found writing since then. In college I wrote juvenile fiction and a memoir my mother had never seen. The memoir was about Roth. I had found my way to move on, but it was the same thing that also dragged me down. My experience had provided me a window into worlds that were silent to others, but sometimes, once I'd entered, the window slammed shut behind me. Writing both freed and trapped me.

My mother tried a different tactic.

"What kind of flowers do you like? Do you want poppies on your grave?"

FAKE SANTA
1986

"Jingle bells, jingle bells, jingle all the way. Oh what fun it is to ride in a one-horse open sleigh..."

The song faded as the carolers continued down the hall, right past our unit.

Christmas was a week away, and already the hospital was starting to resemble Santa's workshop. The carolers stopped to sing at each unit, except ours. Little bands came and played Christmas songs on their instruments, shows were performed in the large hall, and nurses wore Santa pins on the collars of their white uniforms.

"Mom says you're going to be home by Christmas," Anya said. She twirled around my room. "I think Mema will still be there, so dinner should be good," she added.

My sister stopped her twirling and sat down on the edge of my bed.

"Aren't you excited?" she asked. "Don't you want to come home?"

I looked at my sister's eyes. Her eyes got mean when she thought someone was hurting me. She was always looking around, careful not to let anyone sneak up on her, surprise her.

How could I tell my sister I was scared to go home—scared to leave the hospital? How could I explain that her protection was not enough, that I needed more than what a big sister could give me?

I shrugged my shoulders.

"I just don't want to get too excited, 'cause they might change their minds," I said.

"Oh. You think they'd do that?" my sister asked. Her shoulders slumped.

I shrugged again.

"Yeah, I guess you can never count on them," she said. "I guess you never know."

Anya turned away and looked at a puzzle on my chair. "Want to put this horse puzzle together?" she asked.

"We can't," I told her. "Some of the pieces are missing."

Everyone assumed I wanted to go home for Christmas. Funny thing is, no one ever thought to ask me what *I* wanted, how I would like to spend the holiday. I knew I was supposed to want to go home for Christmas, but as the day got closer, I only felt more afraid. Christmas alone in the hospital seemed okay to me.

Santa didn't seem to be that into the holiday this year anyway. He shuffled into the community room looking anything but merry. He lowered his bag and stood in the doorway.

Michelle and I stopped work on our puzzle. We did a lot of puzzles together, mostly of cute baby animals. Chatty Girl turned down the TV, and a pair of diabetic boys exchanged looks of annoyance.

With his hands on his hips, Santa looked more like the Grinch than Jolly Saint Nick.

We were all waiting for the real Santa to magically appear when Amanda entered the community room from the opposite door.

Without stopping to see who else was in the room, she walked right up to Santa.

I was quick to follow. We were the youngest, after all, which meant Santa was supposed to fuss over us the most. My eyes were glued to Santa's face, waiting for his rosy cheeks to light up and his belly to shake with laughter.

"Merry Christmas," Santa said. He didn't sound merry. "And what do you girls want this year?" he asked, pulling up his sagging red pants.

Amanda shrugged and looked at his felt bag. "Do you have presents in there?" she asked.

"Yep."

Santa picked the bag up and pulled out two records wrapped in shiny ribbon. He placed both on the table, waiting for us to take them.

I looked at the plastic singalong records and then at the large bag Santa had now slung back over his shoulder.

"Umm, do you...do you have..." I glanced at the record and then at the big red bag.

"What? Do I have what?" Santa asked. He bent over so he could get a better look at me. "I have to go to the other units," he said. "I don't have a lot of time."

"I was just wondering," I started. His tapping foot was distracting me. "See, I heard you were giving out Teddy Ruxpins this year."

"I am," Santa said. He straightened up and readjusted his bag.

"Could I...could I have one?" I asked quietly.

"They're for the other units."

The real Santa must have been for the other units too.

That year Santa's imposter had even more surprises for me. My Christmas wish of staying in my room over the holiday wasn't going to come true.

"You're going home for Christmas," Sherri said.

She handed me a flat, record-sized present. I barely glanced at it. I'd already received enough records for one holiday.

"You have to promise not to open it until Christmas, okay?" she said.

That wasn't going to be a problem. I nodded my head. Then I remembered what she had just said.

"I'm going home?" I said.

"Oh, sorry," Sherri said. "I mean, just for the day. Early Christmas morning your mother is going to pick you up and take you home. You'll be back here by Christmas night."

Sherri pushed my bangs away from my forehead. "You want to go, don't you?"

I pulled back and shrugged. I wasn't sure what I wanted. I only knew what everyone told me I wanted. Because everyone else seemed to think I should want to spend Christmas at home, I was trying hard to pretend I did, but I hadn't quite tricked myself into believing it yet.

"I know your sister really wants to see you, and your mom is looking forward to it."

I couldn't leave Anya alone on Christmas. We had only ever spent one Christmas apart. It happened when I was around two and my parents had split up for a few months. Mom took me and Dad took Anya. Even though Anya got to go to Indiana for Christmas, she still hadn't forgiven Mom for leaving her with Dad.

I still didn't want to go home, though. I didn't want to be taken out of the hospital, and I didn't want everyone watching me. I didn't want to smell all the holiday food, and I didn't want to sit around while everyone filled their plates and watched me just pick at mine.

Christmas morning found us whizzing down the freeway.

"I've never seen so little traffic on this road," my mother said. She laughed. "I guess that's one advantage to driving at six o'clock on Christmas morning."

I couldn't see any other cars, just empty asphalt all around. I clung to the door. "Mom, can we go a little slower, please."

"There's no one on the road and your sister is waiting for us," my mom said. She didn't turn her head to look at me.

"You mean, she hasn't opened any presents yet?" I asked. My sister, the one who always tried to open all her presents on Christmas Eve, hadn't opened a single gift yet?

"Well, she did open one thing," Mom admitted. "A Nintendo your grandparents got for the two of you."

"I didn't want Nintendo. I hate video games."

"Well, what *did* you want?"

My mom suddenly slammed on the brakes as a truck appeared in front of us.

"Anya really wanted it, and thought you would like it too. Your grandparents wanted to get something nice for you guys."

My mom looked over her shoulder as she moved to another lane. I caught her hurried look before her eyes focused back on the road. Her face showed impatience, an annoyance that wasn't going away.

"Don't you dare say anything bad to your mema about the present, and don't start pouting."

My mom pressed her foot down harder on the gas pedal.

"Your sister has gone through enough for you, spending Christmas morning without me while I go pick you up, spending many evenings without me when I'm visiting you, or because I'm too exhausted to move."

I pulled my knees up toward my chest and looked out at the empty road.

Life was so much simpler within the walls of the hospital.

"Don't you dare ruin this day for your sister, okay?"

"Okay."

If they had just left me in the hospital, there would have been no chance of me screwing up, no chance of me ruining other people's happiness.

I watched a light turn on in the window of a farmhouse along the side of the freeway. I tried to imagine the hand that turned on that light, the kid that was awake and ready to scramble down to the Christmas tree.

When we got home, I entered the living room, a guest in my own house.

My grandma was now more of a resident than I was. I felt like that single glass ornament hanging on a tree, where all of the other ornaments were matching, homemade and unbreakable.

I stood in the doorway a minute too long.

"Hi, Katya," Anya said. She looked up from the TV where she was trying to hook up the Nintendo.

She never called me Katya. I was Woofys, her kid sister.

"Mema and Papa Van gave this to us," Anya said, holding up the Nintendo box.

I nodded my head and shuffled past her toward the couch, where I collapsed and waited to be told what to do next.

It was weird to be home again, without structure or schedules. I didn't know how to live. I didn't know what I was supposed to do.

The long drive had been enough. I was tired, and I wanted to go back to my safe place.

"Mom said I could open it," Anya's voice interrupted my peace. "I know I was supposed to wait, but it takes a while for her to get to the hospital, and she said I—"

"I don't care," I said.

"Oh." Anya glanced over at my mom, who was standing by the TV. Mom didn't say anything.

"Do you want me to show you how to play?"

I shook my head. "I didn't want a Nintendo."

"You didn't want anything, so your grandparents got you and Anya a very nice gift," Mom said.

She walked away from the TV and stood in front of me, her eyes glaring. "Don't ruin this happy day for the rest of us, okay?"

I nodded and scrunched down into the couch.

I shut my eyes and listened to the noises around me. Anya was busy playing with the Nintendo, Mema and Mom were in the kitchen cooking, and Papa Van was hovering over the food, munching on anything he could reach without being shooed away by Mema.

At dinner everyone's eyes were on my plate. The food stuck in my throat, dry and tasteless. The cranberry sauce and mashed potatoes wouldn't even slither down. I managed to eat a few mouthfuls and spread the rest around enough so it looked like I had eaten more.

Papa Van seemed to be the only one who was truly hungry, his loud voice and full plate like echoes in an endless hallway.

After my Christmas visit I knew I didn't want to go home for good; I wasn't ready. I wasn't so sure I was welcome there anymore. I didn't really want to go to a special home, either, which was another option being tossed around.

I didn't know what I wanted. The future stretched no further than the next hour. For now, I wanted to stay safely tucked away in the hospital; beyond that, I didn't know.

When it got too confusing, I escaped the only way I knew how: I left my body. When they started hooking me up to machines, when they pricked me with needles, when pain was inflicted, I went away. Whenever someone started talking about my health or began to show emotion—whether it was fear, anger, or happiness—I would pull back. As the other person reached out for me, I would leave them with my shell, hoping they wouldn't harm it too much. It had taken time, but I had perfected the art of disappearing.

My mom never understood why she couldn't reach me. It was because I wasn't there. Being there was too painful.

I had found that for every person who could make you smile, there were two others who could make you sad. Outside the hospital I had no protection from these people. I wasn't strong enough yet to endure the stares, the questions and the curiosity.

The time was growing close, though.

The blondes had left the hospital long ago, and there was a different batch of diabetic boys there now. Even Stuffed Animal Girl was improving; it wouldn't be long before she got out.

Only a few of my bones still stuck out now. There were no wrinkles on my face, and the skin around my nose no longer sagged.

I didn't like the solid feeling of weight. I liked the springiness of being thin.

Weight tied you to this world. I wanted to float away from it.

HAUNTED GROUND
2018

The etching on the memorial tablet ends with a question: "Is it not haunted ground?" The answer is yes. The ground on which the memorial stands, and where I am standing alongside Tom, the former Roth counselor, is haunted. We are on a grassy corner behind a retirement complex near Stanford University. The tablet used to be located at another corner nearby, just outside the Roth Unit. About the height of a man, the monument was one of the first things children from the Unit would see when they went outside.

"And it used to freak the kids out," says Tom. "If you start to read it, it's a little bit spooky."

I read Felicia Dorothea Hemans's, née Browne's, eerie words aloud.

> *Must I not hear what thou hearest not,*
> *Troubling the air of the sunny spot?*
> *Is there not something to rouse but me,*

Told by the rustling of every tree?
Song hath been here, with its flow of thought;
Love, with its passionate visions fraught;
Death, breathing stillness and sadness round;
And is it not—is it not haunted ground?

The monument includes only part of the poem. The other stanzas talk of phantoms and tombs, whispering breezes and stricken minds. The words seem a fitting endnote to the Roth legacy, part of the Stanford legacy, which in turn is the legacy of a dead child.

I didn't know the last part until Tom brought me here. The 1898 memorial was erected thirteen years after Leland Stanford and his wife Jane established Stanford University in memory of their son, Leland Jr., who died in 1884. A beloved only child, Leland Jr. arrived late in his parents' lives after they had been married almost two decades. The family was on a tour of Europe when fifteen-year-old Leland Jr. caught typhoid. Mary and Leland Sr. moved their son from Rome to Florence for treatment. Doctors and nuns were brought in to treat and care for the feverish boy, who slipped in and out of delirium over a span of several weeks. There were periods of hope and then heart-break, when just two months before his sixteenth birthday, Leland Jr. died. Devastated by the loss of their only child, Mary and Leland Sr. built Leland Stanford Junior University as a memorial to him.

Jane erected the tablet after Leland Sr. died in 1893. The ground was already haunted with the remains of the region's original occu-pants, the Puichon Ohlone tribe. Today few mention the Puichon or the university's full name. There are no known Puichon living, but there are Muwekma Ohlone, the lone survivors of the many native lineages that once lived in the area. If it wasn't for Tom, I never would have known about the dead child and decimated tribe.

Both sound like stories I could have written, what one of my editors once called "tear-jerkers." Instead of a sappy Father's Day piece, I once wrote about a tragic accident that left a father a paraplegic and the son, a caregiver. The father and son grew beyond the accident and professed words of love, but the hurt was still raw, the healing incomplete. I wrote similar stories for "happy" holidays, not just for Veterans Day or 9/11 anniversaries. Grieving widows, homeless parents, soldiers with blood on their hands—all of them opened up to me. Listening, I lost my own distant pain in their more-immediate anguish. It helped them. It helped me.

But it also held me back. I saved my empathy for them and found myself drained when it came to relationships with my own family. My boyfriend complained that I kept him in a neat box. My visits to my mother and stepfather were infrequent. My communication with my father was pretty much nonexistent.

It was different with Anya. We stayed close, until one day, she didn't need me anymore. She became a doctor, and she had her husband and three kids. Her stories about our childhood didn't always match mine. I couldn't listen to hers; it would have meant hating my mother, and that was something I couldn't do.

Because without Anya, my mother was all I had left, from before.

In time I became closer to my mother and stepfather. They needed me in ways my sister did not. These days, regrets keep my mother up at night.

I don't have any. I've learned how to listen for the voices few people hear. I want to hear those voices. I need to hear them. I want to remember how hard it is for children who are forgotten, and I want to tell the story they cannot tell. I want to see the warning signs so many adults overlook. I seek them out and tell their stories. Sometimes I even become part of those stories.

And it all began with Roth. Which is why I am back here now, searching for answers with Tom.

Only it soon becomes clear that we are looking for different things.

Tom didn't bring me here to talk about death and hauntings. He wanted to look at flowers, specifically the wisteria that decorates the outside of the building. The same purple flowering vines used to decorate the entrance to the old children's hospital we both knew so well. The hospital that once stood nearby may have been torn down, but the wisteria was preserved. According to Tom, it's one of very few things from the old hospital that was saved.

We started our tour earlier, across the street from the latest version of Stanford children's hospital, a massive multiple-story structure with valet parking. On top of the building is an abstract metal windmill named "Sleeping Lucy." The windmill can be seen from blocks away, all the way over by the spot where the old hospital once stood, which is where Tom and I end up, back where we started our journey together all those years before.

As we walk, Tom continues to talk, telling me the famous child actress Shirley Temple was from the area, and she donated her doll collection to the hospital. It was displayed in the old hospital's front lobby. Tom doesn't know what happened to the dolls. As we draw closer to the site of the old hospital, he points to a neatly manicured garden with a fountain. This was once a wide-open field where staff from Roth would take the kids at night to watch birds and foxes. Later he mentions an outdoor spot where the staff would eat lunch when they didn't eat in the cafeteria. I'm not sure if he is talking about the same location in the yard. I have trouble keeping up with his tour. He points to the trees; some of the original valley oaks are still here.

"I guess that's one of the reasons I wanted to bring you over here, because even though the buildings are gone, the 'niceness' of it is still here," he says.

He repeats the last part. The niceness. It's part of the hospital I never saw. Not the dolls nor the field, and definitely not the cafeteria. None of the things he has shown me are etched in my memory.

I remember the inside of a single unit, Roth. I remember a window and the view outside.

That isn't entirely true. I also remember the other patients, and ask him about the ones I've always wondered about, the ones who were occasionally sealed away in a room, visited only by staff in full protective gear. The answer he provides isn't what I expected: They were kept isolated because of chicken pox. I had imagined something more exotic. Chicken pox is about as mundane as you can get. Except at a children's hospital, it can be deadly, especially for patients with lung diseases. Chicken pox wasn't why the patients were there; it was just why they were quarantined.

Sometimes the whole unit would be exposed and have to be locked down and covered in plastic sheets for twenty-one days. Once while Tom was working there, the Unit was re-exposed on day twenty, and had to be locked down all over again. Tom took care of one of the girls in isolation. She is the one who writes to him every holiday season. I don't know whether she was the one in isolation when I was there; I never got past the sealed door to find out.

And I never got outside, where Tom finds his niceness. I also don't see it now. What I see is Vi at Palo Alto, the extravagant senior living complex that has replaced the hospital. The upscale community occupies 23 acres and has 388 apartments, 38 assisted-living units, 24 Alzheimer units, and 44 care beds. The minimum entrance fee is $559,100. That only gets you in the door, however; you still need to pay a regular monthly fee that starts at $4,110.

I will never end up here. I wouldn't be able to afford it.

Yet it was a retirement home I was originally headed for after the hospital. That was the plan. There was no room for me at the group home, where the hospital wanted to send me, so they decided to place me in a retirement home until space opened up. I was supposed to end up in what Roth has become, a senior living community.

DISCHARGE
1986

"I thought you were going to release her before the end of the year," my mother said. She straightened up so she could look into Dr. Steiner's blue eyes.

"Yes, I had said we might be able to release her by then," he said. "And that is still a possibility, but I no longer think it's the best course to pursue."

"What do you mean?" my mother said. Her voice was raised now.

I turned away from the puzzle I was working on.

"Calm down, Karla," Dr. Steiner said. "We're just considering all the options. She still isn't at the weight we hoped she would reach by this time. She is still dangerously thin, and refuses to talk with the psychiatrists."

I backed my chair away from the table and moved toward the hallway. I was hoping to sneak back to my room before Dr. Steiner or my mother tried to pull me into their fight.

Dr. Steiner continued: "Katya hasn't shown much enthusiasm for going home, and so—"

My mother cut him off: "Katya hasn't shown much enthusiasm for anything."

"As I was saying, we have been looking into other options, such as group homes," he said, ignoring my mother's comment. "The one we would like to place her in is full right now. There is a home for the elderly where we think we might be able to temporarily admit her."

"An old people's home? You're joking, aren't you?"

I slipped past them and was just about to turn the corner and disappear down the hall when Dr. Steiner spotted me. He didn't miss much. Since the first time he made me talk in the meeting, I had felt him watching me, even when he wasn't there. He didn't visit the Unit often, but I knew whatever I did was reported back to him. Roth was under his control—and so was I.

"Katya, come here, please," he said.

My mom turned around and both she and Dr. Steiner watched as I slowly made my way back to them. I walked past my mom and stood between the two of them, out of arm's reach from either of them.

"Katya, remember what I told you about the home we were thinking of sending you to?"

I nodded. "The one with a swimming pool," I said.

"Yes, the one with the swimming pool," Dr. Steiner smiled. "What do you think about going to live there? Do you remember what you told me?"

Of course I remembered what I had told him; I was the one who'd said it. "It would be fun to live in a place where I could go swimming all the time," I said again.

My mother shook her head. She was looking at Dr. Steiner, not me.

"Great. So you talked her into going to a retirement home because it has a swimming pool?" she said.

Then she turned to me.

"Did Dr. Steiner tell you about the youth home they'll send you to afterwards?" she asked. "Did he tell you it's a home for juvenile delinquents, where they send troubled teenagers who steal and use drugs—and who may be violent?"

I looked from my mom to Dr. Steiner, unsure who to believe.

"Sherri said I couldn't have a hamster there, 'cause the other kids might get jealous and hurt it," I said. "Dr. Steiner said there would be a swimming pool there, too." I shook my head and hunched my shoulders. "I don't want to go anywhere."

With that I headed to my room. I don't know how Dr. Steiner and my mom ended the conversation. It didn't really matter to me. Everyone seemed to have an opinion about what should happen to me. Everyone except me. Which was good, because it didn't look like I was going to be the one deciding. Even though Dr. Steiner asked me what I thought, it was just a trick. He could twist my words to fit whatever decision he made.

It was hard to keep track of who was winning. The fact that my dentist, and not Dr. Steiner, had figured out I had been throwing up was a plus for Mom. The court officials thought this showed that my mom was taking good care of me.

Then there was the other fight, the one with Dad. Being "sent home" meant I would be released to Mom's house. Dad could visit me on weekends, and ask Anya and I to stay with him. If I said no, I was told I would be forced to go. The whole custody battle was one of the reasons I didn't want to go home—that, and the pool they'd promised me at the other two places.

In not wanting to go home, I never thought about missing Mom and Anya. I never thought about missing anyone. If you don't care about people, you don't miss them.

In the end they decided I would live with my mom temporarily, until there was room at the residential home. I was supposed to come back to the hospital for regular weight checks. If I didn't keep gaining weight, I would be readmitted to the hospital.

When I left, Amanda was still in the hospital. She had gained very little weight during the days we had been there together. Her skin still sagged on her bones.

I stuffed my shirts and pants and teddy bear in the bag my mother had brought. As my mom led me to the end of the hall, a stretcher was wheeled in. I stood still as I watched the nurses rush by with heated blankets and thermometers. The stretcher was pushed into the small room, the room I always thought of as Lauren and Sandra's.

Dan walked by, and I tugged at his shirt. "What's going on?" I asked.

Dan looked down at me and then raised his eyes to my mother and slowly shook his head. "Lauren's back. She has pneumonia this time."

"Jesus," my mom said. She grabbed my hand and pulled me toward the end of the hallway.

I kept looking backwards, my feet stumbling as I watched more and more blankets being brought to Lauren's room. When the hospital doors shut behind us, I heard my mother sigh. She thought all that was behind us now.

I knew better. I knew I would never be safe. I had a weapon that would always remain a part of me.

WHAT MIGHT HAVE BEEN
2019

After being in Roth, the children went home—for the most part. In his report Dr. Steiner writes that 80 percent of patients returned to their families. In person he tells me they didn't always stay at home, at least at first. There was the girl who came back twenty-eight times. She was an exception; most just came back once or twice. Even with her, though, Roth was ultimately successful.

"In the long run, it worked," says Dr. Steiner. "Did you come back? I can't remember."

"No," I say.

My reply seems insufficient, so I add an explanation. "My mother and stepfather used a turkey baster to feed me Ensure." I don't say more, reluctant to relive the memory of having my jaw held open while Ensure was forced down my throat one turkey baster squeeze at a time.

"Oh, Jesus Christ," he says. "They clearly didn't learn."

I wonder if that is what he had feared would happen. Or did he worry things might turn out even worse? Whatever the reason, I was supposed to be among the 20 percent of those who weren't sent directly home. Of that group, 11 percent ended up in residential treatment, 3 percent in foster care and group homes, and 6 percent in different hospitals.

In my case, the difficulty was in finding a place that would take me.

"Placing kids like you, with these kinds of medical and psychiatric problems, was always tricky," says Dr. Steiner. "Psychiatric places would say, 'Wait a minute—we're supposed to do *what* with these kids? Caloric intake and what?' And medical places would say, 'What are we going to do with her if she doesn't do what we ask her to?' You're caught in between."

Today a child like me in California might be sent to a special foster home with parents clinically trained to care for them. It would probably be a good fit. That is, it would be, if they could find a place. There is currently a shortage of foster parents. When California began reforming the child welfare system in 2017, they hoped to move around 65 percent of youth from group homes to home placement. A year later, they had dropped their expectations to 35 percent.

Back in 1986 there were only a few places in California that would take kids like me. One of them was in Ukiah, today a rural Northern California city of 16,000. It was full. Despite the hospital's letter to the facility, asking that I be placed on a waiting list and admitted as quickly as possible, I was not. This is how that letter ends.

However, given limitations of the family's insurance and financial resources, continued hospitalization until placement is not possible, so the patient will return home...

The retirement home idea didn't work out, either, probably because they did not want a ten-year-old. Instead, I was released to my mother. My stay at home was supposed to be temporary. It wasn't. My mom filed for full custody after I was released, temporarily, to her custody. She lost the case. The court psychologist said it would be detrimental to my father's health if his children were taken from him.

My mom was awarded full custody in the years that followed. I would see my father once a year or so, for dinner or a movie. I dreaded the visits. And longed for them. My dad moved out of state, and then out of the country. Child support didn't always arrive. When he was late with payments, my mom would encourage me to call him. I wasn't told to ask for money, just to talk to him. I found that just as hard.

By high school I had stopped hoping my dad would love me and started hating him. I was eating again—and angry. That was when I began to write what I couldn't say. I found my voice on paper.

At first, I voiced only my own pain, but later I realized there were others who needed to be heard, and not all of them had the ability to write their stories. I had a mission then, a reason to keep going. I could tell their stories. When I focused on the pain of others, I forgot for a while how much I was hurting.

I never made it to the group home in Ukiah. I wonder what would have happened if I had. It might have helped me heal, or it might have damaged me further. Tough, older kids could have taken advantage of me, or they could have taken me under their wing. My mother believes it would have been the former. I tend to agree. Yet I still wonder. The first letter I find requesting my expedient placement does not name the facility. When I look for group homes that operated in Ukiah during the 1980s, I find only one that matches my criteria, Trinity Youth Services. Later I find a second letter from a social worker at Roth that mentions Trinity specifically.

Trinity closed in 2009, so I'm too late to visit in person. All I have now is a newspaper article about what Trinity once was. The facility itself is described as covering three square blocks. It included a cafe-teria, offices, open space, a swimming pool, and an inner courtyard. Its history of serving children began in 1903, two decades after it was constructed as the Sacred Heart Convent. First, there was a school. In 1904, an orphanage was added. In 1968 the orphanage, Albertinum, was sold to the Greek Orthodox Church. The church converted it into a home for troubled children.

In the news article a policeman says there were many calls from the facility. Most of them were about runaways. A local historian mentions the disruption the children caused, including the time they backed up the sewers after flushing inappropriate things down the toilets. The historian says she understands the need for homes like Trinity; she just doesn't think they should be located in residential neighborhoods—especially her west side neighborhood.

I look her up. Again, I am too late. She died in 2015. Several former employees and a former resident of the home are also mentioned in the article. A search for the former resident leads nowhere. His name is too common, his path and background, too much of a mystery. The two former employees are easier. They are on Facebook. I send them friend requests and messages. I never hear back.

The former director is working at an organization that helps people with disabilities find employment. I e-mail her at work. After a week, when I still haven't heard back, I send her another message. When that e-mail also goes unanswered, I call. Several calls and voicemail messages later, I finally corner her. In a tone similar to the one Dr. Katz used in his e-mails, she tells me she isn't interested in talking to me.

Their phrasing reminds me they have a choice. They don't have to talk to me. They owe me no explanation. They owe me nothing.

I do get her to give me something, though: a name.

Smoke

2004-2005

Matches. I was supposed to remember to bring matches, or a lighter. Patients weren't allowed to have either, but I could bring them. It didn't quite make sense to me, but then, I was getting the information second- and thirdhand. Anastasia told me what she could, but she was the one locked up, a patient in an adult madhouse. Her mother wore T-shirts with cute cats on them and talked about spirits. She didn't seem capable of finding her way to the institution—or remembering the matches. So I drove Anastasia's mom and packed the matches.

At the adult psychiatric facility I placed all I had brought with me on the conveyor belt, to go through the metal detector: keys, wallet, cell phone—and the matches.

Anastasia asked about the matches first. She led us to a balcony so she could smoke a cigarette. After she lit up, I took the matches back. We didn't talk about why Anastasia was there. We talked about the matches and how hard it was to get them at the facility.

Anastasia and I were reporters at the same Kentucky newspaper. I was rigid and disciplined, arriving at work before everyone else. Anastasia was laid-back, arriving late and leaving early. The day she found out about her sister was no different. It was ten in the morning, and Anastasia wasn't at work.

I was in the middle of a call with a source when I saw her cell phone number flash on my desk phone. I clicked over, telling Anastasia that I would call her back in a few minutes.

"Okay," she said.

She sounded a little off, but then that wasn't unusual. Anastasia smoked a lot of marijuana.

After my interview ended, I started typing up my notes. The phone rang again. It was Anastasia. I had forgotten to call her back.

I picked up and started to apologize. Her choked sob drowned me out.

"My sister's dead," she said. For a while that was all she said, over and over again: "My sister's dead."

It still didn't really sink in. We were in our twenties. Sisters didn't die. But Masha had.

Masha had been living in California. Anastasia hadn't heard from her in several days, but she wasn't worried. Not at first.

They found her body a few days later. She had jumped off a bridge.

A week or so after the phone call, Anastasia went to California to figure out what to do with Masha's cats and everything else her sister had left behind. Then she came back to Kentucky—and work.

For a while things seemed pretty normal. I would show up to work at eight each morning and Anastasia would stop by my desk two hours later, on her way to her own workspace. The hours between our arrivals stretched to three, and then four, and then days passed when I didn't see Anastasia. Finally she just stopped coming to work altogether.

When our editor couldn't get ahold of Anastasia, he called me. He wanted me to check on her, to make sure she was still there, still alive.

I would find her at her apartment, getting high. I always found her. Except the time I didn't. She tried to do what Masha did, but with pills. That's how she got locked up. First she landed in the emergency room. After that, they sent her to a mental institution. She was supposed to stay for several days.

I saw her at both places, but it is the institution I remember. It was there that I glimpsed the life I hadn't lived. The life I might have had if I had continued in institutions after Roth—at the retirement home, at the home for troubled children, and then later, at a place like this.

The other patients seemed unhinged in a way the youth I had been hospitalized with were not. Maybe it was the passage of time that had done that to them. Maybe it was a life spent locked away. Or drugs. Or all of the above.

Maybe it was just life.

I wondered if I would've been there with them had I not gotten out of institutions when I did.

Anastasia's mother talked about Masha's ghost. She explained that her eldest daughter had appeared to her as a cat. She didn't seem to see her youngest daughter, the one smoking beside her on the balcony, surrounded by people wearing dressing gowns at two in the afternoon.

I asked about the doctors. Anastasia hadn't seen one. Maybe tomorrow, she said. Therapists and psychiatrists also seemed in short supply.

She wasn't dying here. But she wasn't living either. She was just passing time.

When her dad called me to ask how she was doing, I wasn't sure what to say. He called her "Ana-stay-zhuh." She pronounced her name "Ah-na-stah-ziyah."

I didn't trust a father who couldn't say his daughter's name properly.

A Straight Flush
2019

Camille Schraeder not only worked at Trinity in the 1980s, but was also raised in a similar setting. That is how she first got to know the child welfare system, as an infant in Boise, Idaho. Camille and her twin sister Corinne were placed with a foster family when they were just two months old.

"We were taken away for failure to thrive," she says. "Which means we were starving to death."

Camille, who wears her blonde hair long and free, doesn't dwell on the details. In many cases, she doesn't know them, or doesn't believe what she does know.

"When you have nine ACEs, you don't quite trust everything," she explains.

At first I think she's talking about playing cards. Only later do I understand she is using professional lingo. Adverse childhood experiences, or ACEs, are a measurement of childhood trauma. There are ten of them. Camille experienced nine. She could have, probably should have, ended up in bad shape. Instead, she coordinates mental health care between providers and the county through her business, Redwood Quality Management Company (RQMC). There is also Redwood Community Services (RCS), which offers mental health care. Camille is busy with both, but she is not rushed. She takes time to talk and listen, which is why she tends to run late. In her office there is a framed portrait of Gandhi. In front of it is a curling iron.

Camille is fifty-seven and slightly round at the waist, outfitted in a peach sweater and blue business pants. She has five siblings, all with names starting with the letter C. When Camille and Corinne were taken away, their older siblings were placed with their grandparents. Camille doesn't remember the foster family where she and her twin were placed. She doesn't even remember if there was more than one family. The only vague memory she has is watching a parade while perched on someone's shoulders. There is no way for her to find out anything more, as the records were destroyed in a fire.

Camille was four or maybe five when she returned home. She stayed there for about a decade. It was hell. There was physical abuse, sexual abuse, and poverty, she says. At fourteen or fifteen she was detained again.

Detained is a word I associate with the criminal justice system. That is one definition—to keep someone in custody, often for a crime. The other definition is to hold someone back. I am not sure which one Camille is thinking of when she describes children taken from their families as being detained in the foster care system.

In Camille's case, she was detained because she stole a car. She had also gotten in fights and was failing at school in California, where her family now lived. It was her acting out that got her noticed.

Camille was placed at the Christian commune In Search of Truth (I'SOT) in the tiny rural Northern California town of Canby. Members of the commune, which was founded in the 1960s by E. Marie White, had a license to care for troubled youth. Things were different back then, and when you were placed somewhere, you could end up staying there until you came of age, says Camille. She stayed even longer.

Camille remained with I'SOT in Canby until she was twenty-two. She was indoctrinated, both by the group's methods and their isolation. The majority of the town's several hundred residents were members of I'SOT. Camille believed the group's prophecies, and agreed to an arranged marriage when she was nineteen. Her husband was forty-two. She looked after children who had been sent by the State to be raised by the commune, and donated the majority of her salary back to the leadership.

"They did a lot of things that they should not have done, certainly that would never, ever be allowed in today's environment, and shouldn't be," says Camille.

I'SOT lost their group home license in 1990, following a state investigation concerning complaints of physical and sexual abuse. Camille was one of those who spoke out. Now she tells me that I'SOT also helped her by giving her a sense of significance, a sense of "I matter in the world." Which is why she has trouble telling this part of her story. While I'SOT did bad things, the commune also enabled Camille to become who she is: a successful businesswoman, a wife and a mother. That isn't how people like her usually end up.

My life was supposed to have a different ending, as well. But after college I never again stopped eating for a long period of time. I can't say what worked or what didn't, just that I survived. I lived.

I didn't marry and have two kids and drive a Subaru. Instead I became a journalist and author. My mother refers to my work as a calling. When people ask how I find stories, I tell them I don't; they find me. I write about what I feel compelled to write about, the issues and stories I can't ignore. Crystal and the other girls in the detention facility; teenagers who release their internal pain by cutting themselves; foster children trying to transition to life on their own. I write about their pain and thereby keep my own in check.

Physically I have a few reminders of Roth, most obvious among them my misshapen rib cage. Then there are the other illnesses that "continue to elude diagnosis": pancreatitis, hives, vertigo, and hearing loss. What they all seem to have in common is an unknown cause and an unclear conclusion. There is a physical component, but doctors believe there is also an emotional one. They call me an "enigma," and say I am "never boring."

While food will always be an issue, I eat a relatively normal diet now. The only times I really battle is when I stop my medication, stop taking antidepressants. When that happens, I slip. I struggle to eat. I struggle to work. I struggle to stay alive. I have taken leaves of absence from work and I've had some medical close calls, but after Roth, I have never been institutionalized again. Instead, my mom and stepdad hold me together while I wait for the drugs to work their way back into my system.

The most recent break came when I started working on this book, revisiting Roth. By the time I found Camille, I was beginning and ending my days in tears. In between, I tried to force food down. My eyes were dry the day I met Camille, but I was skinnier than I should have been. She looked at me the same way Sherri once regarded me: with concern and fear. Camille holds on to me as long as she can, letting me lose myself in her story.

Camille left I'SOT at twenty-two in order to offer her baby, Jerusha Victoria, a different life. She had no idea how to budget, how to go grocery shopping, or how to obtain a driver's license. What she did know was how to care for kids. Former I'SOT members were expert at that, which is how Camille ended up at Trinity. The man who hired her in May 1985 was also from I'SOT.

Dressed like a frumpy fifty-year-old, in a long dress, with an old-fashioned hairstyle, Camille took a job as a child-care worker for the senior boys at Trinity. Later she was moved to the coed unit. She worked sixteen-hour days, Wednesday through Saturday, or Sunday through Wednesday. Her husband had trouble adapting to life outside I'SOT, and they drifted apart. Camille later married a therapist at Trinity who now helps run RQMC.

At I'SOT there was a whole philosophy about how to raise children. At Trinity, the only philosophy they followed was what the man in charge, Father Steve, told them to do, which was basically to take good care of the kids.

It was instructions many of the children's families had been unable to follow. The majority of the children at Trinity were detained in the foster care system. I was not, which would have made me unusual. Yet there was something interesting I found in my research: Children in the foster care system suffer from eating disorders at higher-than-average rates. When it comes to bulimia, the rate among alumni of the foster care system is seven times higher than that found in the general population. Other studies have found that a quarter of preadolescent children in foster and kinship care (children in the care of relatives) have significant eating issues—young children, like me, not influenced by age or gender. With so much in their lives in turmoil, they turn to the one thing they can control: food.

That is certainly what I did, which means in some ways, I had more in common with young children in the foster care system than I did with the teenage girls at Roth.

I was not officially detained, but I also was not officially released to my mother. I was temporarily released home with the understanding that if I lost weight, I would be detained. That's why my mother used the turkey baster to force feed me.

Camille calls it tough love. I sense that this is another thing that sets me apart from many of the kids at Trinity. I had a parent with the ability, desire, and means to fight for their child. I would have been unusual in other ways as well. Most of the children at Trinity at that time were boys—only ten or eleven of the seventy residents were female. Although they ranged in age from seven to eighteen, in general the children tended to be in the older age range. They also tended to be "pretty troubled kids" who acted out in ways similar to the way Camille had.

"I'm external and aggressive and all that, so people paid attention because I forced it, good, bad, or indifferent," she says.

The Trinity kids did the same thing. One boy barked like a dog. Others had trouble sleeping, managing school, and regulating their emotions. "We had some who were sick..." She doesn't complete the sentence. Instead she talks about the "little ones," which at ten is what I would have been. Camille worried about one little seven-year-old girl so much that she actually thought about adopting her. She wonders aloud what it would have been like for a little kid like me, mixed in with all the older children, with their external and aggressive behaviors. Trinity had a psychiatrist, a psychologist, and quite a few therapists, but I wasn't the kind of child they were used to treating.

"You were probably too severe for the level of sophistication we all had back then, in my opinion," says Camille.

She remembers it being "very, very difficult" to manage the meals and care for the two diabetic boys they did have at Trinity. Yet they did it, and they might have been able to help me as well. Camille thinks that if my disorder was trauma-based, and an emotional health disorder rather than a mental health disorder, I might have done okay. I am not sure how to separate them, or if you even can.

For years I used a difficult home situation to explain why I chose to starve myself. My father was a mess of a man, and I had exhausted myself trying to care for him. While his problems may have been severe, the situation of a child becoming a caregiver for one parent in joint custody situations is not unusual, according to Dr. Christine B. L. Adams, one of the authors of *Living on Automatic*.

"Children will be called upon to tend emotionally to this parent in a role-reversal manner," she writes.

With joint custody and fifty-fifty custody, "fairness" children "learn to ignore and subordinate their emotional and developmental needs and defer to parents' and judicial wants and needs for this 'fairness,' " she explains. The emotional pressure to please the parent and failure to do so can result in the child feeling suicidal. That is pretty much what happened with me. I needed a way out, and I found one.

But now I wonder if it was something more. After going off Zoloft and failing to function yet again, I have been forced to admit that suffering from depression was not a one-time thing for me. That much is clear. The how and why is harder to determine.

My depression may have developed because of what I went through as a child; the physical effects of starvation; or the emotional effects of my father's behavior. ACEs have been shown to contribute to depression in adults, as well as other health issues. Maybe the antipsychotic drugs the hospital gave me played a role. Or maybe I inherited a sadness from my father's family, the same despair that caused my great-uncle to kill himself and his family. Then there is my father's PTSD and how it might have altered his genes, and mine. Or maybe it is just how I am—and how I will always be.

"It was both," I tell Camille.

Then I tell her more. I tell her about the straitjacket, about the wrist and ankle restraints, about my father. She asks me things few of the other people I have talked to have asked.

"How long were you in the hospital?"

"Did they use the feeding tube?"

"Were you an only child?"

I answer her questions. It is nice to have someone acknowledge the details of how difficult the experience was for me. The surprising thing is that this acknowledgment comes from someone who has experienced so much trauma herself.

In many respects, my story pales next to Camille's and those of the children she has worked with. I may have experienced neglect, emotional abuse, and poverty, but there was also a strong foundation in the middle class, and at least one parent who did her best to fix the situation. I had more than Camille and many other detained kids.

Still, when I was off my medication, I worried that I might end up where Camille and others who have been institutionalized often end up.

To Be Continued
2018

I go to a coffee shop to write. The story I don't tell is that of the man who sits at a corner table by himself, rubber bracelets stretching up his wrist, a notebook filled with carefully diagrammed pages open in front of him. He talks about all the articles he has read on misogyny and involuntary celibates, or incels. He maps out the book he is writing about his late son, his only child, a college student killed by another young man, an incel, in a mass shooting.

The father is always searching for answers. He has met with the father of the young man who took his son's life. Someday he would like to talk with incels who have or are planning to commit mass murder.

Every time we meet in the coffee shop it seems like there is another plastic memorial bracelet on his wrist and another article he has read about mass murder. There are more chapter ideas for his book and more discoveries about incels. There is always more, but never enough. The answer he really wants to hear will never come, because the young man who killed his son is dead. Even if his son's killer was alive, the killer would never be able to answer all of the father's questions.

No one can. He has too many questions for this lifetime. He knows this, but the search keeps him going, keeps him coming to the coffee shop.

The one person I never interviewed for this book is my father. Maybe it's because I know his answers will also be incomplete. Like the father in the coffee shop, the questions I have are too many for one man to answer. Maybe that's why I don't ask. I need to keep looking for the answers on my own, the same way the father in the coffee shop does.

LAS AMIGAS
2019

As Camille drives toward Trinity with me in the passenger seat, she raises the same concern the local historian raised, about the children being housed in this neighborhood.

"I would never put a residential treatment facility here again, ever," she says. Not because of the effect it would have on the residents, but because of the scrutiny it exposes the kids to.

In the early years of Trinity, the 1980s, Camille remembers the community as being supportive. There was a park next to the grounds with a large green area where the children would play baseball and swing on the swings, like any other neighborhood children.

Camille slows down as we approach the first building, a long, two-story, cream-colored structure with red and green trim.

"Okay, here we are," she says.

There are a number of buildings, far more than I expected. I am trying to take it all in—the fence, the open space in the middle, the numerous structures—when Camille points to a long, low building.

I imagine there are rooms inside, lined with bunk beds. Camille tells me everyone had their own room; at least they did after a staff member reported that sexual acts were occurring in the shared rooms.

The streets are empty so Camille can drive as slowly as she wants, and she does, pointing out the school, the gym, the kitchen, the dining hall, and the offices. She gestures to a tall brick building. That was the coed unit where Camille worked. Downstairs was Los Hermanos, with ten boys. Upstairs was Las Amigas, with eleven girls. Camille was responsible for both, a total of twenty-one kids.

"You would have been in my unit, Las Amigas," she says.

I think I would have liked being with Camille.

We talk about collaborating. I am eager to continue the relationship. Everyone else I interviewed gave me pieces, but it is Camille who shows me how to put the puzzle together. Camille could keep doing what she is doing, and I could help her by telling the story of what she does. But Camille worries I won't be able to handle the heartache of too many tragic foster care stories. I worry she might be right.

In telling this story I have exhausted myself. I am not sure I have enough left to give to children who are already lost in the system.

From the passenger seat of Camille's car I glance at the second floor of the building, where I would have lived. I had always imagined I would have shared a room. In reality it is just the bathroom I would have shared. There would also have been a living room with a television, a multipurpose room for activities, and a quiet room, as well as a few offices, including Camille's. Meals were taken in the dining hall, with all the children from the various buildings. At some point the older boys may have eaten separately. Weekends offered a chance to get away on outings.

We round a corner. "And then this was the church sanctuary," Camille says, pointing to a church building next to the brick one. "We didn't go in there very often, but we had plays, stuff like that in there."

She gestures toward another feature, a marker on the wall that says "The Albertinum Dominican Sisters." It's not unusual that Trinity had its start as a convent and orphanage. According to *The Chronicle of Social Change*, a non-profit independent news site covering child welfare, many group homes started as orphanages. By the early 1900s, almost 125,000 children were living in institutions in the United States.

Some kids had parents and returned home when their families were able to care for them again. Others were raised in the orphanage. Sometimes their parents visited; other times they didn't. Poverty wasn't the only reason they ended up there. According to Camille, broken marriages and mental illness—usually on the part of the mother—also factored in.

She remembers meeting former residents of the orphanage, older men and women who would stop by to see the home where they grew up.

The word *home* is deceptive. In terms of mental health, children in group homes and other institutions are among the most vulnerable. According to *The Chronicle of Social Change*, the very nature of institutional care results in poor lifelong outcomes. Research has shown that children in group homes have lower graduation rates than their peers in other forms of foster care, and an increased propensity to be involved with the justice system.

It isn't all bad. A former Trinity resident credits the group home with turning his life around. In a newspaper article that ran when Trinity closed in 2009, the former resident says that the home helped him see there was more out there in life. Today he works as an advocate for the developmentally disabled.

Camille remembers Trinity a bit like Tom the counselor remembers Roth. The first people to work at Trinity were the peaceniks of the 1960s, coming from a place of real desire to serve, she says.

Still, she is a realist. "As you become more knowledgeable about the roots of trauma, the effects of trauma, and all those things, you also realize you're going to do the very best you can, and it may not be enough," she says.

Camille left Trinity in 1995 and started her own agency that focused on finding foster families for children in need.

We turn another corner and Camille points out a playground. "This was a pool back when I was here," she says. The pool was paved over and turned into a playground when the insurance became too expensive to maintain.

It was the pool that had initially convinced me I wanted to come here. My only hesitation was over whether I would be allowed to have a hamster. I have a feeling pets weren't allowed.

Camille thinks I could have fallen in love with Trinity. Like her, I was a caretaker, and there were plenty of kids I could have taken care of at Trinity.

I was far younger than Camille was when she ended up at I'SOP. I also didn't act out. I was one of the quiet ones, the ones they worry about, the ones who get lost in the system.

That is probably what Camille is thinking when she tells me what she tells me next.

"I'm glad you didn't go there," she says.

We are toward the end of the tour. There is another sign on the wall that Camille points out. I read it out loud. Dharma Realm Buddhist University.

"Now it's a meditation center," says Camille. "I just think it's the most wonderful thing, don't you? From taking care of kids to taking care of souls. Sort of."

I agree, sort of.

Camille and I don't do wonderful; we do real life. We do "sort of."

What happened to me at Roth and at home afterwards wasn't all good. It also wasn't all bad. It is what happened, though, and it's why I am here today, just as Camille is here in part because of I'SOT.

"I'm sitting here," she says. "So, what do you do about that, right?"

I'm sitting here, too. That is why I am here, why I am writing this—because others aren't here.

Yet sometimes I feel like I shouldn't be here. I feel like I belong neither to those who have made it nor to those who have failed. I belong to a place in between. It's as if Camille and I are shadows of the real thing. Maybe that is what allows us to straddle both worlds, a foot on each side. We bridge the gap for ourselves, and, if we are lucky, for a few children that cannot cross alone.

AFTERWORD
2021

Stanford medical students used to mail me surveys when I was still a child. I asked one student to connect me with other former patients. She said she had talked to one of them I might know, Sandra. She couldn't give me Sandra's contact information, but she promised to give my information to Sandra. If Sandra wanted to contact me, she would. She never did.

I don't know what happened to Sandra and the others, those who were in the hospital with me, those who I would have known at Trinity, just as I don't know what happened to the thousands of other children institutionalized each year in the juvenile justice system, the foster care system, and the mental health-care system.

The only ending I know is Crystal's. The slight teenage girl from Kentucky is now twenty-eight. In the picture of her I find online, she looks barely changed from the sixteen-year-old girl I knew at the youth detention facility, the kid who insisted the dog she was training blinked once to let her know he wanted to be called Rascal. A girl with a slightly lopsided, open-mouth grin.

In the image she is smiling the same way, which is strange, because it's a mug shot.

I track Crystal down on KOOL, the Kentucky Online Offender Lookup—a misfit of an acronym if there ever was one. She is still slight, just four-foot-eleven and 115 pounds. She is an adult now, though, so there is no hiding what she has done. She is in a pretrial diversion program. Her charges include tampering with evidence, public intoxication, and possession of a controlled substance, heroin.

I write to Crystal. She doesn't write back.

The window that once opened for me has closed. In the silence I realize maybe I need to start earlier, before children get taken away.

That is when I decide to volunteer as a mentor. I ask the organization for a younger child between the ages of eight and twelve.

The girl I get is ten. Annie is sweet and happy and seldom complains. She talks a mile a minute. But she can also be quiet. Because of the COVID-19 pandemic, she has been studying at home, isolated from the world. She misses school. She misses basketball. She misses her best friend. All she wants to do is go outside, which she can't do very often, as her mother works and her older brothers are busy. I meet her mother once via video chat, while she and Annie are taking a walk. Annie is bubbling with energy, running ahead to point out the flowers, the spot where a porta-potty once stood, the statues in a church yard.

Most of the time we meet while Annie is at home. When I go to open the video application for our date each week, she is already there waiting. We play charades, work on her school essays, and learn dances. She doesn't talk about her father, and I don't ask. She has a handful of brothers and a mother she adores. When we make door-knob decorations, she gives hers to her mom. The stick-on supplies I bring her are old and we have to use glue to make them work. When

I help her with her essays, I make them more complicated than they need to be. The bookmarks we make need far too many staples to hold them together.

I worry she will get bored with me, tired of yet another video meeting. Then her mother sends me a text. She tells me she is grateful for me coming into Annie's life, and that I have made Annie very happy.

The organization has warned me that this is the honeymoon stage. In a few months Annie may push back, challenge me. I realize that is coming. When it does, I will remember her mother's words.

Because this isn't Annie's ending.

Notes

The Prisoners

Juvenile Justice Center, San Leandro, CA. Volunteer, The Beat Within. Alameda County, 2012.

The Patients

Kanner, L. (1960). *Child Psychiatry*. Springfield, IL: Charles C. Thomas.

Schowalter, J. E. (2003). *A History of Child and Adolescent Psychiatry in the United States*.

Cahalan, S. (2019). *The Great Pretender: The Undercover Mission that Changed Our Understanding of Madness*. Grand Central Publishing.

Lipsett, D. R. (2003). Psychiatry and the general hospital in an age of uncertainty. *World Psychiatry*.

Summergrad, P. (1994). Medical psychiatry units and the roles of the inpatient psychiatric service in the general hospital. *General Hospital Psychiatry*, 16, 20–31.

The Prince

INS. (1953). "Whiting Man Beats Wife, Two Children to Death with Meat Grinder, Kills Self." *Palladium-Item*.

Staff. (1953). "Scenes of Triple Murder and Suicide." *Hammond Times*.

Steiner, H. (1982). "The Socio-Therapeutic Environment of a Child Psychosomatic Ward." *Child Psychiatry and Human Development*, 1321, 71–78.

———. (1983). "A Psychosomatic Unit for Children and Adolescents: Report on First Year and Ten Months." *Child Psychiatry and Human Development*, 14 (1), 3–15.

His Subject
Interview with Dr. Hans Steiner. Stanford Faculty Club, CA. June 25, 2018.

Interview with Dr. Hans Steiner. Office, Palo Alto, CA. December 12, 2018.

A Very Special Category
Children's Hospital at Stanford. Records for Katya Cengel. Number 090 71 51: history, physical examination; discharge summary, psychiatry; clinic visits; community meeting notes.

Back Behind Bars
Cengel, K. 2008. "Rehabilitating Rascal." *Courier-Journal*: Features.

Number 090 71 51
Interview with Dr. Iris Litt. Mademoiselle Colette, Menlo Park, CA. December 13, 2019.

Cole, S. (1986). "Sex Discrimination and Admission to Medical School, 1929–1984." *American Journal of Sociology*, 92, 549–67.

Sexson, S. B., and B. B. Kahan. (1991). "Organization and Development of Pediatric Medical-Psychiatric Units, Part I: Administrative, Financial, and Political Issues." *General Hospital Psychiatry*, 13, 296–304.

Little Difficult One

Kahan, B. B., and S. B. Sexson. (1991). "Organization and Development of Pediatric Medical-Psychiatric Units, Part II: Clinical Management Issues." *General Hospital Psychiatry*, 13, 391–98.

Antipsychotic

Interview with Dr. Bernard Kahan. Phone. November 29, 2018.

Interview with Dr. Richard Shaw. Phone. November 5, 2019.

The Storyteller

Interview with Tom McPherson. Stanford, CA. November 8, 2019. Phone, December 18, 2018, and several e-mails.

By Proxy

Kahan, B. B., and B. Crofts Yorker. (1990). "Munchausen Syndrome by Proxy." *Journal of School Health,* 60.

Everybody Loves Dan

Interview with Dan. Starmont Winery, Napa, CA. December 29, 2018.

The Comprehensive Care Unit

Interview with Mary Sanders. El Camino Hospital. Mountain View, CA. December 12, 2019.

Staff. (2016). Our History. https://supportlpch.org/blog/our-history: Lucile Packard Children's Hospital, Stanford website.

Dremann, S. (2017). "New Lucile Packard Children's Hospital Is a Habitat for Healing." *Palo Alto Weekly.*

Haunted Ground

Johnston, T. (July/August 2003). "About a Boy." *Stanford Magazine*: Features. https://stanfordmag.org/contents/about-a-boy.

Leventhal, A., D. DiGiuseppe, D. Grant, K. Reinhart, R. Cambra, M. Arellano, S. Guzman-Schmidt, G. Gomez. M. O. T. o. t. S. F. B. Area & O. F. C. Services. 2016. Report on the Recovery, Analysis and AMS Dating of Ancestral Muwekma Ohlone Human Remains Recovered from the Horše 'Iššéete Ruwwatka.

Vi at Palo Alto. https://www.retirementliving.com/vi-at-palo-alto.

What Might Have Been

Steiner, H. (1983). "A Psychosomatic Unit for Children and Adolescents: Report on First Year and Ten Months." *Child Psychiatry and Human Development* 14 (1), 3–15.

Loudenback, J. (2019). "California's Sweeping Group Home Reform Falters Without Key Supports for Youth." *The Chronicle of Social Change*.

Anderson, G. "Ukiah Youth Home Shuts Its Doors." *Press Democrat*. July 31, 2009.

A Straight Flush

Interview with Camille Schraeder. Office in Ukiah, CA. December 17, 2019.

Staff. "I'SOT Loses Child Placement License." *Modoc County Record*. September 13,1990.

Adams, C. B. L. (2019). "Shared Physical Custody: What Children Discover and Suffer." Psychology Today website.

Pecora, P. (2010). "Why Current and Former Recipients of Foster Care Need High Quality Mental Health Services." Springer Science + Business Media online. March 14, 2010.

Tarren-Sweeney, M. (2006). "Patterns of Aberrant Eating Among Pre-Adolescent Children in Foster Care." *Journal of Abnormal Child Psychology.* October 4, 2006.

ACKNOWLEDGMENTS

I owe thanks to those who kept me alive, chief among them the staff of the Roth Unit at Children's Hospital at Stanford and Dr. Hans Steiner, who died October 17, 2022. My sister, mother, stepfather, and countless friends, family members, and mentors also deserve credit.

Then there are those who made this book possible by trusting me with their stories. I owe the greatest debt to Tom McPherson, whose passion for Roth allowed me to see the magic I had missed.

A highlight of the reporting process was tracking down Dan and realizing he was just as wonderful as I remembered. I was also able to meet others whose hearts are just as big, including Camille Schraeder and Mary Sanders. Then there are the doctors and experts who took the time to talk to me: Dr. Steiner, Dr. Litt, Dr. Kahan, and Dr. Shaw.

Quincy Troupe first saw the promise in my story, and numerous writing friends took it from there, including Leza Lowitz, Robert McNally, Lisa Coffman, Melissa Fraterrigo, Julia Bricklin, and Dallas Woodburn. Thank you to the members of the Word of Mouth Bay Area group (WOM-BA) and Bob's writing group for writerly insights and support. Thank you to my agent, Delia Berrigan, for making everything easier and more enjoyable. Miranda Heyman and David LeGere at Woodhall Press were fantastic editors and Melissa Hayes did a wonderful job as copyeditor. Any errors are my own.

ABOUT THE AUTHOR

Katya Cengel is the author of Independent Publisher Book Award (IPPY) and Foreword INDIES winner *From Chernobyl with Love* and two other non-fiction books including *Exiled: From the Killing Fields of Cambodia to California and Back.* She has written for *New York Times Magazine, Smithsonian* and *Marie Claire* among others.